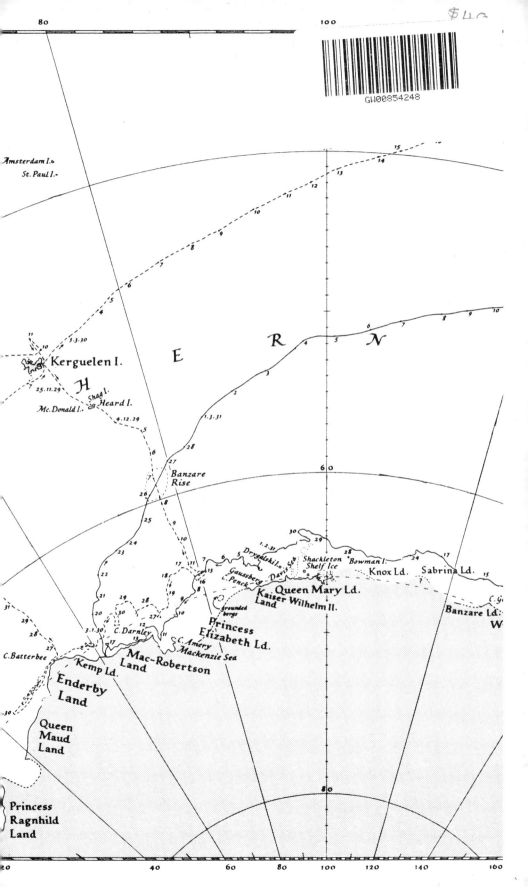

ANTARCTIC DAYS WITH MAWSON

The author on the voyage south as assistant zoologist. Mawson said of him, "His jovial disposition and fine physique proved an asset at all times."

ANTARCTIC DAYS WITH MAWSON

A personal account
of the British, Australian and New Zealand
Antarctic Research Expedition
of 1929–31

by
Harold Fletcher

ANGUS & ROBERTSON PUBLISHERS

ANGUS & ROBERTSON PUBLISHERS
London . Sydney . Melbourne

First published in Australia by Angus & Robertson Publishers in 1984
First published in the United Kingdom by Angus & Robertson (UK) Ltd in 1984

Copyright © Harold Fletcher 1984

National Library of Australia
Cataloguing-in-publication data.
Fletcher, H.O. (Harold Oswald), 1903–
  Antarctic days with Mawson.
  ISBN 0 207 14889 9.
  1. British, Australian and New Zealand Antarctic
  Research Expedition, 1929–1931. 2. Antarctic
  regions. I. Title.
919.8'904

Typeset in 11 pt Goudy Old Style Roman
by Graphicraft Typesetters Limited, Hong Kong
Printed in Hong Kong by Everbest Printing Co., Ltd.

This book is dedicated to the
memory of
Sir Douglas Mawson, O.B.E., D.Sc., F.R.S.,
scientist and explorer,
1882–1958

" . . . in him we have an Australian Nansen,
a man of infinite resource, splendid spirit,
marvellous physique and an indifference to frost
and cold that was astonishing — all the attributes
of a great explorer . . ."

Edgeworth David, 1909

Contents

Preface

Although half a century has passed since the BANZARE voyages, a full and personal narrative of life and activities ashore and on board the expedition vessel *Discovery* has not been published. Several abbreviated and concise narratives have appeared. A paper written by Sir Douglas Mawson on the expedition was read before the Royal Geographical Society of London and published in their journal of August 1932. A comprehensive and official history, based on the Mawson papers, together with controversial issues raised at the time was written by A. Grenfell Price, C.M.G., D.Litt., in *The Winning of Australian Antarctica*, published in 1962. Lady Mawson devoted a short chapter to the BANZARE voyages in her book, *Mawson of the Antarctic*, published in 1964.

This book is an attempt to make known the everyday experiences and the more intimate domestic life and feelings of the expedition's 37 members, always in close contact with one another on board the relatively small vessel *Discovery*. It is a story of a concerted effort in which everyone worked together as a team in a spirit of comradeship always more accentuated when conditions became most trying and hazardous.

Many of the expedition members have passed on. No excuse is offered in recording the many incidents, thoughts and reactions of my colleagues, which were largely forgotten until brought again to mind when reading my diaries for the first time since they were written more than 50 years ago. In writing the historical chapters in this book frequent references were made to publications of early Antarctic expeditions; also to A. Grenfell Price's book, *The Winning of Australian Antarctica*. Many incidents in his book, recorded from Sir Douglas Mawson's notes, are included in my diary and usually in more detail. Reference was also made to notes written by Frank Hurley during the second voyage of BANZARE, given to me many years ago. Extracts are acknowledged.

I am deeply indebted to the Antarctic Division, Department of Science and Technology at Kingston, Tasmania, and to the Mawson Institute of Antarctic Research, Canberra, for photographs and permission for them to be reproduced. Some photographs were taken by Stuart Campbell during both voyages of BANZARE.

Thanks are due to Mrs Nancy Gunn and Miss Jean Easthope for advice and encouragement. Also to Miss Margaret Ryan, my daughter

Ann and my son Ian for meticulously checking the final manuscript. Ian is no stranger to Antarctica, having on two occasions carried out research at the Amundsen–Scott South Pole Station.

Introduction

The Antarctic Continent, although never seen, appeared on maps of the 16th century as a great southern landmass named Terra Australis incognita. Centuries later there was proof of its reality when it was sighted for the first time in the year 1820.

Interest in the great southern land was reawakened and expeditions representing many nations sailed south in further attempts to make landings, lay claims and investigate its potentialities. A major breakthrough in Antarctic exploration was made in 1831 when Sir James Clark Ross forced his vessel into a virtually ice-free sea, which was later named after him. He discovered a spectacular mountain range stretching the whole length of its western shore. Strangely enough this most interesting area received little attention for about 60 years.

Following exploration by British expeditions in the eastern sector of the Antarctic continent, Britain claimed sovereignty over the territory lying between the 45th and 160th degrees of east longitude with the exception of Adélie Land. Further extensive geographical and scientific knowledge within this territory was made known by the two Australian expeditions organised and led by Sir Douglas Mawson during the years 1911–14 and 1929–31.

An Act of Parliament in 1936 passed this territory to the Australian Government to control and administer. It consists of almost one-third of the continent and is now recognised as Australian Antarctic Territory. Australia has not taken its responsibilities lightly and many millions of dollars have been made available in establishing permanent Antarctic stations, their equipment and staffing. The record of exploration and research in many scientific disciplines successfully carried out is an imposing one.

Australia can be justly proud of its achievements in the past 50 years. In the near future it is almost certain that present territorial claims will be challenged. If so, Australia will be in a strong position to refute any challenge against its right to its claimed Australian Antarctic Territory.

It is hoped that readers of this book will gain an insight into the importance and significance of Antarctica. It is a continent of extreme moods, generally inhospitable and brutal, but as the roar and strength of gales and hurricanes subside it emerges as a breathlessly silent land of astounding beauty.

Early Unveiling of Antarctica

Learned men of the 15th century were emphatic in their view that a great southern continent must exist to balance continents of the northern hemisphere. In the 16th century, cartographers of that time showed on their maps a vast continent covering the base of the globe. To the north it was delineated as extending high into the three great oceans of the southern hemisphere and connecting with South America and South Africa. Based solely on man's credulity the great south land, named Antarktos by early Greek philosophers, remained unseen. It was virtually a mythical continent for several centuries.

Its connection with South Africa was dispelled when Vasco da Gama sailed around the Cape of Good Hope in 1497 with no sign of land to the south. Twenty-three years later, Magellan passed through the strait which now bears his name near the tip of South America. The adjoining land of Tierra del Fuego was hailed as part of the great south land. However, Sir Francis Drake, in 1577, sailed south of Tierra del Fuego to the 56th parallel without sighting land.

Another early navigator, Abel Tasman, was the first to reach a reasonably high latitude when, in 1642, he sailed across the Indian Ocean as far south as latitude 49°. Continuing into the Pacific Ocean, he discovered Tasmania and New Zealand. This voyage relegated the south land to a position much farther south than postulated by the early cartographers. Tasman's discoveries excited interest but it was almost a century later before determined efforts were made to discover Antarktos or prove its non-existence.

In 1739, Pierre Bouvet, a French naval officer, was commissioned to sail south in an attempt to discover the continent. He sailed his ship into the Southern Ocean to latitude 54° south. Bouvet sighted land before continual bad weather forced him to return. He named it Cap de la Circoncision thinking it was part of the south land. It was later renamed Bouvet Island.

Another French navigator, Lieutenant de Kerguelen-Tremarec, sailed south in 1771 in command of the frigate *Fortune*. On January 17, 1772, he sighted through fog and rain, an extensive mountainous landmass in latitude 49° south. Gale-force winds prevented a landing. He boldly concluded that he had discovered the great southern continent and, without any further investigations, returned to France with a highly coloured version of his discovery. This romantically minded navigator reported it to promise "all the crops of the Mother Country ..." and to "... furnish marvellous physical and moral spectacles." He was hailed as a national hero.

The following year he was despatched in command of two vessels to explore his landfall and claim it for France.

De Kerguelen-Tremarec reached his discovered land in December 1773. He very soon realised that his discovery was only a large island. He stood off the coast for almost a month and, strangely enough, made only one landing. A ship's boat reached shore in a sheltered bay where a bottle, containing a proclamation claiming the island in the name of France, was deposited in a hurriedly erected cairn.

On his return to France the government did not accept de Kerguelen-Tremarec's report with great enthusiasm. Feeling imposed upon, the authorities had him thrown into prison where he remained until his death. While dying he expressed a wish that his discovery be named the Isle of Desolation; a wish not fulfilled since it is now known as Kerguelen Island.

In the same year Kerguelen Island was discovered, another French navigator, Marion du Fresne, after rounding the Cape of Good Hope, sailed south-east and discovered what is now known as Marion Island. Continuing east he then came across the Crozet Islands, 3000 kilometres away. Both islands are in about 46° south latitude.

Why these intrepid seafarers hastily returned to their homeland after sighting land is difficult to understand. Bad weather alone would not have prevented them from waiting to consolidate their knowledge and prove the accuracy of their claims. They were tough seamen and they would hardly have been influenced by the plague of superstitions surrounding the newly discovered Southern Ocean.

It remained for the great British navigator, Captain James Cook, to reach high southern latitudes and cut the still unseen southern land down to actual size. In 1772, Cook was commissioned by the British Admiralty to sail south in an attempt to circumnavigate the continent, if it existed. Early in January 1773, after a fruitless search for Cape Circoncision (Bouvet Island), he sailed south-east and came in contact with waters covered with broken pack-ice and studded with numerous large icebergs. Undaunted, he forced his ship south and crossed the Antarctic Circle, latitude 66°33′ south, on January 17. Cook wrote in his Journal, "At a quarter past 11 o'clock we crossed the Antarctic Circle and are undoubtedly the first o and only ship that ever crossed that line." Persisting on his southern course he reached 67°33′S, 39°35′E, a position about 100 miles north of what is now known as the Princess Ragnhild Coast.

Faced by impenetrable pack-ice, Cook swung his ship and set a course north to Kerguelen Island where he hoped to make a landing. A week's search in thick fog yielded no sign of the island. Cook then headed south-east, reaching a latitude 61°53′ south, about 300 miles north of what is now Wilkes Land. Heavy pack-ice conditions prevented further southing and after sailing east just north of the 61st parallel, he turned the ship and set a course for New Zealand.

Cook left New Zealand late in November 1773, to continue his circumnavigation of the southern land. On December 15, the ship sailed into waters packed with many large icebergs which threatened the safety of the ship. Undismayed by the severe ice conditions and bitter cold, Cook persisted on an easterly course and six days later crossed the Antarctic Circle north of what is now Marie Byrd Land. On Christmas Day, more than 200 large icebergs were recorded. The ship's deck was covered with snow and ice, the rigging festooned with glistening icicles.

Officers and crew began to show evidence of suffering from the severe cold and Cook sailed north for a short respite in warmer conditions. Several weeks later he again sailed south to renew his attack on the unseen continent. On January 26, 1774, the ship crossed the Antarctic Circle for the third time. Four days later, Cook reached his most southerly point, 71°10'S, 106°54'W, off what is now called the Walgreen Coast. Distance from the South Pole was a little more than 1600 kilometres.

Further progress south was barred by solid pack-ice extending away as far as the eye could see; bergs surrounded the ship in all directions. To the relief of all hands, Cook turned the ship north, planning to return in the summer months to complete his exploration. He had traversed three-quarters of the globe in high latitudes without sighting land.

On his final voyage into the Southern Ocean he passed Cape Horn on December 28, 1774. Several weeks later, he sighted a large mountainous island which he described as, ". . . ice and snow-bound, bleak and barren". He named it South Georgia. A month later he discovered a series of smaller islands and took formal possession of them for Britain, naming them the South Sandwich Group.

Cook, not greatly impressed by these desolate islands, continued his circumnavigation of the globe, finally crossing the track of his first voyage towards the coast in December 1772. He then set a course for Cape Town and sailed into Table Bay on March 21, 1775. Cook was justly proud that he had conquered the effects of scurvy, a dreaded disease among seafarers of those days, by carrying ample supplies of limes. During his voyages of three years and 18 days, he lost four of his crew — only one by sickness. His vessel *Resolution*, a barque of 469 tonnes, carried a crew of 110 men.

Cook was quite sure a great continent did exist. On several occasions, from his most southerly points, he was strongly tempted to record sightings of the continent. In this assumption he was no doubt correct as he described heavy impenetrable pack-ice extending south, followed by unbroken ice rising in level until it disappeared from sight in the distance. A typical description of the continent. At the conclusion of his incredible voyages, overcoming the worst weather in the world and surviving navigation in ice-strewn waters, Cook wrote, "I can be so bold to say no man will venture further south than I have done, and that the land to the south will never be explored."

Following Cook's voyages there were no further exploratory expeditions of importance to the Antarctic for almost half a century. Towards the end of the 18th century British and American sealers and whalers ventured south to exploit the rich harvest of life populating newly discovered subantarctic islands. Sailors, their imaginations fired by reports of untold numbers of seals and whales, sailed into virtually unknown waters in search of this untapped source of wealth. Suffering extreme hardships and in constant danger, they soon developed and established a most lucrative industry which has continued to the present day.

Several of the whaling companies, notably Enderby Brothers of London, interested in new discoveries, at times instructed their captains that when conditions were suitable and the safety of their ship was not threatened, all efforts should be made to reach the southern continent.

First sighting of the Antarctic continent has been credited to Nathaniel Palmer, a 21-year-old captain of the 14-metre sloop, *Hero*. Early in the summer season of 1820–21, while in the vanguard of an American sealing fleet searching for fur seal colonies, he saw and recognised land slightly north of the Antarctic Circle, what is now known as Graham Land. Edward Bransfield and William Smith, two British captains of fur sealing vessels operating in the same area late in 1820, also claim the first sighting of land.

During the years 1819–21, Captain Thaddeus Bellingshausen, in command of a Russian expedition of two vessels, the *Vostock* and the *Mirny*, successfully circumnavigated the Antarctic continent in high southern latitudes, but without sighting land. He crossed the Antarctic Circle on six occasions.

Late in 1820, Bellingshausen had reached 69°06′S, 1°11′W, from where on several occasions he sighted high ice-cliffs extending east and west. These were almost certainly coastal ice-cliffs of the present Kronprinsesse Martha Land. Continuing west, Bellingshausen could hardly believe his eyes when, in January 1821, through heavy mist, he sighted nine sealing vessels at anchor off the rocky western coast of what is now Palmer Land. Sealers were on shore slaughtering a prolific fur seal population, much sought after for their valuable pelts.

Inviting the young Captain Palmer on board his vessel, Bellingshausen learned the extent of his land discoveries. He is recorded as saying, "What do I see and what do I hear from a boy. That he is commander of a tiny boat the size of a launch of my frigate, has pushed his way through storm and ice and sought the point I have for three

17

long weary anxious years searched for day and night. What shall I say to my master [Czar Alexander I]; what will he think of me?"

During the next few years several notable expeditions were despatched to the Antarctic coast by the public-spirited firm of Enderby Brothers. In 1823, they despatched a small brig, *Jane*, accompanied by a cutter, *Beaufoy*, under the command of James Weddell, to look for land below South Georgia and the South Sandwich Islands. Crossing the Antarctic Circle at approximately longitude 32° west, his vessels were confronted by a sea covered by heavy pack-ice and innumerable bergs. For days he forced his way south, finally emerging into open ice-free water. Sailing on, he reached latitude 74°15' south, the farthest south so far attained by any navigator. Open sea still persisted but sickness amongst the crew and diminishing food supply forced him to give up. He had entered and discovered a large indentation of the continent later named the Weddell Sea.

Seven years later, Captain Biscoe, in command of the *Tula*, a schooner of 150 tonnes, and the cutter, *Lively*, of 50 tonnes, was sent south. His instructions were to make every endeavour to reach an entirely unknown part of the Antarctic coast on the opposite side of the continent to the Weddell Sea. On February 25, 1831, Biscoe sighted land south of 66°29'S, 45°17'E, near the western border of the present Australian Antarctic Territory. Sailing west for several days he observed an extensive mountain range and many peaks projecting through the ice-covered continental slope. This was a momentous discovery. For the first time the actual rock mass underlying the continental ice-cap was seen.

Biscoe named his important discovery Enderby Land and six of the highest peaks were named after members of the Enderby family but strangely enough these names have disappeared from present-day maps and charts. Biscoe tenaciously fought continual blizzards and heavy pack-ice in an endeavour to land on the rocky coast, but without success. Most of his crew were down with scurvy and reluctantly he was forced to turn north. The two vessels had parted company some time previously. The *Tula* arrived at Hobart with only a few of the crew able to carry out their duties; several had died. The *Lively* reached Westernport, Victoria, with a death roll of seven of her crew from scurvy.

Members of the scientific staff. Top row: Professor T. Harvey Johnston (senior biologist), Dr W. Ingram (medical officer), the author (assistant zoologist). Middle row: R. C. Simmers (meteorologist), Sir Douglas Mawson (expedition leader), R. A. Falla (ornithologist). Bottom row: E. Douglas (aviator), A. Howard (hydrologist), S. Campbell (aviator).
(By courtesy of the Mawson Institute. Photo: F. Hurley.)

The Enderby Land coast remained unsighted for the next hundred years until it was revisited by the BANZARE voyages of 1929–31 when several landings were made.

In 1833, the Enderby Brothers sent out a square-rigged vessel, *Magnet*, commanded by Captain Peter Kemp, in search of land east of Biscoe's discoveries. He reported the appearance of ice-covered land rising into the interior of the continent. On present-day maps, the sector is named Kemp Land.

A final Enderby expedition of two vessels in charge of Captain John Balleny left England in 1837 to explore the unseen coast between longitudes 150° and 100° east. South of the Antarctic Circle he discovered the Balleny Islands. Sailing west, he reported the doubtful appearance of ice-covered land away to the south. Three weeks later the smaller of his two vessels, *Sabrina*, was lost in a gale with all hands. To commemorate its loss, Mawson, in 1931, added the name Sabrina Coast to his chart while off the coast.

It was now quite apparent that a great continent covering the base of the globe did exist. Nations of the world, now extremely interested, began to send well-equipped expeditions to the southern continent, still shrouded in mystery. The first of these was a French expedition under the leadership of Jules Dumont d'Urville. On January 19, 1840, when in a position 66°S, 140°E, he sighted an extensive coastline of high ice-cliffs. Sailing closer he anchored his ship off an area of ice-free land, rocky headlands and a group of small islets. A party landed and returned with a collection of rocks — first knowledge of the geological structure of the landmass.

Dumont d'Urville named his discovery Adélie Land, after his wife, and claimed the territory in the name of France. On the return journey, his first port of call was Hobart, Tasmania, where he had an edict, claiming the land, published in the *Hobart Town Courier*.

America now began to take an interest in Antarctic exploration. Following exhaustive planning, an expedition comprising six vessels under the command of Captain Charles Wilkes, left Chesapeake Bay, USA in 1838, on a four-year voyage of exploration. The expedition spent a year in the Pacific before reaching Sydney where the ships were refitted. During their stay, geologists collected some of the first invertebrate fossils to be found, in an outcrop of rocks of Permian geological age, in the Hunter Valley of New South Wales. These are now housed in the American Museum of Natural History.

Wilkes, in the *Vincennes*, a vessel of 792 tonnes, sailed south in December 1839 and reached a position near the recently discovered Balleny Islands in January 1840. Sailing south-west, he sighted the Adélie Land coast on January 21, two days after its discovery by Dumont d'Urville. Keeping mainly in open water north of the pack-ice edge, Wilkes repeatedly charted and laid claim to mountainous land to the south. Later it was proved that most of his sightings did not exist and the accuracy of his observations was widely questioned. It would appear that Wilkes, with little experience of Antarctic conditions, was consistently misled by distant icebergs many kilometres in length, which in the usual poor visibility give a false impression of land. Controversy regarding the validity of his land claims still persists. It must be recognised, however, that Wilkes's expedition was an impressive and important one.

Perhaps the most important expedition to Antarctica was carried out by Sir James Clark Ross. Under instructions from the British Admiralty, his objectives were to carry out magnetic observations and make determined efforts to reach the Antarctic continent. Sailing south from Hobart in November 1840, in command of two vessels, the *Erebus* and *Terror*, he passed north of the Balleny Islands and crossed the Antarctic Circle at longitude 171° east. Here he was confronted by a sea studded with immense icebergs and heavy pack-ice extending south to the horizon. By no means intimidated he maintained his southerly course. For nine days he battled his way against ice and gale-force winds until suddenly his ships broke through into an ice-free open sea.

Sailing south-west over what is now called the Ross Sea, he sighted a spectacular mountain range which he traced south for 800 kilometres. It had an average height of 2400 metres with peaks rising to 3000 metres, and to a great extent it was free of ice. In latitude 77½° he observed two volcanoes, 40 kilometres apart, which he named Mt Terror and Mt Erebus. The latter, 4020 metres high, is still active. To this newly discovered land he gave the name Victoria Land.

In about the same latitude, Ross came across a great ice barrier stretching away to the east. Its cliff face ranged in height from 15 to 30 metres. He sailed along this for 400 miles to where it joined the east coast. Ross named this great field of ice the Great Barrier, but it is now known as the Ross Ice Shelf. During his stay in this remarkable new area, Ross made only one landing, on an offshore island near Cape Adare which he gave the name Possession Island.

It can be said that Ross was the first to really discover the Antarctic Continent. Crashing his way into the Ross Sea he opened a gateway providing access to an enormous area of exposed continental rock and a coast suitable for landings and establishment of base huts for future expeditions, an ideal starting point to probe into the continent's unknown hinterland.

For the next half century, nations lost interest in Antarctic exploration and no further important knowledge was sought or gained. It was not until January 1895, that Captain Christensen of the whaler *Antarctic*, finding the sea remarkably free of pack-ice, reached the coast at Cape Adare, the western headland of the Ross Sea. A party went ashore but stayed for only a few hours.

In the same year, Captain Adrien de Gerlache's vessel became frozen in and was trapped in the heavy pack-ice while exploring off the Graham Land coast. Drifting with movements of the pack through the long, dark winter months, the ship was not released until the following summer when the ice broke up. Gerlache and his crew were the first to have the doubtful honour of experiencing a winter in high southern latitudes. On board, the Norwegian explorer Roald Amundsen, destined to be the first to reach the South Pole, had a narrow escape from death during the ship's long drift.

In December 1898, C. E. Borchgrevink, a young Norwegian, led an expedition to the Ross Sea in the vessel *Southern Cross*. A party of 10 men landed at Cape Adare, erected a hut and spent the following winter there. They were the first men to spend a winter on the continent. Little knowledge was gained, as the party was hemmed in by high ice-clad mountains, later named the Admiralty Mountains.

In the meantime, Borchgrevink, a member of the *Antarctic* expedition four years earlier, sailed south in the Ross Sea and reached the ice-cliffs of the Ross Ice Shelf. A small party landed and travelled over it on foot to reach latitude 70°50′ south — the most southerly point so far attained.

Assault on the South Pole

It seems that polar exploration exercises a strange fascination over men who participate in it. Refusing to heed extreme hardships and narrow escapes from death, many have returned again and again to compete against the hazards of the inhospitable ice-covered continent. In some cases it finally claimed their lives.

At the end of the 19th century, existence of the Antarctic Continent was well established. The vast interior, however, was still shrouded in mystery. In fact, so little was known that at a meeting of the Royal Geographical Society in 1893, the Duke of Argyll remarked that more of the planet Mars was known than Antarctica. But this lack of knowledge was soon to be overcome.

The importance of scientific research in the unique south polar environment was strongly stressed by scientific societies and, as a result, future expeditions included scientists. For the first fourteen years of this century, expeditions visited the Antarctic Continent. Five were British, two German, and France, Norway, Japan and Australia each sent one.

Apart from scientific investigations, the main objective of expeditions led by Scott, Shackleton and Amundsen was the planning of long sledging journeys with the ultimate goal of reaching the South Pole.

The honour of breaking open the unknown interior belongs to Captain Robert Falcon Scott, R.N. In 1901, leading a British expedition composed of naval and scientific staff, he was instructed to sail into the Ross Sea and explore Victoria Land. On February 8, 1902, Scott entered McMurdo Sound and anchored his ship, *Discovery*, in a small sheltered bay below the south-western slopes of Mt Erebus. The ship, used later for the BANZARE expedition, remained frozen in at its anchorage for the following two years.

A hut was erected on shore and after settling in, preparations and training began for long sledging journeys planned for the summer months. Scott's hut, because of its historic interest, was completely restored to its original condition in 1960. It stands on Hut Point alongside enormous fuel tanks of America's McMurdo Base, established in 1957.

In November 1902, Scott and two companions, Ernest Shackleton and Dr Wilson, set out to sledge south over the Ross Ice Shelf. With dogs hauling their sledges, they reached latitude 82° 16' south on December 31. At this stage the extremely rough surface of the ice shelf, strong winds and bitter cold had undermined the strength and health of the party. Tainted food had caused the death of some dogs and others died from exhaustion, leaving only six from the original team of 19.

Scott decided to return to the main base. Shackleton's health deteriorated to such an extent that he had to be hauled on a sledge for most of the journey. Finally surviving a punishing task, the party arrived safely back at the hut on February 3. Altogether they had travelled 1545 kilometres in 94 days.

At the end of the winter months, Scott set out from the hut on October 12, 1903, with two supporting parties, to climb the mountain range of Victoria Land and reach the ice plateau which covers most of the continent. Manhandling their sledges, they reached the plateau surface, 2980 metres above sea level, on November 22. The supporting parties now turned back while Scott, with Petty Officer Evans and Stoker Lashley, continued west across the ice-sheet. While traversing a glacier on their ascent they came across the carcasses of two Weddell seals at a height of 1500 metres above sea level. How these slow, lumbering creatures could have climbed to such a height and so far from the sea is beyond understanding.

Scott and his companions continued their march west against appalling conditions. Fighting their way against constant strong winds, interspersed with blizzards and gale-force winds, they reached a position 480 kilometres west of their base at longitude 146° 13' east. During the journey, temperatures never rose above freezing point, usually about minus 30°C, and often reaching minus 40°C.

The party set out on the return journey on December 19. Arriving at the base hut on Christmas Day, Scott found only four men in residence; the remainder were still out on prearranged sledging journeys. Scott's party, on their western trip, had marched 1766 kilometres in 81 days and had climbed heights totalling 6000 metres. This important sledging journey gained knowledge for the first time of the vastness of the polar ice-cap. It also brought home forcibly the frightful conditions that would have to be endured in any attempt to reach the South Pole — 2800 metres above sea level.

The *Discovery* had to be freed from its imprisonment by surrounding ice before returning to England. With the aid of ice-saws and explosives, she was released, after weeks of arduous work, on February 16, 1904. Shackleton, because of illness, had been sent back to England by Scott on the relief ship *Morning*. The ship had brought provisions to the base late in December 1902, and had become frozen in. She was unable to sail for England until March 2, 1903, when she was freed from the ice by explosives.

Shackleton was lionised on his return to London. He was one of the three men who had reached the farthest position south — only 8° from the South Pole. Taking advantage of his popularity, he set about organising an expedition of his own. Finance was soon forthcoming, but it was not until late in 1907 that he sailed south in the *Nimrod*, a former sealing vessel. His objective was to land and form a base at King Edward VII Land, about 650 kilometres east of McMurdo Sound. He was forced, however, to land at Cape Royds, about 32 kilometres north of Scott's base, where a hut was erected. His hut, like Scott's, was restored in 1960. Clothing and footwear used by Shackleton's party still hang on the walls. Equipment, magazines and unopened cases of tinned food-stuffs, all perfectly preserved, give, as one visitor wrote, "an eerie atmosphere of timelessness".

Members of Shackleton's expedition included three Australians: Mawson, David and MacKay. In November 1908, Shackleton and three companions, one of whom was Frank Wild, set out to achieve his ambition of being the first to reach the South Pole. Hauling their sledges they marched across the Ross Ice Shelf and passed Scott's farthest south position of latitude 82°16' on November 26. The party then found a high range of mountains which extended east across their path.

Shackleton ascended the present Beardmore Glacier, an enormous river of ice 190 kilometres long and 65 kilometres wide. They gained the ice plateau at a height of 2000 metres. Continuing south, they marched 320 kilometres to reach latitude 88°23' on January 9, 1909, 3060 metres above sea level and only 156 kilometres from the

South Pole. At this point Shackleton decided it would be suicidal to continue. Recurring winds of gale force, low temperatures and fatigue had brought the party to a state of almost complete exhaustion. It was a wise but heartbreaking decision.

Shackleton and his companions finally reached their base at Cape Royds after experiencing terrible hardships. It was an epic sledging journey as they pioneered a route to the plateau surface and the South Pole; a route followed by Scott on his second and ill-fated expedition.

A year later, following Shackleton's return to England, Scott set out to reach the pole. He also realised that scientific results were equally important and planned an ambitious scientific programme to augment research carried out during his first expedition. He included four biologists, three geologists and two physicists in the expedition's personnel.

On January 4, 1911, his vessel, *Terra Nova*, forced her way through heavy pack-ice into the Ross Sea and reached McMurdo Sound. Here he established his base in the shadow of Mt Erebus at Cape Evans on Ross Island where he organised sledging journeys. One of the most arduous was a visit to a known emperor penguin rookery at Cape Crozier, east of Mt Erebus. The object was to study the birds during their egg-laying season which, unlike all other penguin species, is in midwinter. Leaving on June 25, 1911, a party of three, led by Dr Wilson, hauled two sledges and struggled through continual darkness under the most harrowing conditions to reach their objective. Returning to Cape Evans on August 2 after an absence of five weeks, they told of terrifying experiences. With only a small tent for shelter they had endured blizzard after blizzard with temperatures averaging from minus 38°C to minus 55°C. Cherry-Garrard, a biologist on the journey, later wrote an account of their adventures in a book entitled *The Worst Journey in the World*.

In the meantime, Scott's plans for his dash to the South Pole were well advanced. He was anxious to leave as early as possible in the spring, knowing that Amundsen was sailing south with the one objective — to reach the pole. At Amundsen's last port of call on his way south, Scott received a telegram with a terse message, "Madeira. Am going south. Amundsen."

On his journey of about 1280 kilometres each way, Scott planned to make maximum use of ponies, dogs and the newly invented tractors. These were to carry supplies and establish food depots across the Ross Ice Shelf as far as the Beardmore Glacier — a distance of 640 kilometres. From that point, two parties would man-haul their sledges on to the ice plateau and Scott's party would then march to the pole.

Tractor-hauled sledges left Cape Evans on October 24, 1911. They were to proceed as far as possible, thus easing the load on the pony-hauled sledges which would leave later. It was not an auspicious beginning to the long journey. The tractors made only a little more than one kilometre an hour, with continual assistance from the crews. Three days after reaching the Ross Ice Shelf they broke down beyond repair. Abandoning the tractors, the crews marched on hauling heavily laden sledges.

Scott, with the pony sledges, left Cape Evans on November 1 and was joined by the faster travelling dog teams six days later. The already established One Ton Depot, 210 kilometres from Cape Evans, was reached on the 15th. Both parties then continued, meeting up with the tractor crews on the 21st. After rearranging sledge loads the tractor party returned to the main base. The remainder reached the foot of the Beardmore Glacier on December 10 with only five ponies surviving the cruel conditions. These were killed and most of the flesh stored at an established Lower Glacier Depot for the return journey of the South Pole party.

So far, the parties had been dogged by bad weather. Crossing the Ross Ice Shelf, they had experienced heavy falls of snow, bitterly cold southerly winds and a rough ice surface which called for superhuman efforts to make progress. Ponies plodding through heavy snow suffered badly from frostbite. Dogs burrowed in the snow to escape the cutting winds, apparently suffering no ill effects.

Lower Glacier Depot now became the parting of the ways. Scott sent the dog teams back to the base at Cape Evans while he and eleven men, hauling three sledges, set out on their march to the south on December 9. They struggled up the Beardmore Glacier and on the 22nd reached the ice plateau at a height of 2400 metres. As planned, three men with a sledge left this camp, No. 44, to return to the base, a relatively easy journey, following the line of food depots already laid down.

Battling on over a rough, uneven ice surface, the hauling of the sledges became a nightmare. The party also had to contend with strong icy winds and freezing temperatures. On January 4, 1912, at Camp 57, Scott detailed another three men to return to Cape Evans. Scott, Oates, Bowers, Wilson and Evans, hauling a heavily laden sledge, marched on the final stage of their journey, passing the latitude that Shackleton had reached two years earlier. Visibly weakened from cold and fatigue, they laboured on, finally reaching the South Pole on January 18. One can imagine their agonising distress when they sighted a black flag attached to a sledge runner amidst the remains of a camp. Attached to the flag was a record of the arrival of Amundsen and his four comrades, on December 16, 1911.

Scott wrote in his diary, "Great God, this is an awful place and terrible enough for us to have laboured to it without the reward of priority." He estimated its altitude to be 2895 metres, close to the now known elevation of 2799 metres.

Amundsen's dash to the pole was the acme of perfect planning. His base camp, Frandheim, was established at the Bay of Whales near the eastern extremity of the Ross Ice Shelf. From this point his party left on their southern journey with 52 well-trained dogs to haul their sledges.

Pioneering a new route to the pole by ascending the Axel Heiberg Glacier, about 120 kilometres east of the Beardmore Glacier, Amundsen reached the South Pole in 55 days. The return journey took only 38 days. He arrived at his base camp in perfect health with 12 dogs and a surplus of food. Amundsen had planned to arrive back at his base on January 25, 1912, and did so after sledging 2800 kilometres.

Scott's party was now faced with the overwhelming task of retracing their steps to Cape Evans, more than 1280 kilometres away. They set out on January 18. On that date Scott wrote in his diary, "Now for the run home and a desperate struggle. I wonder if we can do it." Prophetic words. The return journey is now a saga of history. A story of profound courage, intense suffering and unsurpassed tenacity of purpose to combat appalling odds as they staggered back step by step. Following the death of Evans and Oates, they struggled on until they pitched a tent on March 21, 30 kilometres from the safety of One Ton Depot. Fate now stepped in. A blizzard made further progress impossible. Eight days later, food and fuel gave out and they perished.

Early in the spring, a search party noticed a mound of snow under which they found the tent containing the bodies of Scott, Wilson and Bowers. The last pathetic entry in Scott's diary read, "It seems a pity, but I do not think I can write more ... for God's sake look after our people."

On their sledge was found some 15 kilograms of geological specimens, collected by Wilson from exposed sandstones and shales near the top of the Beardmore Glacier. At no time did the party, even for a moment, consider reducing weight by jettisoning the specimens.

It seems that Scott had an underlying prejudice against full use of dogs on his expedition. Before leaving England, he visited the famous Norwegian polar explorer Dr Fridtjof Nansen. When Scott was about to leave, Nansen's parting remark was, "Don't forget — dogs, dogs and dogs."

End of the Heroic Era

Enshrined in the history of Antarctic exploration are the names of Amundsen, Mawson, Scott and Shackleton. Men of indomitable courage and unbelievable endurance, they made incredible sledging journeys into the ice-covered continent. Hauling heavily laden sledges, they persevered under appalling conditions, exploring the unknown interior and pioneering routes to the South and Magnetic Poles.

Sir Douglas Mawson, an idol of the Australian public, was born in Yorkshire in 1882 and arrived in Australia with his parents when he was a child. In 1905, he became lecturer in mineralogy and petrology at the University of Adelaide and was appointed professor of geology and mineralogy 15 years later. Knighted in 1914, he died in 1958.

Mawson's introduction to polar exploration was gained as a member of Shackleton's first expedition to the Antarctic continent in 1908. In March of that year, Mawson, with Professor Edgeworth David and Dr Alistair MacKay as companions, all Australians, set out to climb Mount Erebus, the only active volcano on the continent. They reached the summit, 4075 metres above sea level, and were the first men to scale the treacherous icy slopes. They had fought every inch of the way and were trapped in their tents by a blizzard for two days. But they were amply repaid for their heartbreaking climb of six days as they gazed into a vast crater of simmering heat and steam, 275 metres deep and 800 metres wide, with steam explosions from openings on the bottom.

Shortly before Shackleton left on his attempt to reach the South Pole, plans had been completed for David (the leader), Mawson and MacKay, to proceed on a sledging journey to the location of the South Magnetic Pole. The small party, hauling a sledge half a tonne in weight, left the main base at Cape Royds early in October 1908. After a hazardous journey of two months, north-west along the Ross Sea coast, they reached the Drygalski Glacier. Turning inland at this point, the party dragged their sledge 900 metres up the glacier, finally reaching the vast ice plateau which covers more than two-thirds of the continent. Continuing their march to the north-west over a constantly rising surface, they reached a position where the magnetic needle dipped 89°45'. The Magnetic Pole was reached the following day at 72°25'S, 152°16'E, 2240 metres above sea level. The North and South Magnetic Poles are the two points on the earth's surface where the lines of magnetic force are vertical.

The party was now faced with the long return haul of 420 kilometres to the Drygalski Glacier. Arrangements had previously been made for the expedition's ship, *Nimrod*, expected to arrive at Cape Royds on January 16, to steam north and pick up the Magnetic Pole party on the coast on about February 1. To keep this appointment David and his comrades had to travel 21 kilometres a day. They were weakened by their physical efforts on the outward journey with months of living on meagre rations. David, more weakened than the others — he was 50 years of age — was finally smitten with snow-blindness and handed the leadership over to Mawson who proved to be a most able navigator. Making forced marches, the party eventually arrived at the top of the Drygalski Glacier on January 31 with only two days' food left. Completely exhausted, they hoisted a flag which could be seen from sea.

Early next morning they were awakened by the sound of guns. Rushing out of the tent, they were greeted by the sight of the *Nimrod*, steaming slowly through pack-ice to an anchorage. Although partly planned, the meeting was a remarkable coincidence. The ship's officers had only a vague knowledge of the party's whereabouts and sighted the flag flying high on the glacier.

This sledging trip must rank as one of the most outstanding in polar exploration. The party travelled 2030 kilometres in 122 days. Professor David spoke in glowing terms of Mawson's leadership. He later wrote, "Mawson was the soul of the march to the Magnetic Pole. In him we have an Australian Nansen, a man of infinite resource, splendid spirit, marvellous physique and an indifference to frost and cold that was astonishing — all the attributes of a great explorer."

Mawson was then 26 years of age. Seemingly, perils, hardships and incredible discomforts, synonymous with polar exploration, acted as a challenge rather than a deterrent. He was inspired to dedicate his future to the further unveiling of the Antarctic continent.

He later organised and led the Australasian Antarctic Expedition of 1911–14. His plans were to explore the continent between Cape Adare and Gaussberg, about 3200 kilometres of coast lying south of Australia. The expedition's vessel, *Aurora*, was a 35-year-old sealing vessel, commanded by Captain John K. Davis.

On the way south a party of six men with equipment to establish a radio relay station was landed on Macquarie Island. On January 8, 1912, after battling through the ice for days, an exposure of rock was sighted in a position immediately east of Adélie Land. It was an ideal situation for the establishment of a main base. Preparations immediately began to transport the many tonnes of provisions and equipment ashore. The hut was finally erected on what was named Cape Denison in Commonwealth Bay.

On January 19, the *Aurora* sailed west to establish a second base to be manned by a party of eight under the leadership of Frank Wild. Frequent blizzards, with winds of 80 to 110 kilometres an hour, were encountered and the ship was held up on many occasions by heavy pack. A landing point could not be located and time was beginning to run out. Coal stock was dangerously low for the ship's return to Hobart, 2300 miles away.

In a desperate last bid, Wild and his companions decided to land and form their base on what is now known as the Shackleton Ice Shelf.

This immense sheet of ice, stretching 320 kilometres east and west, extends about 20 kilometres over the sea from the continental ice-cap. Over the next four days, 36 tonnes of stores were landed on the ice shelf, 48 metres above sea level. The ship left on February 19 to return to Hobart.

During the following summer months, sledging journeys totalled almost 1000 kilometres. On one occasion a party of men sledging to the south-west were confined to their tents for 17 days by continual blizzards and heavy falling snow. The newly discovered land, so well explored and charted, was named Queen Mary Land.

In the meantime, a party left for Gaussberg. On the way they discovered and named Haswell Island and Masson Island. They finally reached Gaussberg, an extinct volcano discovered by a German expedition led by Drygalski in 1902. The volcanic peak, rising 425 metres above sea level, is joined to the mainland ice-cap by an ice causeway 180 metres high. Climbing to the summit, the party found a cairn erected by the German party.

Away to the east at the main base, Mawson and his party of 17 companions had settled in. During the dark winter months, continual scientific observations were recorded, at times under terrible conditions. Mawson aptly named Adélie Land the Home of the Blizzard. It is the windiest spot on earth with an average wind velocity, recorded in 1912, of 78 kilometres an hour. This figure included calms and the milder summer months. During the months of May and August the average strength of the wind was 95 kilometres an hour. The worst day was May 14 when, for 24 hours, the average was 145 kilometres an hour.

Early in the spring, sledging parties started to leave the base. First away, on November 9, 1912, were Mawson and his two companions, Lieutenant Ninnis and Dr Mertz. They set out to explore the ice plateau away to the east towards Cape Adare, the western headland of the Ross Sea. Food and equipment were packed on three sledges each weighing 770 kilograms. Seventeen dogs hauled the sledges.

Four weeks later they had reached a point 480 kilometres from the main base. Disaster struck on December 14 when Ninnis, following in the track of Mawson and Mertz, broke through a weakened snow-bridge and plunged to his death with sledge and dogs.

Hurrying back, Mawson and Mertz found a gaping opening, about four metres across, in which they could see only black depths. On a narrow shelf about 30 metres down, a bag of food and two dogs could be seen — one was dead and the other died minutes afterwards. Stunned by the sudden tragedy, Mawson and Mertz later took stock of the situation they now faced.

The loss of Ninnis's sledge and its contents was a catastrophe. Following behind was usually considered the safest and so the best dogs were used. The sledge had contained their only tent, poles, most of the provisions and other important items. Mawson and Mertz were left with food for 10 days and practically none for the remaining six dogs which were in poor condition.

In a state of shock and with the barest of resources, they set out to return to the main base, a distance of 480 kilometres. An improvised tent was made from spare canvas with supports cut from a discarded sledge. Its erection each night after a day's exhausting march, particularly in a strong wind, was almost beyond their combined efforts. In their hearts they must have thought they faced a hopeless task but their talk was always of survival.

On December 17, the last of the six dogs died in its harness from starvation. This source of food which augmented their meagre provisions came to an end. The tough and stringy meat was cut into small pieces and mixed with pemmican, biscuits and raisins, all boiled together. It helped to appease their hunger, but they were always painfully hungry.

Mertz, who had never really recovered from the shock of Ninnis's death, could not stomach the food and was eating less and less, although Mawson gave him a larger ration of the emergency supply. His health began to seriously deteriorate at the beginning of the new year. On January 7, 1913, he was in a shocking condition, suffering from severe frostbite, continual fits and delirium. He could not walk unaided. Mawson helped him into his sleeping bag and he passed away several days later.

Mawson, now alone, was still 200 kilometres from the Commonwealth Bay base. To add to his physical discomfort, skin was peeling from his body, leaving raw painful flesh surfaces. The hardened soles of his feet separated and had to be bandaged back in position. Never faltering in his decision to march on, oblivious to pain, he cut his sledge in half and set out on what was to be an incredible journey. Stumbling and staggering on, defeating death on many occasions, he miraculously reached the safety of Aladdin's Cave on February 1. This was an outpost base, eight kilometres from the main base. His arrival was not a day too soon. A blizzard raged for the next seven days without even a slight let-up and he could not continue. Here, he sheltered with ample food and warmth.

Mawson anxiously waited for the blizzard to cease. On the seventh day the wind had dropped to 50 kilometres an hour, so he decided to fight his way to the main base. Still in a very weakened condition, each kilometre seemed an eternity; each step on his padded feet racked him with pain. Staggering on, he reached a point about a kilometre from the hut where he would be able to see the *Aurora*. It was not at its anchorage. One could well imagine his thoughts. Had the party left, presuming he and his companions had perished? He then saw figures moving around the hut. It seemed ages before he was seen. The first to reach him was Frank Bickerton, one of five men who had volunteered to remain for another year in case the party returned. Mawson's ordeal was over; he had survived against impossible odds.

Bickerton was shocked at the ragged and emaciated appearance of Mawson. Normally weighing 90 kilograms, he was down to half his weight. His face was ravaged by intense suffering and he had completely lost his hair. His features had altered to such an extent that Bickerton at first glance could not recognise him.

A wireless message was sent to Captain Davis on the *Aurora* which had left only the day before to relieve Wild's party at Queen Mary Land, 2250 kilometres to the west. The *Aurora* turned back only to be faced by a full gale which prevented her from entering Commonwealth Bay. After beating up and down for many hours in huge seas with no sign of the gale lifting, Captain Davis decided it was imperative he proceed to the relief of the western party. It was a difficult decision but a correct one as later events proved. Ice was rapidly closing in on the Queen Mary Land coast when the western party was relieved. It is possible that they could not have survived another winter. The *Aurora* then sailed to Australia.

Mawson and his companions, Bickerton, Bage, Madigan, Hodgson and Dr McLean, were now resigned to another long, dark Antarctic winter. Fortunately, they had comfortable quarters and an ample supply of food. Under the care of Dr McLean, Mawson's health improved during their enforced stay, but he had by no means recovered when the party was picked up the following summer on December 12, 1914.

Mawson's battle against most appalling odds was described by Sir Edmund Hillary as, "probably the greatest story of lone survival in polar exploration". A complete account of his remarkable journey was splendidly written by Lennard Bickell in his book *This Accursed Land*, published in 1977.

Apart from the expedition's successful geographical activities, a most ambitious scientific programme was also completed. So much so, it is recognised as one of the great scientific expeditions of its day.

The grand finale of the Heroic Era was Shackleton's adventurous plan to sledge from the head of the Weddell Sea to Cape Evans in the Ross Sea — the first trans-Antarctic crossing. Dogged by ill fortune his expedition is a magnificent story of superb leadership, human endurance and courage.

Late in 1914, Shackleton in his vessel, *Endurance*, entered the Weddell Sea and sailed south to reach the coast of ice-cliffs at its termination. There, he planned to land with a party and establish a base where the crossing party would start out on their sledging journey. Within 30 miles of his objective, the *Endurance* became firmly frozen in thick pack-ice and all efforts to free her failed. Then began a zigzag drift of 281 days covering 1500 miles and finishing up 570 miles north-west of her original imprisonment. Ice pressure and a 160-kilometre-an-hour blizzard crushed the ship to such an extent that she sank below the ice on November 21, 1915.

Realising his ship was doomed, Shackleton had established a camp on the ice with material salvaged from the ship, including three ship's lifeboats. Drifting north, the pack-ice began to break up, forcing the party, time and again, to take to the boats. Finally freed from the pack and with little food remaining, the 28 men, including 11 scientists, survived stormy seas to reach the safety of Elephant Island on April 15, 1916. The men were all suffering from lack of food, bitterly cold winds and incessant snowstorms. Most were suffering from severe frostbite. The future held nothing but despair and chances of their rescue were remote.

Shackleton, realising his men would slowly perish, decided to set out on a rescue bid. On April 24, with five companions, he left Elephant Island in a six-metre-long ship's boat to sail to the inhabited whaling stations on South Georgia, 800 miles to the north-east. It was a perilous voyage against adverse currents and terrifying gales with little chance of success. Twenty-two men, under the leadership of Frank Wild, remained on the desolate island to await the outcome.

Sixteen days later, after a daily struggle to keep themselves alive, the six men were thrown ashore on South Georgia on the opposite side from its whaling stations. With no other alternative, Shackleton, with two companions, Worsley and Crean, set out to cross the almost impassable 2700-metre-high mountain range to organise rescue for his men. Climbing and sliding, mainly in darkness, the three men finally reached the Stromness Whaling Station emaciated and on the verge of collapse. While the other three men were being picked up on the other side of the island, plans were being set in motion to rescue the marooned men on Elephant Island. Three vessels, unsuitable for penetrating heavy pack-ice, failed in their attempts to reach the island. Shackleton's frenzied persistence induced a fourth attempt which was successful. A Chilean trawler reached Elephant Island on August 30, 1916 to find all the men still alive.

On the oppposite side of the Antarctic continent, the *Aurora*, carrying the supporting party for Shackleton's trans-Antarctic attempt, had sailed into the Ross Sea and landed a shore party at Cape Evans in January 1915. A blizzard then blew the ship northward where she later became trapped in solid pack-ice. She drifted for 1200 miles before finally breaking free nine months later when she sailed to New Zealand.

In the meantime, the shore party left at Cape Evans had successfully established food depots on the Ross Ice Shelf. After laying the last depot at the foot of the Beardmore Glacier, latitude 84° south, tragedy struck the party. One man died from scurvy while two others, completely exhausted, were temporarily left at a camp while the remainder sledged to the base for help. Finally rescued, the two men soon regained their health. In May 1916, tragedy struck again. The leader, Dr Macintosh, and a companion, left the base to sledge across sea-ice on a short journey. Shortly after they left a blizzard suddenly swept down from the mountains probably causing the sea-ice to break up and rapidly drift north away from the land. They were not seen again. The survivors of the party were rescued by a relief ship in January 1917, two years after their landing.

The Heroic Era ended on a note of tragedy and also one of unexampled leadership, human endurance and the will to survive under soul-destroying conditions of near starvation and freezing temperatures. Shackleton's unsuccessful but epic expedition received little public notice because it coincided with war in Europe.

The Mechanical Era

The decade after the cessation of hostilities in Europe saw the beginning of the Mechanical Era which was to completely revolutionise Antarctic exploration and scientific research. First came light aeroplanes used for reconnaissance work from ships during the BANZARE and Norwegian expeditions from 1929 to 1931. The first flight over the South Pole was made by Rear-Admiral Byrd in November 1929.

The American Operation High Jump expedition was launched on a grand scale. It arrived in the Ross Sea in 1946 with 13 ships and 4000 men. McMurdo Station was established on Ross Island and is now a township of more than a hundred buildings with laid out and well-lighted streets. It has all essential amenities, a cinema, telephones and a hospital. It also provides laboratories for 10 research teams of visiting scientists. In summer the population is about 1000 men and women, and in the dark winter months there are approximately 200 personnel. Frequent flights to McMurdo Station from Christchurch, New Zealand, are made by giant cargo planes. Ice-breakers and other ships make regular visits to McMurdo between early January and March.

The International Geophysical Year, 1957–58, brought about a great impetus to research in the Antarctic. Scientists concentrated on a programme of coordinated research, embracing biological, medical, earth, and atmospheric sciences. By the early 1950s, nations which had claimed territories had established research stations. Today, there are about 40 research stations scattered over the continent, usually with a change of personnel every 12 months.

Among its other five research stations, the United States has one located at the South Pole, 2799 metres above sea level, established in 1957. Its winter personnel is usually about 20. The Australian Government insists on the validity of its claim to a large sector of the continent, the Australian Antarctic Territory, and its declaration of a 200-nautical-mile fishing zone. In consolidation of its claim, its three research stations, Mawson, Davis and Casey, have been active for many years.

On March 10, 1980, the Soviet Union completed the establishment of a research station, Russkaya, on the coast of Marie Byrd Land. This new station almost completes the encirclement of the continent by Soviet bases. They now consist of seven on the coastline and one, Vostok, well inland.

Most research stations are equipped with almost every conceivable type of mechanical equipment for labour saving and progression across ice, including planes, helicopters, huge ice-moving tractors, snow-cats and motor toboggans. Most of them have interior heating. Long, man-hauled sledging journeys are now only a memory of the painful, heroic past. Air-conditioned tractor trains are now used and have successfully covered long distances over all types of ice and snow terrain for periods of up to three months. Distributed among the vehicles is ample space for food, fuel, equipment and, most important, comfortable living quarters.

At the conclusion of the very successful International Geophysical Year, interested nations drafted an Antarctic Treaty of acceptable rules which would be of benefit to all those actively engaged on the continent. On October 15, 1959, a conference convened at Washington, USA, was attended by Argentina, Australia, Chile, France, Japan, New Zealand, South Africa, Russia, the United Kingdom and the United States of America (the host nation). Belgium and Norway also attended although at that time they had no bases. The terms of the Treaty, unanimously agreed to, were finally ratified on June 13, 1961.

Important items were that Antarctica shall be used for peaceful purposes only; nuclear explosions or disposal of waste materials are prohibited; facilitation and cooperation and free exchange of all scientific investigations; complete freedom of entry to any area south of the 60th degree of latitude. An item of great importance was that all territorial claims be held in abeyance for a period of not less than 30 years. Up to the present time there has been a real and sincere desire of the concerned nations to adhere to the terms of the Treaty.

However, conditions do change over the years and whether the concerned nations will completely adhere to the high ideals of the Treaty remains to be seen. There is already some dissension concerning the validity of claimed lands and the exploitation of mineral possibilities and life in the surrounding seas. Let us hope that reason will finally prevail and the future of the great southern continent will be safeguarded for all time.

PART ONE

FIRST
VOYAGE

October 19, 1929 to April 1, 1930

Planning the Expedition

A T AN IMPERIAL CONFERENCE held in London in 1926, the importance of further exploration and scientific research in the Antarctic quadrant claimed as British Territory, was strongly stressed. It was pointed out that a vital need was to continue and extend exploratory and scientific activities to solidify Britain's territorial rights to what constitutes almost one-third of the continent, extending between the 45th and 160th degrees of east longitude, excluding Adélie Land.

Already Mawson, during his Australasian Antarctic Expedition, 1911–14, had explored and charted at least 1600 kilometres of previously unknown coastline on the eastern part of the claimed British Territory. Scientific results were also outstanding. Following this expedition, Mawson's strong desire to continue his work to the western border beyond Enderby Land was always paramount in his mind.

In July 1927, an Antarctic Committee was set up, supported by the Australian National Research Council. Following several meetings it was decided as a matter of urgency that an Australian Antarctic expedition be planned with Sir Douglas Mawson as leader. The area defined for investigation was the entire coast of the territory over which Britain claimed sovereignty.

The expedition was to consist of two summer cruises. Provision had to be made in the event of the ship being trapped in the ice and frozen in during the winter months.

One of the first major problems was finding a suitable ship; one which could combat heavy pack-ice conditions with some degree of safety. The expedition was extremely fortunate in that the famous historic vessel, *Discovery*, was made available by the British Government. Built in Dundee and launched in 1900 it was expressly designed for the British National Antarctic Expedition of 1901–04. It has been said that the leader, Lieutenant Robert Falcon Scott, did not take her on his second ill-fated expedition because of her extreme rolling propensities. As later events proved during the BANZARE voyages, this could very well be true.

After the return of the Scott expedition the vessel was sold to the Hudson Bay Company for trading purposes. In 1922, she was purchased by the British Government for oceanographic research in waters around the Dependencies of the Falkland Islands. Before being lent to the Australian Government she was refitted at a very high cost, the work taking several years.

As an added aid to the proposed expedition the New Zealand Government provided substantial financial assistance. Because of help given by both countries the expedition received the name British, Australian and New Zealand Antarctic Research Expedition — in short BANZARE. Much needed and welcome financial donations were also provided by private individuals and business firms, chief among them being Mr Macpherson Robertson of Melbourne. He was later knighted and also received an additional honour in having a sector of Antarctica named after him — Mac Robertson Land, lying between the 60th and 73rd degrees of east longitude.

Plans and organisation of the expedition were completed by June 1929. The *Discovery* by this time had moved in and was moored alongside the East India Dock, London. Installation of equipment began and included winches and all gear necessary for the running of complete oceanographic stations. An echo sounder, loaned by the British Admiralty, was also installed. The ship was already equipped with two other depth recorders: an electrically driven Kelvin machine and a steam-driven Lucas machine. Marconi wireless equipment and a short-wave telegraph transmitter would enable communication with the outside world. It was hoped the *Discovery* would be ready to put to sea about August 18.

In command of the *Discovery* was Captain John K. Davis who was also second-in-command of the expedition. He was at that time Director of Navigation under the Commonwealth Government but had received leave of absence from his official duties. Captain Davis was no stranger to the Antarctic as he had been Chief Officer on the *Nimrod* which was Shackleton's vessel on his 1907 expedition. He was also in command of the *Aurora* during Mawson's 1911–14 expedition to Adélie Land and Queen Mary Land.

Ship's officers were: First Officer K. N. MacKenzie, Second Officer W. R. Colbeck, Third Officer J. B. Child, Chief Engineer W. J. Griggs, Second Engineer B. F. Welch and Wireless Officer Petty Officer A. J. Williams, seconded to the expedition from the British Navy. The crew consisted of eight able seamen, not all of them greatly experienced in sail. An outstanding crew member was J. H. Martin, who, we understood, had resigned a commission in the Guards Regiment to join the expedition. He possessed a magnificent physique, about 193 centimetres tall, and amazing strength. Naturally, he was known as "Lofty" and although inexperienced as a blue-water sailor he quickly mastered the intricate ship's rigging and handling of sails. His acquired sailing knowledge was such that he was appointed bosun on the second voyage — a position he well merited. His great strength proved a considerable asset and on several occasions incidents were averted by him which could have resulted in nasty situations.

Also on board the *Discovery* in England were two members of the scientific staff: R. G. Simmers of Wellington, New Zealand, the expedition's meteorologist, and J. W. S. Marr, a hydrological and plankton specialist. Marr was very experienced, having served as chief scientist for several years on the research ship *Discovery II*. He was one of the two Orcadian Scout Patrol Leaders selected by Shackleton to accompany him on the *Quest* to the Antarctic in 1922. On that expedition Shackleton died and was buried at South Georgia.

Frank Hurley, the expedition's photographer and cinemato-grapher — no stranger to the Antarctic — also joined the *Discovery* in England.

Back in Australia the remaining scientific staff — all Australians and New Zealanders — were advised they would be leaving Australia with Sir Douglas on the Blue Funnel liner *Nestor* on September 9, 1929. The *Discovery* would be joined at Cape Town from where she would sail for the south on October 19.

My appointment as assistant zoologist came in a roundabout way. I had been reading with interest press statements concerning Mawson's second expedition to the Antarctic. Early in March 1929, I suggested to the Director of the Australian Museum, at that time Dr Charles Anderson, that our institution should be represented. He agreed and later spoke to Sir Edgeworth David, a member of the Antarctic Committee and also a Trustee of the Australian Museum. I had put myself forward in the hope of being selected as a member of the expedition. I thought my training as one of the scientific staff of the museum would be in my favour. I had also carried out a good deal of field work, including many trips on the state trawlers, collecting and preserving marine life brought up in the nets.

Some time later I was interviewed by Sir Edgeworth David and Dr Orme Masson. Nothing further was heard until early in July when I received a redirected telegram while in Yass, NSW, on field research. Dated July 9, it read, "Antarctic Committee offers you post Assistant Zoologist with special reference taxidermy — salary rate three hundred pounds per annum — please telegraph whether you accept — letter follows giving further details. Rivett for Chairman." Naturally, I lost no time in accepting. My remaining time before departure was devoted mainly to learning the art of skinning birds. The death of a seal at Taronga Park Zoological Gardens was timely. It gave me an opportunity of skinning one of these creatures which I would meet up with during the expedition. It was a laborious task as every vestige of fat has to be removed before the skin can be safely preserved.

Other expedition personnel on the *Nestor* with Sir Douglas

Mawson were Professor T. Harvey Johnston, chief biologist, from South Australia; Dr W. Wilson Ingram, medical officer; Commander Morton H. Moyes, cartographer; A. Howard, hydrologist, from Queensland; R. A. Falla, ornithologist, from New Zealand; and myself. Flying Officer S. C. Campbell and Pilot Officer Eric Douglas were seconded from the RAAF, to fly the two-seater de Havilland Moth seaplane. It would be used for reconnaissance flights to determine pack-ice conditions, and for tracing the Antarctic coastline.

A message from Captain Davis in England informed Sir Douglas that the *Discovery* had completed loading and was leaving London on August 12 to coal at Cardiff. Leaving the dock in boisterous weather the ship was barely clear when a strong gust of wind swept her heavily against South Quay. Fortunately, only very slight damage resulted.

High grade coal briquettes were stowed in every conceivable corner of the ship. Space for the stowage of coal consisted of holds under the wardroom and bunkers flanking the engines on both sides. This normal stowage space for coal allowed for only slightly more than 200 tonnes, inadequate for a long voyage even though sails were the main means of progression. Coal was stacked on the decks almost to gunwale level. Briquettes are made up of compressed anthracite coal with a small amount of pitch to bind the powdered coal together. The blocks — each weighing 11 kilograms — are formed under high pressure in a special press at the Crown Coal Company works at Cardiff.

The *Discovery* left Cardiff for Cape Town on August 18, 1929. Apart from a handful of people on the quayside the *Discovery's* departure in misty rain created little interest. Dock workers cheered and ships' sirens screeched a farewell as she steamed out on her voyage to Cape Town.

Before the ship left the dock Captain Davis ordered a search to be made for stowaways; none were found. However, shortly afterwards a young boy of fourteen years was discovered hiding in a ship's boat tucked well forward under a covering tarpaulin. He was transferred to the pilot ship and returned to shore.

In Sydney, on September 9, 1929, Commander Morton Moyes and I joined the *Nestor* en route to Cape Town. Sir Edgeworth David was among the many friends to say farewell. Punctually at noon the *Nestor* moved away from the wharf and slowly steamed out into the harbour. My last sight was that of Sir Edgeworth, who walked to the very end of the wharf and continued to wave until the ship was lost to view. A cherished possession of mine, now stained by salt water seeping into my cabin on the *Discovery*, is Rudyard Kipling's book *The Day's Work*. It was presented to me before the *Nestor's* departure. Written on the flyleaf was "September 10th, 1929 — Wishing you 'Bon Voyage' and 'Au Revoir' — T. W. Edgeworth David."

At Melbourne, four other members of the expedition boarded the *Nestor*: Flying Officer Campbell, Pilot Officer Eric Douglas, Dr Ingram, who had arrived from Sydney by train, and R. A. Falla from New Zealand. As the ship cast off from Princes Pier an aeroplane of the RAAF swooped low, almost to mast level, and dropped a message of farewell.

Arriving at Adelaide we linked up with Sir Douglas Mawson and Professor Johnston. Expedition members from Australia were now together for the first time. Here I met Sir Douglas, not without some degree of nervousness, but I was soon put at ease by his cheerful greeting and welcoming remarks.

As the *Nestor* steamed across the Indian Ocean to Durban to her first port of call, the *Discovery* was sailing south and following a course down the Atlantic Ocean to Cape Town. We learned later her voyage of 50 days was uneventful, arriving off Cape Town on October 7. According to the local press she was a most picturesque sight approaching Table Bay with all sails set and filled with a moderately light breeze. Sails were lowered and furled as she was met by a tug and towed to No. 1 Berth. It was said she recalled the days when Cape Town docks were filled with sailing vessels of all nationalities, the whole waterfront being a forest of masts and spars.

The *Nestor* entered Table Bay several days after the *Discovery* had arrived from England. As she steamed slowly up the bay, expedition members lined the rail for our first sight of the vessel which was to carry us south to battle against the Antarctic gales and blizzards. When she was sighted there was a general feeling of apprehension. Completely dwarfed by nearby overseas ships she appeared to be very small for the task ahead. The newly arrived members were lodged in a city hotel so that work being carried out on the *Discovery* would not be impeded.

After settling in there was a concerted move to look over the *Discovery* and meet other expedition members who had sailed in her from England. We were met at the dock with a scene of complete confusion. Decks and nearby wharf space were covered by stacks of an indescribable array of packages, cases and general equipment. Simmers and Marr stopped momentarily to greet us and explained that the task of stowage was well under control. When completed, prepared lists would indicate the approximate position of any particular item. "At least," said Simmers, "that is the general idea."

The ship herself was undergoing a final overhaul. The whole organisation of the docks had been most generously placed at the disposal of Captain Davis. We had no chance of meeting the crew as they were scattered over all parts of the rigging, checking and replacing anything which showed signs of wear. Our offers of assistance were gently refused. In the packed atmosphere our presence would no doubt have been a hindrance rather than a help.

I was happy to meet my old friend Frank Hurley. He was jubilant at going south again and determined to make an outstanding photographic record of the expedition. His equipment included five cine-cameras, including one for microscopic shots of marine life. Also 6000 metres of cine-film, 2000 photographic plates, an aerial and a panoramic camera and four other types. It will be remembered that Hurley, at the conclusion of the BANZARE voyages, produced a full-length feature film entitled *The Siege of the South* — an official film of the expedition. It was well received and successfully screened throughout Australia and also overseas.

Several days later, when loading and stowage activities had quietened down, First Officer MacKenzie showed me over the *Discovery*. After a study of her sturdy construction and quarters below decks she appeared to magically increase in size and my original feelings of disquiet at first sight of her were quickly dispelled.

It is doubtful whether present-day tradesmen could build a wooden ship similar to the *Discovery*. Trimming of the timbers called for men skilled in adze work — almost a forgotten art these days. The *Discovery* is 54.5 metres in overall length, a beam of 10.3 metres, and sides of exceptionally strong construction. Its frames are of English oak beams, 28 centimetres thick, grown in form wherever practicable. The main outer planking is 15 centimetres thick of pitch pine or Canadian elm according to position. Covering this is an outside sheathing of greenheart about 10 centimetres thick, and an inner lining of Riga fir, 10 centimetres in thickness.

Spaces between the frames and the inner and outside layers of planking are filled with rock-salt which pickles the wood, preventing dry rot and other forms of wood decay. The rock-salt needs renewing about every three years to remain effective.

The important ice-battering bow section of the ship is of enormous strength. It consists of a network of strong timber girders and struts all firmly held together by bolts — some 2.5 metres long — running almost entirely through the timbers. The forward section of the forecastle is a solid reticulated mass of strong wooden girders. The bow is further strengthened and protected by an outer armour of steel plating extending some distance back on both sides of the stem.

The *Discovery* sailed from England to Cape Town as a barque — a three-masted vessel, square-rigged except for the mizzen mast which was fore and aft rigged. At Cape Town, yards and topgallants were taken down from the mainmast and she sailed south as a barquentine — square-rigged on the foremast and fore and aft rigged on the other two masts. This was done to present as little wind resistance as possible when fighting gale-force winds off the Antarctic coast.

The *Discovery* was powered with a triple expansion steam engine, completely auxiliary to the sails, capable of sending the ship along at a speed of about six knots. To conserve our limited coal supply the engines were to be used only when manoeuvring close inshore, in heavy pack and iceberg-strewn waters, and maintaining headway when riding out raging southern storms.

At the conclusion of the BANZARE voyages the *Discovery*, on her return to England, was finally moored alongside the Thames Embankment. She became a floating museum for relics of Scott's Antarctic expedition and was also used as a training ship for Sea Scouts. Half a century later it was discovered that her wooden hull was rotting because of a fungus in her inner hull shell. Deterioration was so rapid it was considered that the ship would be beyond repair in a few years. The cost of repairs was estimated at £350,000, a sum which, at the time, her owner the Defence Ministry could not afford. A decision concerning her repairs was temporarily set aside. The famous vessel is now being restored in St Catherine's Dock, London, and will join the Maritime Trust's national collection of historic ships, open to visitors in the East Dock.

On the same day that the *Discovery* arrived in Cape Town from England, Captain Lutzow Holm, one of Norway's famous airmen, also arrived by passenger ship. He immediately transferred to the Norwegian oil transport ship *Thoroy* which sailed south that afternoon, accompanied by three whale chasers. They were to join the factory ships *Thorshammer* and *Thor* which were carrying out whaling activities in the vicinity of Bouvet Island. In a press interview Holm said his plans were to join Captain Riiser Larsen who had sailed direct to the Antarctic on the *Thorshammer*. They would then transfer to the *Norvegia*, a small wooden vessel of only 305 tonnes, equipped by the Norwegian Government for whaling research. The *Norvegia* carried two aeroplanes, an American Lockheed, adaptable as either a sea or land plane, and also a seaplane loaned by the Norwegian Navy.

Larsen and Holm were officers of the Norwegian Air Service. The former was navigating officer of the *Norge* in the Amundsen–Ellsworth expedition when that airship flew from Spitzbergen to Alaska. He and Holm were the first to fly to the relief of General Nobile and his crew when their airship *Italia* crashed in the Arctic.

The arrival and hurried departure of Captain Holm from Cape Town naturally aroused considerable speculation, particularly when it became known that their planned activities were virtually in the same area of Antarctica to be explored by Mawson's BANZARE cruises. Sensational articles appeared both in South African and English newspapers with startling headlines suggesting that a race had developed, with the Norwegians planning to raise their flag along the

Antarctic coast ahead of Mawson's expedition.

During his interview with the press at Cape Town, Captain Holm stated that while BANZARE intended to explore some 3200 kilometres of coast, he and Larsen would concentrate their work in a much more limited field. He qualified his statement, however, by adding that they did not definitely know what they were going to do. They were to await further instructions. It does not fall within the scope of this book to record the repercussions resulting from the newspaper publicity and the following rather terse messages at a high diplomatic level which passed between Norway and England. On January 14, 1930, the *Discovery* and the *Norvegia* met by chance off the Enderby Land coast. Both Norwegian airmen came on board and a long, amicable discussion was held with Mawson concerning their activities and future plans.

The programme of the British, Australian and New Zealand Antarctic Research Expedition was fully outlined in instructions issued to Sir Douglas Mawson on September 12, 1929, by the then Prime Minister of Australia, Mr S. M. Bruce. The instructions were as follows:

Being in all respects ready for sea, and having embarked all necessary personnel, equipment and stores, you are to leave Cape Town on October 15th or at the earliest possible date thereafter, and to proceed to Kerguelen Island, calling at the Crozet Islands at your discretion. Having completed coaling at Kerguelen Island you will proceed to the western extremity of Queen Mary Land (west of Mt Gauss), calling at Heard Island en route if you deem it advisable to do so. From thence you will cruise westward to Enderby Land following the coast or ice barrier as circumstances permit to longitude 45° east, and, at your discretion, if conditions are favourable to 40° east. You will then cruise back along the coast eastward to Kemp Land and then to Queen Mary Land and Knox Land, subject to any change of course which you may find it necessary to make either by reason of coaling requirements or otherwise. When conditions make further cruising in Antarctic regions impracticable you will proceed to Australia, calling first at such port in the Commonwealth as may be convenient.

You will use your best endeavours to make a hydrographic survey of the coast and its contiguous waters between the western extremity of Queen Mary Land and Enderby Land at 45°–40° east, such survey to comprise the correct location and charting of coasts, islands, rocks and shoals.

On such lands or islands within the area specified in the preceding paragraph you will plant the British flag wherever you find it practicable to do so, and in so doing you will read the proclamation of annexation as set out in Annexure A to these Sailing

Orders, attach a copy of the proclamation to the flagstaff and place a second copy of the proclamation in a tin at the foot of the flagstaff. You will keep a record of each such act of annexation in the form set out in Annexure B.

During the course of the expedition you will carry out to the best of your ability all scientific work and investigations which it is practicable for you to do in respect of all the matters falling within the competence of the scientific staff which has been selected to accompany you, comprising, amongst other things, meteorological and oceanographic observations and investigations concerning the fauna, notably whales and seals, of the seas, and lands, visited by you, and all matters connected therewith which may assist in the future economic exploitation of such fauna. All written records made, and all specimens of whatever sort taken and preserved, and all negatives and photographs made during the course of the expedition will be the property of the expedition, and you will be responsible that no improper use is made of them by any member of the expedition.

On your arrival in Australia you will furnish the Commonwealth Government with a full report of the work which you have carried out in respect of each and all the objects of the expedition as set out above.

(signed) S. M. Bruce
Prime Minister

BANZARE's programme of work was successfully carried out. In retrospect, however, it is certain that if the ship's captains, on both voyages, had cooperated more fully with Sir Douglas, far more would have been achieved. On the first voyage Captain Davis had been over-anxious for the safety of the ship. He was reluctant to force her through pack-ice when it was reasonably apparent that good southing was possible towards the Antarctic coast. Although Captain Davis showed little enterprise on such occasions, his seamanship in open waters inspired the utmost confidence during violent weather conditions. As winds increased to gale and hurricane force, producing mountainous seas, his normal gloomy and unfriendly manner would be replaced by one of rapt enjoyment as he spent long hours on the bridge until conditions improved. It was also rumoured he had been heard to burst into song.

Captain Davis was not available for the second voyage of BANZARE and command was given to MacKenzie who was Chief Officer on the first voyage. MacKenzie on that voyage left little doubt in the minds of listeners, particularly Sir Douglas, how he deplored Davis's determination not to take the *Discovery* into heavy pack-ice. If only he were in command! His appointment as Master on the second voyage was thought to be a good choice but later events proved this was certainly not the case. Responsibilities of his first command appeared to weigh heavily on his shoulders and he began to depend to a great extent on his officers. He withdrew into himself, practically ignored his friends among the scientists and developed a nervousness which became very apparent in bad weather.

The safety of a ship and her personnel must naturally be the first thought of her Captain. On voyages of exploration, however, certain calculated risks must be taken to accomplish and fulfil planned activities and achieve good results. I could well imagine Sir Douglas's feelings of frustration on occasions when his suggestions to push through heavy, but penetrable pack-ice, towards sighted, unknown land were overruled by the Captain. Particularly as the *Discovery* was constructed to cope with such conditions.

During our stay in Cape Town, members of the scientific staff were officially signed on as able seamen with a wage of one shilling a month. Although our wages were never received we all prized our seaman's discharge with its notation "Conduct Satisfactory". Our duties as seamen were sought only during bad weather and always restricted to deck activities, such as swinging the yards, raising and lowering sails and assisting the helmsman as "lee-man" on the manually controlled helm.

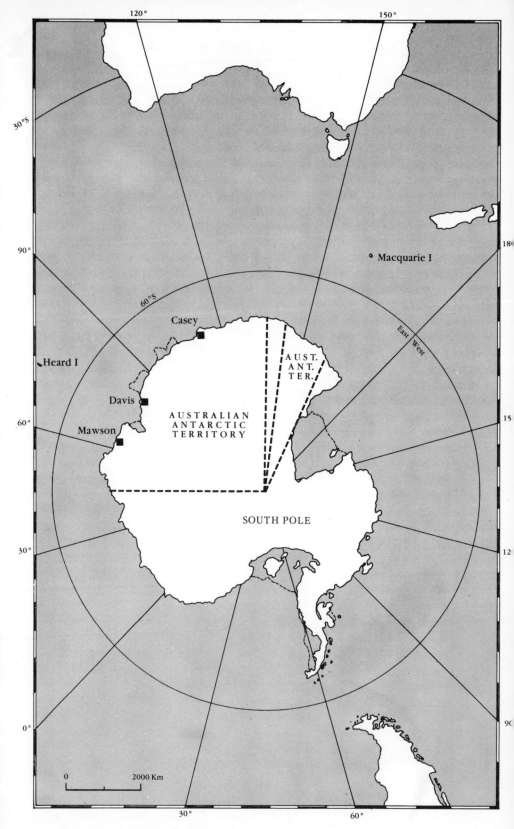

(By courtesy of the Antarctic Division.)

The Antarctic Continent

W E WERE ABOUT to set sail for the inhospitable ice-covered continent. From the combined efforts of earlier expeditions, there had emerged a fairly accurate picture of the vast extent of Antarctica. Large areas of the interior were yet unsighted and many kilometres of its coastline remained unknown. With an area of about 13 million square kilometres, the continent is approximately the size of Europe and the United States combined. The actual continental rock mass, its geological features and mineral wealth, is still undetermined and lies submerged under an immense ice-cap of 29 million cubic kilometres. In places at least three kilometres deep and with an average thickness of two kilometres, it forms an immense plateau surface covering most of the continent, ranging from 2700 to 3600 metres above sea level, with its margins descending rapidly to the coast.

The Antarctic ice-cap controls the safety of the world's coastal cities. If it melted, there would be sufficient water to raise the oceans' levels by 60 to 90 metres.

The ice, under terrific pressure, is forced out to sea to form narrow prolongations or peninsulas of ice, referred to as ice tongues or glacial tongues. Still attached to the continent, they may extend out to sea for up to 150 kilometres. Floating ice extensions surround most of the continent's 20,000 kilometres of coast and have a thickness ranging up to half a kilometre. These tremendous ice tongues may at times give a false impression of the coastline. Early navigators plotting areas as land were later found to be in error because of them.

Each year many millions of tonnes of ice break away from the ice shelves and, driven by wind and currents, drift north as icebergs. Coastal waters are crowded with bergs of varying sizes. Some range up to 320 kilometres long and 100 kilometres wide. Bergs are tabular shaped when calved, generally about 35 metres high and a depth of eight to nine times that under water. As they drift north, weathering produces beautiful and fantastic shapes and designs. Many resemble floating frozen mediaeval castles complete with turrets, battlements and perfect spires.

Each year thousands of millions of tonnes of ice break away from the floating edge of the ice-cap. This astronomical loss of ice is, to a great extent, restored by heavy falls of fresh snow. Indications are that the ice-cap at one time in the past was 300 metres higher than it is today. Ice brought to the surface from a depth of 900 metres, in the form of cores, was deposited as surface snow 51,000 years ago.

With the coming of winter, the sea surrounding the continent begins to freeze. Floating fragments of ice from disintegrated bergs and remaining pack-ice become welded together until the continent is effectively sealed by solid ice for distances of 500 to 650 kilometres from its coast. With the advent of summer (late November and December) the frozen sea ice begins to break up and is navigable for stout ships and ice-breakers.

Antarctica is without doubt the coldest and stormiest continent in the world. Lowest temperatures, averaging about minus 56°C, are experienced on the high inland plateau surface. The average temperature along the coast is about minus 20°C, rarely rising above freezing point even during the summer months. In 1983, the lowest temperature ever recorded was minus 89.6°C at the Russian base, Vostok, located about 1000 kilometres inland at a height of about 3200 metres.

Cold is intensified by deeply chilled winds sweeping down the plateau slopes to the coast. Gathering momentum and force in their descent, they develop unbelievable velocities, lashing the coast as they roar north. Coastal waters are transformed into a raging inferno with spray thrown high in the air to form a dense cloud. It is a wonderful but terrifying sight.

For a large part of the summer months, Antarctica experiences 24 hours' daylight. The sun, when visible, rises slightly above the horizon and after travelling in a great circle at the same angle, sinks from where it emerged 24 hours earlier; a few minutes later it rises again. Later, in the winter months, it disappears below the horizon and the continent is shrouded in darkness for several months.

Knowledge of the ancient life of Antarctica has increased a hundredfold since the Shackleton and Scott journeys. Perfectly preserved fossil plant remains have been collected from rocks of Permian geological age at a number of localities. These sediments were deposited about 225 million years ago.

The richness of the fossil flora is clearly revealed in a sedimentary sequence in the Ohio Range, West Antarctica. This includes numerous coal beds, four metres thick, while the bedding planes contain a profusion and variety of beautifully preserved leaves. Large petrified tree trunks as much as seven metres in length and 60 centimetres in diameter are also embedded in the sediments. A fossil flora such as this suggests a warm, humid climate in which it flourished, forming forests in a swampy environment. Fossil floras of Permian age from all localities in Antarctica are identical with those found in India, Madagascar, South Africa, South America, New Zealand and Australia.

Other interesting finds of ancient life in Antarctica include a fragment of a lower jaw of a primitive amphibian, collected from rocks of Triassic age in the Transantarctic Mountains in 1967. These extinct amphibians, known as labyrinthodonts, were the first known land-living, or terrestrial, vertebrate animals found on the continent. Two years later a skull was found of a creature belonging to an extinct group of mammal-like reptiles. Identified as *Lystriosaurus*, it is identical with other members of the genus found in rocks of the same geological age in South Africa.

Today, Antarctica is an isolated continent, but its geology, fossil flora and fauna tie it very closely with surrounding continents in the southern hemisphere. Plant and animal genera of the past are identical with those in continents thousands of kilometres away. The accepted theory today is that South America, South Africa, India, Madagascar and Australia were once joined together to form an immense continent known as Gondwanaland. In Jurassic times, 145 to 170 million years ago, it is thought that great tectonic stresses cleaved the landmass into four large divisions. They gradually drifted apart through the years, to their present positions.

It is fitting that Antarctica should possess a unique and fascinating bird population. All are sea birds. Most important are two species of penguins — the Adélie and the emperor. Other birds that nest on the continent are restricted in species but occur in large numbers. Nesting places and penguin rookeries are confined mainly to rock outcrops and naturally these areas have a large congregation of bird life in comparison with the greater ice-covered areas.

There are no vertebrate land-living animals endemic to Antarctica. At least five species of seals frequent the coast but rarely venture far inland. Their breeding grounds are usually the surrounding subantarctic islands. Antarctic waters contain an incredible wealth of invertebrate marine life. Rich in plankton, the dominant species is *Euphausia superba*, a small shrimp-like crustacean which serves as the staple diet of most Antarctic animals.

Various whale species, including the massive blue whale, frequent the Southern Ocean. For almost the past two centuries whaling operations have resulted in the killing of a very large number of whales. The day of reckoning, however, is near at hand because today these giant creatures are heading for extinction.

A Great Farewell from Cape Town

O N OCTOBER 19, 1929, the *Discovery* was ready to sail south as planned. Before sailing, a representative of the crew approached Captain Davis with a request that canvas dodgers be fitted over railings surrounding the navigation bridge. Completely uncovered, the helmsman and officers on watch had no protection against the elements other than their heavy, thick clothing. The request was refused with the remark, "Captain Cook didn't have dodgers on his ship and neither will we." This appeared to be a harsh decision, but no doubt Captain Davis with his experience in navigating through ice-strewn waters considered a clear, uninterrupted, all-round view essential. However, on the second cruise, dodgers were fitted; they offered no difficulties and proved a great comfort.

Coal briquettes had been stacked in every corner of the ship including the bathroom and even the bath. It was assumed that not too many expedition members would be indulging in cold plunge baths even if fresh water was available. At the last moment dynamite was taken on board and stored in a safe place. It would be used as a last resort to free the ship if she were trapped in frozen pack-ice with little prospect of release. Finally 15 sheep were manhandled on board and penned on a raised decking. Sufficient feed to keep them alive was stacked nearby until we reached low temperatures. Many cases of oranges and eggs were stowed on the poop deck. Some time after leaving Cape Town, eggs produced at meals were politely but firmly refused, having reached a stage which caused strong symptoms of nausea at close quarters. The cases later became covered with snow and were forgotten.

At the stroke of 10 A.M., ropes were cast off and the S. Y. *Discovery*, assisted by a tug, moved out into Table Bay. She was flying the burgee of the Royal Thames Yacht Club, the Blue Ensign aft and a white flag hoisted at a masthead, indicating an Antarctic voyage.

Many messages of goodwill and Godspeed were received by Sir Douglas Mawson. The *Cape Times* in their morning edition bid the expedition farewell, stating that the gallant enterprise would be followed with the deepest interest and the good wishes of the whole of South Africa. Messages were received from Australia, New Zealand, Britain and other countries. Finally, a message from the King: "The Queen and

I send you and all members of the expedition our best wishes for your success and safe journey." Sir Douglas had already paid a tribute to South Africa's interest in the expedition and said that if it had been their own expedition they could not have given more assistance.

We were given a great farewell as the *Discovery* moved out from the dock. Every steamer gave blast after blast on their sirens. Responding to the cheers and singing of "Auld Lang Syne" by visitors on the quayside, Sir Douglas led responding cheers. Frank Hurley recorded the farewell scene on cine-film from high in the rigging, where we later found he was just as much at home, even in the most boisterous weather, as in his darkroom.

Reaching midstream, the tug's towline was released and the *Discovery* steamed out of Table Bay on the start of her long southern voyage. For the first time the 37 members of the expedition were together. Most of the scientists remained on deck as we steamed at half-speed down the coast. Our last farewell was from Robert Blake who had entertained some of us at Cape Town. Flying his Gipsy Moth, he circled the ship several times before dipping its wings in salute and heading back home. At noon, the ship had covered 12 miles and our first midday position was 33°55'S, 18°17'E. At 4 P.M., the ship was swung and the compasses corrected for deviation. She was then headed on a south-easterly course for our first objective — Marion Island.

Scientists, or passengers, as Captain Davis called us, had disappeared below deck and were busily engaged in unpacking and settling into our various allotted cabins. Professor Johnston and I shared the cabin used by Scott on his 1901 Antarctic expedition. Regaining the deck, I found Falla already there, complete with binoculars, identifying birds circling and following the ship. As I was to assist him in this undertaking he informed me that he planned a daily record of bird identifications, their frequency and numbers. He proposed to make a count at each hour between 8 A.M. and 5 P.M. Resulting observations over the whole oceanic regions traversed would provide interesting information, particularly on the distribution of species.

Since leaving Cape Town we had passed many large flocks of coastal birds. Most abundant were cape cormorants, locally known as "ink drinkers" because of their general black plumage. In Table Bay, thousands of these birds frequented the water in pursuit of small fish. They are important as guano producers and on the offshore Robin Island large deposits are controlled by the government. Throughout the day large flocks followed the ship but next morning none were in sight.

Other coastal species included great numbers of jackass penguins excitedly porpoising around the ship, Dominican gulls and greater shearwaters. The only species with a southern distribution was a solitary giant petrel. Several terns which could not be specifically identified were seen standing on a large dead eel floating on the sea.

Campbell and I assisted Sir Douglas in checking packing cases, with a stowage list, in the scientific equipment hold. Markings on each case had to be checked, necessitating many movements — an exciting procedure in a hold with little spare space, in semi-darkness and the always present risk of cases becoming lethal missiles as the ship rolled. This task was the forerunner of many checkings and rechecking of cases in various holds during the voyage.

Later in the afternoon, several tonnes of coal briquettes, from those stacked on deck, were moved to a bunker by Sir Douglas, Simmers and myself. As coal was consumed it was left to the scientists to fill the bunkers, usually Sir Douglas, Ingram, Campbell, Simmers and myself. This was carried out by members of the coal gang forming a chain and briquettes being thrown one to the other. According to distance of movement others would be invited to lengthen the chain. Even though a briquette weighed 11 kilograms, one suffered loss of face if one was dropped, no allowance being made for the erratic rolling of the ship.

I had read of the rolling propensities of the *Discovery*, but was not prepared for her behaviour in a comparatively light swell and calm sea. My misgivings at what could be expected in heavy seas were later borne out. Rolls of up to 40 degrees were commonplace and at times 50 degrees were experienced. Our only casualty from seasickness was "Doc" Ingram.

The next morning was perfect with a light breeze and calm sea. Coastal birds were left behind and subantarctic species began to make their appearance. Cape hens were with us all day, usually in flocks of about 40 and never less than 10 in number. A single wandering albatross continually followed the ship. We never tired of watching its effortless, graceful flight. Yellow-nosed mollymawks were regularly sighted until 10 days out at sea and were not seen again until our return to the Australian coast. They have a temperate range. Small flocks of terns and prions (whale birds) were noticed feeding but too far off for accurate identification.

At noon, the ship had covered 79 nautical miles under sail since midday the previous day. In the late afternoon the wind freshened from the south-east bringing with it light squalls of rain. The penned sheep were standing up very well to their exposed position and rolling of the ship although looking rather dejected. One was killed to replenish our diminishing fresh meat supply.

Campbell had not been at all well and retired to his bunk. During our stay in Cape Town he had contracted a severe attack of influenza from which he thought he had recovered. However, his temperature was 40.5°C and Doc Ingram, diagnosing pneumonia, was worried about his condition.

Perfect weather conditions continued into the following day, a warm sun, light breeze and a very calm sea. Whales were sighted for the first time. Six finners and a sei, 9 to 12 metres in length, cruised slowly past the ship. I spent most of the day with Sir Douglas and "Babe" Marr in the scientific hold. Cases were opened, their contents checked and repacked, then they were stowed so that those with essential equipment would be readily available when required. It reminded me of a game of chess.

Campbell's illness was casting a gloom over the ship; his temperature remaining dangerously high. Doc Ingram was in constant attendance and was satisfied with his condition. No one was allowed to visit Campbell in his cabin.

At noon the ship had logged 113 miles and reached latitude 36°49′ south. During the afternoon a plankton tow net with a mouth opening of one metre was lowered over the ship's stern and towed obliquely for 30 minutes at a speed of two knots. The resulting haul of plankton was sorted later in the deck laboratory according to their zoological classifications and preserved in a four per cent solution of formalin and sea water. Each container was labelled with the exact position of the netting, latitude and longitude, and recorded as Station 1.

Plankton is a term given to an immense population of floating, swimming or drifting marine life as distinct from coastal and bottom-living forms. On many occasions when the sea was flat calm, I would lie on the safety net under the bowsprit and watch the never ending variety of plankton organisms streaming past in the clear surface water. The galaxy of prolific, fantastic creatures was beyond description.

The morning of the 22nd broke fine and sunny. A light breeze from the west freshened during the morning, later veering to the south and increasing in violence. Early in the morning, about four tonnes of coal briquettes were moved from part of the forward deck to an empty bunker.

By midday the wind had increased to gale force. The ship pitched and rolled in the heavy seas, the decks flooded by huge waves crashing over the forecastle head and gunwales. Each extra heavy roll was at times followed by the noise of articles — thought to be well chocked — coming adrift and sliding and bumping in most cabins. Scientists were called upon to assist in swinging the yards, slackening and hauling in on the braces. Waves sweeping over the gunwale repeatedly lifted us off our feet. Floating and grimly hanging on to a brace, we waited for the wave to recede when, regaining our feet, we continued hauling. To prevent the yard swinging free and out of control as we floated, Lofty Martin jammed his fist holding the brace between the two rollers on the gunwale, thus preventing movement. An exciting introduction to our first storm at sea.

Sailing with most sails set, the ship's speed had increased to seven knots. At noon, our position was 37°33′S, 21°35′E, after a distance run of 127 miles. No new bird arrivals were recorded during the day. Wandering albatrosses, however, had increased in number.

Next morning the wind had eased slightly although a heavy sea was still running. Good progress was being made under sail. During the night, to gain assistance from the southerly wind, the ship's course was altered to the north-east making easting at the expense of mileage on our south-easterly course.

At midday 142 miles had been covered during the past 24 hours, but because of changes in our course, our run to Marion Island was only 85 miles. The ship was still rolling heavily and occasionally seas swept on board. Scientists were issued with rubber sea boots — a great comfort as the decks were frequently awash.

Early in the afternoon the ship's course was altered to south-east and we headed directly for Marion Island. Sails were taken in and we proceeded under steam. A sheep in a very weakened condition was killed.

A small flock of black-bellied storm petrels was an addition to the ship's usual bird followers. This species has a strange habit of occasionally turning over sideways when in flight. Hurley caught an immature albatross on a fishing line with a shining triangular piece of metal attached at the end. With the metal caught in its beak the bird was hauled on board. Its wingspread was 3.1 metres and it weighed 7.25 kilograms. It was the first of many birds that would be skinned during the course of the expedition.

There was good news concerning "Stu" Campbell. Doc reported an improvement in his condition and he was well on the way to recovery. We were given permission to visit him. It would have been of great benefit to him to leave the fug of his cabin and enjoy the beautiful germ-free fresh air on deck.

On October 24, the wind had dropped to a moderately light breeze with an overcast sky and occasional glimpses of the sun. Later in the morning the wind veered to the west and began to increase in strength. Sails were furled and we continued on our south-easterly course under engine power. The last of the coal briquettes stowed on deck were moved into a bunker from which coal had been consumed.

At noon our distance covered since midday the previous day was only 84 miles and we had reached 38°09′S, 23°48′E. A depth of 4770 metres was recorded on the echo sounder. Progress had been slow. Since leaving Cape Town, five days earlier, we had covered only 400 miles.

Later, the wind had increased considerably in strength. Sails were again raised and the ship, appreciating a following wind, ploughed through the rising sea at between six and seven knots. Very soon the wind was blowing at almost gale force. Big seas repeatedly swept on board and once again the decks were awash. The *Discovery* was by no means a dry ship. She rolled continuously at about 30 to 35 degrees — a crazy habit we were getting used to as we gained our sea legs.

Shortly before midnight, Captain Davis ordered sails to be taken in and furled. It was an awe-inspiring sight on deck. Pitch black, except for a ghostly phosphorescent glow; huge waves crashed over the bow and gunwales, made even more eerie by the high-pitched scream of the wind as it whipped through the rigging. In the midst of all this, crew members climbed aloft to take in and furl sails. Immediately lost to sight in the darkness, one was reminded of their presence when they later dropped, one by one, on deck. Remarking to one of the sailors on his unenviable task under such terrible conditions, he said, "Why, this is only a light breeze, no worry at all."

The weather improved the next morning; wind had dropped considerably and the sea was moderately calm. A heavy swell, however, ran in from the west. At the height of the storm earlier on, most of the cabins occupied by the scientific staff were inundated by sea water forcing its way through unsuspected openings. My cabin, shared by Professor Johnston, received more than its fair share, particularly my bunk, and a drying out of the contents took some time.

Our motor boat engine was checked by Eric Douglas and found to be in perfect condition. About 5.5 metres in length, the boat had a small cabin forward which could be detached. It was specially constructed by a Tasmanian boat builder who had provided similar types for use in the Australian light house service. It was shipped to Cape Town and housed together with the Moth seaplane on a grating above deck, in a space usually occupied by the two ship's lifeboats which were left behind.

Bad weather made little difference in the number of birds following the ship. Albatrosses revel in boisterous conditions, and they were a source of great admiration as they skilfully utilised the wind to their advantage in flight.

We were informed by Sir Douglas that owing to our slow passage he had decided to bypass Marion Island and proceed directly to the Crozet Islands, about 1100 miles away on an easterly course.

By midday the next day we had reached latitude 40°27' south after a distance run of 256 miles over the past 48 hours. We had now entered the degrees of latitude known as the Roaring Forties. Seas in this belt of ocean, recognised as the worst in the world, run free and almost uninterrupted right around the globe. Prevailing westerly winds, usually at gale force, create seas of phenomenal size.

Early navigators who ventured into these waters told of mountainous seas which threatened time and time again to engulf their small ships. These stories were received for the most part with disbelief and treated as exaggerated seafarers' yarns. In January 1931, towards the end of our second voyage, we sailed into the Forties north of Enderby Land during a westerly gale. Seas of colossal size were encountered which all hands estimated to be at least 60 metres from trough to crest. A further description of these waves is included later in this narrative.

During the afternoon sails were lowered and the engines started, to enable a tow netting to be carried out. When the net was ready to be lowered over the stern Doc Ingram said he would ask Captain Davis to reduce speed to two knots. Hurrying on to the bridge and before he could speak he was met with a shouted order of "Get off the bridge." Somewhat subdued, Doc quickly regained the deck, realising he had encroached on hallowed ground. The skipper, a most delightful friend on shore, was a martinet at sea.

Finally, speed was reduced and the net was towed for 20 minutes at two knots. A good plankton catch resulted, keeping Marr and Johnston occupied for the remainder of the day.

This was our first Saturday night on board since leaving Cape Town. Following tradition, Sir Douglas produced two bottles of Australian port and we solemnly drank a toast to "our wives and sweethearts, may they never meet". Mellowed by a single glass of port, the evening continued with a variety of songs, mainly ditties and reminiscences of past experiences. All most interesting, but it soon became obvious that many stories were embellished from vivid imaginations. Our best and most amusing storyteller was Doc, who had an inexhaustible supply which he related in his own inimitable style. Saturday nights were always looked forward to as an evening of complete relaxation and enjoyment.

October 27 broke with a heavy, overcast sky and persistent rain. Antarctic clothing and oilskins were issued to the scientific staff. Before leaving Australia measurements of each member had been forwarded to the manufacturer and fittings of most garments were satisfactory. However, in a few cases alterations were necessary with occasional startling results by unskilled needle operators. A record distance run of 142 miles was logged and our position was 41°20'S, 30°52'E.

Birds followed the ship in considerable numbers. Wandering albatrosses had increased and as many as eight consistently followed in our wake. Large flocks of prions had appeared including the medium-billed prion and the broad-billed prion — species which breed on the Marion and Crozet Islands.

Through the night and the next morning a strong westerly wind had been driving the ship along at a steady six knots. At midday we had covered 157 miles, beating the previous day's record run. Later in the afternoon the barometer began to fall rapidly. In readiness for the expected blow, the upper fore topsails were taken in.

At 10 P.M., the wind had increased to gale force from the north-west with a following heavy sea, causing the ship to continually swing away off course. It took the efforts of two men on the manually controlled helm to keep her steady. Once again seas were constantly shipped and the decks covered with swirling sea water. Several rolls of 35 degrees were recorded.

The weather began to moderate early the next morning, although the wind was still blowing in strength from the north-west. During the night, an extra heavy roll of the ship hurled Professor Johnston from his bunk on to a writing desk before landing on the deck. He was visibly shaken, but escaped with only severe bruises. He later asked Doc for something to anoint these with and also treatment to ease an attack of lumbago. Doc arrived with several pads and some liniment and advised Professor Johnston to turn in for the rest of the day. In the throes of seasickness Doc lay down on Johnston's bunk and immediately went to sleep. We wakened him several hours later to make way for his lumbago patient.

Campbell was well on his way to a complete recovery. He had been on deck and was almost his old self again.

Three of the sheep, suffering from continual exposure to the weather and particularly the previous night's gale, were put out of their misery and their carcasses hung in the rigging. The remainder were in reasonably good condition. It was planned to put them ashore on Kerguelen Island, if they survived that long, to recuperate before we left for the Antarctic.

The first appearance of a sooty albatross was recorded by Falla. These birds have a beautiful gliding flight and make slow turns by using the outspread webs of their feet as brakes. A wandering albatross was captured by Hurley, again using a baited triangle attached to a line. When the bait is taken a steady strain on the line keeps the triangle jammed in the bird's beak. Hauled alongside, it was lifted on board in a landing net. Most sea birds are infested with lice and other parasites. Professor Johnston, a specialist in parasitology, zealously searched the feathers for lice and the intestines for other parasites. A second albatross was captured and kept alive until Falla could take measurements next morning. It was left wandering around the deck and disappeared in the night, helped over the side by a Cockney stoker who claimed that while going on duty he was attacked by "the bluidy voolture".

Helped along by the strong westerly, the ship covered a distance run of 165 miles. Our position at midday was 42°38'S, 37°50'E, about 100 miles directly north of the Marion and Prince Edward Islands. At our present rate of speed we would arrive off the Crozet Islands in about five days.

It rained on and off throughout the following day with a light, bitterly cold wind. It was October 30 and driving sleet and falls of snow were experienced for the first time; the deck and rigging were covered with a white mantle. Woollen gloves and balaclavas were brought into constant use when working on deck.

About 20 small-finned whales, also known as blackfish or pilot whales, cruised for some time close to the ship's side. They were readily identified by their general black colour, a whitish patch behind a small, narrow, pointed dorsal fin and a narrow band of white extending from the mouth to the flippers. Birds following the ship were essentially the same. Black-bellied storm petrels were appearing in large flocks. The species breeds in the Antarctic and subantarctic in the summer and moves north during the winter months.

Early in the morning the wind swung to the east and was slightly retarding our progress but, nevertheless, 146 miles were logged for our 24-hour run. Our position at midday was 43°36'S, 41°03'E. A heavy swell was still running from the west. Strong winds, once again from the west, gradually increased during the next day, accompanied by sleet and snowstorms. Deck temperature was 2°C.

Sir Douglas, Marr and I made an attempt to continue our task of checking contents of cases in the scientific hold. Erratic movements of the ship as she wallowed on her way through the heavy seas made the handling of cases too dangerous and we beat a hasty retreat. Little work could be accomplished under the stormy conditions; even reading was difficult.

At midday on November 1, 317 miles had been covered during the past 48 hours and a position had been reached about 70 miles NNW of Hog Island, one of the most westerly of the Crozet Group. A course was kept well to the north and the echo sounder was in continual use as we were in uncharted waters. Soundings registered a depth of 2760 metres at 5 P.M. Three hours later a reading of 560 metres was recorded. Sails were taken in and furled during the night and we proceeded under engine power. Our objective was to reach Possession Island, 73 miles to the east, where it was proposed to land and stay for several days.

Nearing the island the number of birds had increased. A new arrival was identified by Falla as the blue petrel, a species which we later found was concentrated around the Crozets, Kerguelen and Heard Islands.

Next morning a fairly strong wind was blowing from the north-west with bright sunshine and a moderately calm sea. On course to Possession Island, the largest of the Crozet Group, we passed Hog Island and the Apostle Rocks. Moyes later reported that hourly soundings had proved that a deep underwater channel separated those two prominent features from Possession Island.

At 5 A.M., while on watch, MacKenzie sighted what he concluded to be an island in a position not shown on the chart. Its bearing was about 20 miles north-east of Hog Island. He had made a rough sketch of its outline and pointed it out to the helmsman. He did not call either Captain Davis or Sir Douglas to verify his sighting. An island in that position is not shown on a chart completed several years before by a French expedition which had established a base on Hog Island. It was finally decided that MacKenzie must have seen a local dense fog patch or a large northerly drifting iceberg.

Steaming close inshore past the western end of Possession Island, a high pinnacle of rock was observed to be penetrated by a large opening or archway. This interesting example of erosion is aptly named Perforated Rock. Coastal cliffs around the island rise sheer from the sea and landings are only possible at American Bay, where we were heading, and Ship Bay on the east coast.

The Crozet Group consists of five main islands: Hog, Apostle Rocks, Penguin, East and Possession. The last named is the largest. Roughly rectangular in shape it is about 22 kilometres long by 11 kilometres wide. Snow-capped highlands include two mountains towering to about 1500 metres above sea level.

At midday the *Discovery* steamed into American Bay on the north-east coast. As we rounded the western headland a cry from the look out, "Ship on the starboard bow," caused a great deal of surprise. At the time, however, all attention was being devoted to anchoring the ship, a task which was finally completed at 2.30 P.M., in 64 metres.

HMV artists entertain officers and scientific staff aboard the Discovery. *(By courtesy of the Mawson Institute. Photo: F. Hurley.)*

Slaughter on Possession Island

W HILE ANCHORS were being lowered and checked to be holding, hasty preparations were in progress to land a shore party of scientists to make the most of the remaining daylight. A heavy swell created difficulties in boarding the motor boat, already lowered over the side together with a small dinghy. In the meantime, the ship anchored nearby was identified as the *Kilfinora*, a sealing vessel flying the house flag of Irvin and Johnston of Cape Town. Most of her crew were ashore.

As the last of the shore party clambered on board the motor boat, we set off for the beach with Sir Douglas at the tiller. The dinghy being towed behind was leaking badly and quickly filled with water and had to be bailed out. The motor boat was anchored outside the first line of breakers. Several trips were made through the heavy surf, miraculously without capsizing, and finally all hands and their gear were safely onshore. Everyone was soaked to the skin from the waist down and had their sea boots full of water.

On shore we were greeted by some of the sealers with hands dripping with blood from their task of flensing slaughtered sea elephants. We were told it would be at least another two days before their work was completed. The beach was a scene of carnage — an appalling sight with dead and dying sea elephants covering the black volcanic sands of the beach.

We learned the sealers start at one end of the beach and with high-velocity rifles shoot the large bulls and cows. Followers, armed with clubs, kill the smaller cows and pups. In the wake of the killers, flensers strip the thick layer of blubber from the still-warm carcasses. The blubber is then tied together in large bundles and floated out to the sealing vessel for later treatment. From a fully grown bull sea elephant the yield of blubber is approximately 900 kilograms which, when boiled, produces almost half a tonne of oil.

Killing was still going on at the far end of the beach, judging from the rifle shots heard. It was not hard to guess that when the sealers left, not a single sea elephant, young or old, would survive. The sealers were obviously poaching because the French Government had for many years proclaimed the Crozet Islands, together with Kerguelen Island and other possessions in the subantarctic, as national parks of refuge for marine mammals and penguins.

Adding to this macabre scene of utter destruction were the

gruesome activities of giant petrels and skua gulls. Both species prowled over the sea elephant carcasses probing and digging their strong beaks, with a strange air of obscene detachment, into the intestines. They obviously revelled in their feasting, hopping around and flapping their wings and quarrelling amongst themselves.

Giant petrels, also aptly known as "stinkers", are large birds, varying in colour from black to shades of brown. Their flight, although somewhat laboured, is powerful and graceful. Landings are clumsy. When they are about to land they beat their wings furiously to cut speed and alight awkwardly and stiff-legged. When feasting they gorge themselves to bursting point, so much so that it is impossible for them to take off. When alarmed they waddle along the beach in an erratic, grotesque manner, frantically beating their wings in an attempt to lift from the ground. Flight is achieved only after the stomach content has been disgorged.

Southern skuas were living up to their reputation as "scavengers of the south". Extremely pugnacious they will repeatedly dive-bomb intruders within the vicinity of their nests — a nerve-racking experience.

Bull sea elephants begin arriving at the subantarctic islands early in August, the females or cows following about a month later. Most of the summer season is then spent ashore; beaches and low-lying marshy areas becoming crowded with them to such an extent it is almost impossible to walk between them.

Bull elephants may attain a length of from five to six metres — almost twice the length of an average female — and may weigh up to three tonnes. The name is derived from a fleshy prolongation of the nostril, giving the appearance of a trunk. Bulls show their displeasure when disturbed by raising themselves on their front flippers and adopt a threatening attitude with wide open mouths and loud roaring; the trunk is also dilated to a great extent. If the intruder still stands his ground they will attack by propelling themselves forwards by muscular undulations of the body.

Early in the summer season, each bull elephant gathers together about 20 to 30 cows and herds them in a circle where he then jealously guards his adopted family. Any attempt by another bull to take over his harem results in prolonged fierce and bloody fights.

Most of our party had moved inland, but Professor Johnston walked along the beach to an area not yet reached by the sealers. He was interested in observing the mating habits of sea elephants. We learned later that while determining the body temperatures of several cows he inserted long glass thermometers into the vagina. On two occasions the cows twitched during the process, breaking the thermometer, and the broken half was left deeply embedded. It was perhaps fortunate that there were no survivors from the slaughter otherwise some unlucky bull would have received a severe and unpleasant shock.

As Falla, Ingram and I wandered inland, we came across many sea elephant wallows beyond the beach and some distance inland. Used by sea elephants over the years they consist of large areas of soft mud, of sufficient depth and consistency to make it difficult to extricate oneself if unfortunate enough to walk or fall into one.

Our first introduction to the subantarctic penguin species was when we came across a breeding colony of about 40 Gentoo penguins. Attractive medium-sized birds, weighing about seven kilograms, they have a black back, white front and white patch over each eye, joined by a thin band of white across the head. A number of them walked across to inspect us at close quarters, showing no signs of fear. Their stately walk and dignified demeanour were most impressive. Young birds covered with down were as large as the adults, but beginning to moult. To reach that stage, egg laying must have commenced in July or August. Altogether, five rookeries of Gentoo penguins were found at American Bay; one was about a kilometre from the beach at an elevation of about 60 metres. The total number of Gentoos seen was estimated at about 250.

Falla and I decided to make for a low hill on the eastern side of the valley in search of nesting birds. Crossing the valley proved to be an exciting and hazardous journey. On many occasions we sank to our knees in the soft, boggy surface covered with dense, low vegetation. Several swift-flowing streams carrying thaw water from the ice-clad mountains to the sea were crossed by wading waist high. In no time our Burberries became frozen on the outside but our woollen underclothing kept us reasonably warm.

Reaching the summit of our objective, a heavy fall of snow completely blotted out the landscape. When the snow cleared we were greeted by a magnificent panoramic view of American Bay and Ship Bay away to the east. Nearby was an extinct volcanic crater, its eastern wall well preserved but weathering over many years had completely disintegrated its western side. Surrounding lava had been eroded into numerous cave-like depressions with very sharp edges. The whole rocky summit, coloured brick red, was a conspicuous landmark.

Near the cliff edge a colony of giant petrels were showing their displeasure at our presence by a great flapping of wings and loud squawking. Young birds were all covered with down. Climbing around the cliff face we came across a large nest occupied by a young snowy albatross. The nest was surrounded by a rampart of bird excreta built up over the years by a succession of occupants. To some extent it served as a protection from the incessant bitterly cold winds. The young bird, about the same size as an adult, was not greatly alarmed and kept facing us as we circled the nest. It made a continual clacking noise by opening and closing its large mandibles. It had fledged its down and was almost ready to make its first flight. We left it in peace.

Returning to the beach, we arrived at the stipulated time of 7 P.M. only to find that several of the party had not yet shown up. Shots were fired to hurry them along. It was a dismal scene, light was fading, snow falling and an increasing sea had produced a heavy surf. When the latecomers arrived Sir Douglas signalled the occupants of the motor boat to bring the dinghy ashore. They were not in a happy frame of mind having had a long wait in the wildly tossing boat. After three hair-raising trips through the surf, all hands, soaked to the skin, were safely on board and we set out for the *Discovery*.

As the motor boat closed in on the ship there was complete silence as we contemplated the task of gaining the deck. She was rolling almost to the gunwales and to make matters worse the rope ladder was lowered on the weather side. Circling the ship several times, Sir Douglas finally shouted for a ladder to be lowered on the lee side. The answer from the bridge was, "What for?" After this helpful reply from Captain Davis the motor boat was manoeuvred alongside the rope ladder and secured by fore and aft lines. A line was hurriedly thrown on deck from the dinghy and it was dragged away from its determined efforts to land in the motor boat's cockpit.

The motor boat, as it rose and fell with the waves, out of rhythm with the ship's rolling, repeatedly crashed against the side making it difficult for the occupants to stay on their feet. One by one, at opportune moments, we jumped for the ladder and then hurriedly climbed it, before the boat rose again to help us on our way. All aboard safely, not without some near misses, we assisted in hauling the motor boat and dinghy inboard. Hoisting the dinghy on board caused some alarm. A seaman, Mathieson, lowered into it, fastened fore and aft ropes to the central block and tackle line. While hauling, a heavy roll crashed the dinghy against the ship's side; the aft line broke causing the hauling rope to slip forward so that the dinghy, now suspended from its bow, kept swinging wildly and pounding against the ship's side. Mathieson, as he was being thrown out, grabbed the hauling line and hung on while the dinghy was hauled on deck. Fortunately, he was unhurt and the dinghy received only minor damage.

The sealing vessel had left her mooring and had moved around to Ship Bay to a more protected anchorage. We learned that she did this each evening and returned to American Bay early the following morning.

Heavy falls of snow persisted through the night and on the morning of November 3, decks and rigging were covered with a white mantle. The previous night's strong wind had subsided, seas had moderated and bright sunshine favoured a perfect but cold day. Immediately after an early breakfast the shore party left and landed on the beach without trouble.

A very common bird species on the island is the Kerguelen pintail duck which flies in large flocks. Sir Douglas suggested that Doc and I, during our day's wandering, should shoot as many as possible to augment the ship's food supply. This presented no difficulties. Later in the morning, sighting several pintails feeding on the ground a short distance away, we made all the appropriate noises to make them fly. Our sporting instincts prevented us from shooting sitting birds. On their refusing to fly, Doc walked over and nudged one with his foot. It took off, he fired and missed. We found the tameness of the birds most disconcerting and finally had to select ones sitting at a distance before firing. Naturally, our bag was large and for days afterwards we had duck served up to us, cooked in every conceivable way.

Pintail ducks build well-constructed nests under tussocks of vegetation and lined with down. As we neared the site of one nest the sitting bird fluttered away dragging a wing as if maimed in an attempt to lure us away from its nest. This is a common device among many ground-nesting birds.

Nearing lunchtime, we began to return to our landing place on the beach. It had been planned that we would all return there for lunch of sandwiches and tea. Snow had been falling most of the morning and was still continuing. Rifle shots from the far end of the beach indicated the sealers were still busily engaged in the slaughter of the few remaining sea elephants.

During lunch we were pestered with the persistent attention of cheeky, overfriendly sheathbills, commonly known as paddy-birds. Mention of them has not been made previously but, from our first arrival on the island, we had all been trailed by these attractive birds who have all the habits of farmyard chickens. White in colour except for black legs and beak and about the size of a bantam, they have completely lost the power of flight. Sheathbills are numerous on most subantarctic islands and on each island they are specifically distinct.

Their curiosity was never satisfied. Quickly running in all directions amongst members of our party, everything in sight was subjected to a close examination and a severe pecking. Nothing was safe from their attentions. One of Hurley's cameras left on the ground was damaged when its small red viewing window was pecked out. A biscuit tin soon lost its paper covering and for hours afterwards birds took it in turn to savagely peck at their image mirrored on the shining tin surface. With feathers ruffled they savagely pecked at what they no doubt thought was an attacking bird.

Admiration for the sheathbills was lost as their habits were studied. Wounded or helpless birds of their own kind were ruthlessly torn to pieces and eaten. They were also seen on scavenging expeditions amongst the sea elephant carcasses. They feed a great deal on penguin eggs during the nesting season. Working to a studied plan in rookeries, two birds work together. One slowly approaches, from the front, a penguin sitting on eggs while its fellow conspirator unobtrusively makes its way to the rear of the nest. The sheathbill in front with head lowered creeps closer and closer to the sitting penguin now showing alarm and furiously pecking at the intruder. The penguin finally leaves its nest to attack and immediately the other sheathbill dashes in, stabs and lifts an egg in its bill and carries it a short distance away. The two sheathbills together devour the egg. The penguin returns to its nest and makes itself comfortable, giving no indication that it realises an egg has disappeared. This method of obtaining food by the sheathbills is common practice and was seen on many occasions.

After lunch, Moyes, Falla and I decided to walk across to Ship Bay. On the way we were intrigued by a number of skua gulls swimming and splashing in a creek, obviously washing off blood accumulated on their feathers while feeding on sea elephant carcasses. They were so engrossed in their task that our presence was completely ignored.

The beach at Ship Bay was crowded with sea elephants but no doubt these would be slaughtered when the sealers' activities ceased at American Bay. Sheathbills walking over their bodies were feeding on external parasites. Several rookeries of Gentoo and rockhopper penguins near the beach were investigated and observations recorded by Falla. It was here we had our first introduction to the delightful small rockhopper penguins. There were only a dozen or more birds and apparently they had not started nesting.

As it was getting late we started on our return journey to American Bay. From the top of a cliff, Moyes sighted through his binoculars a large iceberg away to the north-west resembling in shape and size what MacKenzie had earlier thought was an island.

Arriving at American Bay, we found two of the party had not yet arrived. The motor boat was anchored outside the line of breakers with Eric Douglas waiting for a signal to bring the dinghy ashore. In the distance a strange sight was approaching. It turned out to be Doc Ingram staggering along under the weight of a large albatross. Clutched in his arms, the bird's large wings were flapping and its long bill was continually snapping at Doc's head, presenting an unforgettable sight. It appeared that Doc had been wandering around on his own and had come across a nest containing a young albatross. Assuming it would be of interest to Falla, he captured the bird and set off for the beach with it in his arms. It was immediately recognised as the young snow albatross Falla and I had seen the previous day and had left in peace. Sir Douglas had also seen and photographed it while collecting rock specimens. After all the attention devoted to the young bird it was unlucky to be literally baby-snatched by Doc in the cause of science. It was added to the collection of birds.

We were now all present and ready to board the motor boat. The dinghy had survived two trips in the surf without mishap and it returned for the final trip. Sir Douglas was in the throes of hurrying the stragglers when he noticed that Professor Johnston was standing by with the extraordinarily large genitalia of six bull sea elephants dangling from his hand. He was promptly ordered to "throw those ——— things away", which he reluctantly did. The choice of the expletive, never before heard from Sir Douglas, was most apt and whether by accident or design left no doubt regarding the natural functions of the discarded objects. All climbed into the dinghy with Simmers and Doc holding the bow on to the incoming waves with spaces left for them to jump on board. Safely negotiating the surf, we saw Simmers and Doc swimming alongside with only their heads above water; they had missed the jump. We had no difficulty climbing on board the *Discovery* on arrival.

Our stay at the Crozet Islands had ended and we were now ready to sail to Kerguelen Island about 800 miles due east. Darkness had set in and Captain Davis decided to remain at anchor until early next morning. The day finished on a happy note when later in the evening we drank a toast to our wives and sweethearts.

Kerguelen Island

ON NOVEMBER 4 at 9 A.M. anchors were weighed and the *Discovery* moved out of the bay under steam. Flags were dipped as we passed the *Kilfinora* at her anchorage. Leaving the island astern a course was set for Kerguelen Island and we were well on our way. At 4 P.M., all hands were called on deck to assist in hoisting sails; the ship responded immediately to an increased speed as the sails filled with a moderately strong following wind. Depth soundings gradually increased from 142 metres at midday to 3875 metres at midnight.

Zoologists began preparations to deal with the extensive collections made during our stay on Possession Island. Johnston was busily searching the vegetation for small insects, and bird skins for external parasites. He also had a large series of parasites to preserve which he had collected from sea elephant intestines on shore. Falla and I began the task of skinning a fairly large series of birds. Marr sorted and preserved a variety of marine specimens collected from between tide marks on the rocky coast. For the first time since leaving Cape Town the laboratory was a hive of industry. We were generally assisted by Doc, who was again beginning to feel the effects of the ship's motion. Work continued until midnight.

The sky was very overcast the next morning, but clearing. Wind had veered to the north easing in strength and the sea was fairly calm. Several small icebergs were sighted from the bridge by the officer on watch. Later in the morning the barometer, which had been steadily rising, began to drop alarmingly. A sudden strong increase in the wind, however, proved to be of short duration.

Zoologists continued with their work. Falla and I persevered with bird skinning without any noticeable decrease in those yet to be completed. Frank Hurley, who had retired to his darkroom after leaving Possession Island, appeared with beautiful negatives covering a variety of subjects he had photographed when ashore.

At noon our position was 46°45′S, 55°09′E, after a distance run of 144 miles and an additional nine miles logged before noon the previous day. A single depth reading taken during the day was 4175 metres.

The engines had been started late in the morning to help the ship along in the light breeze. They were stopped when a loud knock developed. The cause was very soon found and corrected.

Late in the afternoon, a South Georgian diving petrel, flying over the ship, hit the rigging, broke its neck and fell to the deck. This was Falla's first record of the species. Later, a second diving petrel flew on board and was captured. It was identified as a Kerguelen diving petrel. These small, stumpy birds fly swiftly over the waves with fast-beating wings. When diving for food the wings continue beating and propel the bird under water. Emerging with wings still fluttering, they momentarily glide before diving into the sea again. Gentoo penguins, unusually far from land, were seen porpoising around the ship.

For the past few days, Wireless Operator Williams had been unable to communicate with Australia although he could hear them constantly calling and suggesting a definite time for him to transmit. Efforts to locate the trouble were unsuccessful but he was able to contact the *Gloucestershire* en route from Bangkok to Colombo. They relayed a message to Australia informing the station we were experiencing difficulties with our wireless. The fault was finally traced and messages were again being freely transmitted and received.

The wind slowly increased in strength the next morning. Seas had risen from a low swell to short steep waves. The ship's movements changed from a steady roll to a series of sudden convulsive lurches; an entirely new experience. The first few lurches brought forth a medley of crashes and rattles from the galley as pans, dishes and a hot meal, in course of preparation, ran riot. Above the din the cook's plaintive voice beseeched all and sundry to explain "why of all places do I find myself on board a sailing ship in southern seas?" That was a censored version. Actually those within hearing were astonished at his command of language, hardly once repeating his choice of expressive curses.

Zoologists were finding it difficult to carry on with their work because of the heavy rolling of the ship. This was particularly the case while skinning birds.

On the morning of November 7, it was estimated the ship was about 400 miles from Kerguelen Island. Under the benign influence of a strong westerly wind the ship, under full sail, was making good headway. At noon a run of 177 miles was logged for the 24 hours. Two readings on the echo sounder recorded that in 12 hours the sea floor had risen from 3744 metres to 1049 metres — a dramatic shallowing. Soundings from now on would be followed with keen interest.

The strong westerly wind persisted through the night and was still blowing next morning. Under its influence the ship logged 173 miles. Our position was 47°59'S, 67°31'E. We expected to sight the mountains of Kerguelen Island early next morning. Soundings taken during the day recorded the depth of the sea floor at 559 metres early in the morning, gradually rising to 201 metres at midnight.

Since leaving Possession Island, "Bonus" Child had devoted most of his time to preparing a chart of the island's coastline, traversed by us, from bearings taken from the bridge. Showing his completed work to Captain Davis, a gust of wind blew it out of his hands and over the side. I happened to be near the bridge watching two blue whales spouting and saw the chart disappear overboard. Captain Davis turned his back and walked away without a word. Colbeck, standing nearby, looked as if he was about to dive in after it while Child's face, as he watched the chart float away, was a study of disbelief.

Hurrying on deck next morning, I was met with a thick blanket of fog which had reduced visibility to 200 metres or even less. Sails had been taken in during the night. Engines were slowly turning over and the ship was practically drifting. Our exact position in relation to the island was doubtful although the ship's officers' calculations placed us off Hillsborough Bay on the south coast. The sea was calm with a low swell and light rain was falling.

Taking advantage of our enforced drift, a heavy iron-framed dredge, with an opening 122 centimetres by 30, was attached to the cable of the main winch and lowered over the stern. The depth was 146 metres and we watched as cable was paid out. The dredge was then towed for 20 minutes at a speed of one knot. Hauled inboard by Campbell driving the winch, the dredge was covered with green mud. The catch was good, consisting mainly of echinoderms (heart-urchins, crinoids and sea-cucumbers), univalve and bivalve shells and a variety of marine worms (nemerteans and polychaetes). The laboratory again became a scene of activity as specimens were extricated from the clinging green mud.

Later in the day an amazing incident took place. Suddenly, out of the thick fog, a whale-chaser appeared raising a Red Ensign. Ranging alongside, her skipper hailed the bridge, "Where are you bound for?" For some strange reason Captain Davis made no reply. After waiting a few minutes the skipper raised his cap in salute, rang down for engines, and minutes later disappeared into the thick blanket of fog. We were staggered. There we were, fogbound, and a vessel appearing as if by magic was ignored. Obviously, the skipper of the chaser, well acquainted with the waters, would have piloted our ship into Royal Sound, our destination. As later events proved this would have saved a great deal of trouble.

Towards evening, as the fog showed no signs of lifting, the ship was headed north-west away from the coast into safer waters.

Sir Douglas received a wireless message from Captain Firth of the S. S. *Canberra* wishing the expedition every success. It had been transferred for despatch on October 22, but the *Discovery* could not be contacted until almost three weeks later. We enjoyed another Saturday night with an issue of two glasses of port and our usual toast.

The fog had lifted slightly by the next day but a falling barometer presaged bad weather. Shortly after breakfast a violent wind suddenly swept in from the east, later veering south and finally reaching hurricane force with wind velocities of 95 to 120 kilometres an hour. With sails furled the ship ran before the wind which continued without easing throughout the day and into the night.

Mountainous seas developed and crashing waves swept the decks with such force that lifelines were rigged to safeguard crew members as they carried out deck duties. Visibility was reduced by falling snow. Racing following seas swung the ship in the deep troughs — a nightmare to the two helmsmen — while rolls of up to 42 degrees were recorded. For the first time members of the scientific staff were assigned to watches, ready to be called for deck duties, extra lookouts and stints on the lee-helm.

In the evening, we received a special issue of port to drink "Sparks" Williams's health. It was his birthday, celebrated under conditions when voices could barely be heard above the noise of thundering waves and the shrieking of the wind as it swept through the rigging.

At 11 P.M. the wind had eased sufficiently to turn the *Discovery*, and with engines running at full speed she began to make slow progress back towards Kerguelen Island. One hundred miles had been covered running before the hurricane.

The next day, at 4 A.M., Campbell and I were called to stand by during our two-hour watch. Our assistance, however, was not required. Weather had improved; the wind still coming in from the east had dropped considerably and the sea was moderate with a heavy swell. The ship was forging ahead at a steady three and a half knots. Since the ship was turned, 89 miles had been gained and once again we were in close proximity to Kerguelen Island.

Five tonnes of coal briquettes were transferred from a forward hold to empty bunkers. Later, Sir Douglas, Marr and I continued unpacking and checking contents of cases in the equipment hold. Sparks was again communicating with Australia and receiving messages.

On the 12th, at 6.30 A.M., all hands were ordered on deck by Sir Douglas. The ship was pushing her way through an area of giant kelp with a depth sounding of only 23 metres and there was every possibility of her striking a submerged reef. It was an extraordinary sight with no sign of the sea; only a close, writhing mass of kelp extending away in all directions as far as the eye could see. The kelp produced an unpleasant swishing sound as it rubbed against the ship's side. Giant kelp is a type of algae; its fronds are recorded as growing to lengths of up to 200 metres.

Finally passing through the vast area of kelp we continued on course. Several hours later we caught a momentary glimpse of Kerguelen's mountains before the thick mist and light falling snow again blotted out sight of the island. Wind began to increase in strength and a rising sea caused some anxiety as ship's officers had so far been unable to take sights or bearings to indicate our exact position.

As the mist began to clear, a small sealing vessel, the *Plough*, appeared and coming alongside her skipper asked Captain Davis if he had any mail for them and offered to pilot him into Royal Sound. Receiving a curt "no" to both requests he swung his vessel away and departed. Expected bad weather did not eventuate and in clearing conditions we steamed down the coast and passed through the heads of Royal Sound at 11 A.M. in bright sunshine.

As Royal Sound opened up before us, we were greeted by an incredible scene of picturesque beauty. The Sound itself is an excellent harbour. Although exposed to most winds it offers many safe anchorages. It is an immense stretch of water studded with many small islets. Spectacular fjords lead from it into extensive inland waterways. In the background, mountains averaging 1200 metres in height were overshadowed by Mt Ross, an extinct volcano towering to 1865 metres. Bright sunshine reflected the whiteness of snow covering the heights and glaciers on the mountain slopes. I learned later that we were most fortunate to have our introduction to Kerguelen Island under such ideal conditions. Only on rare occasions is the typical boisterous weather of the island interrupted by light easterly winds which disperse the usual heavy clouds — conditions which last no more than 24 hours and are followed by gale-force winds, snow and sleet.

Slowly steaming inland over a millpond surface we made for a deserted whaling base known as Port Jeanne D'Arc, 26 miles inland on the Buenos Aires Channel.

Bird life was prolific. Large flocks of many species crowded the air, continually swooping over the ship and screaming loudly as if resenting our presence. Penguins swam and porpoised alongside. Flying low at great speed over the water were flocks of stormy and diving petrels. It was truly an ornithologists' paradise.

Passing through the narrow, magnificent fjords of Davis Strait and Hydrography Channel, we entered the much wider and longer Buenos Aires Channel. A Norwegian crew member was heard to say, "Why, these fjords are far grander than those of Norway." Some distance up the channel we arrived at the deserted whaling station. The ship, after some time, manoeuvred alongside a rather broken-down wharf. Mooring ropes were fastened to the wharf and some on shore. As an added precaution anchors were lowered.

While the crew were making the ship snug, scientists went ashore

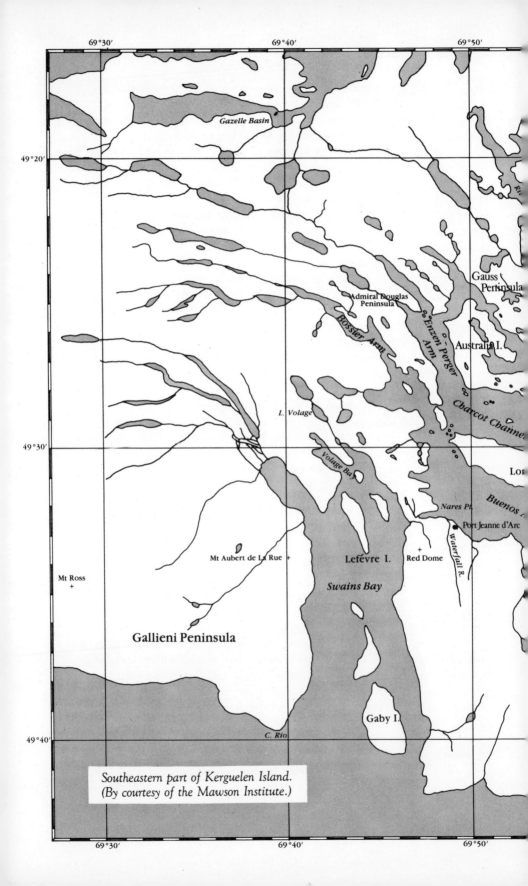

Southeastern part of Kerguelen Island.
(By courtesy of the Mawson Institute.)

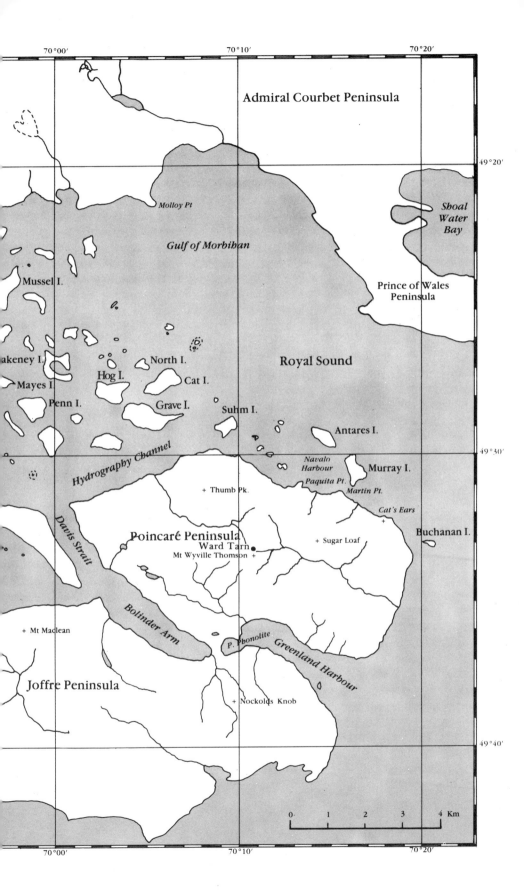

to inspect the whaling base. It was found to be in a state of almost complete disrepair. Huge boiling-down vats and steam digesters were rusted and useless. Timber buildings containing living quarters and offices were still habitable but they urgently required attention. On the walls were writings in the languages of many countries, all with the same theme — a craving to return to a better and more civilised life. The last occupants, seemingly not so long ago, simply walked out leaving even uncompleted meals on the table. Furthermore, we discovered the whole area was overrun by large grey rats, apparently thriving under the island's climatic conditions.

Our first evening at Jeanne d'Arc still remains a pleasant memory. There was a light breeze. A half moon in the cloudless sky illuminated the calm waters of the channel. Surrounding snow-clad mountains were a glorious sight in the moonlight. Occasional loud booming noises in the distance had me puzzled. Later, I learned they were caused by avalanches of snow and ice as they thundered down the steep mountain slopes.

Kerguelen Island is one of the larger subantarctic islands, 145 kilometres long and with a width of 129 kilometres. It is so heavily indented by incursions of the sea that a veritable network of waterways covers a large part of the island. These waterways are so extensive that the land area is estimated to be only 6475 square kilometres. Almost continual winds sweep across the island, usually from the north-west, frequently at gale and hurricane force. Fjords act as funnels through which winds increase in violence, whipping surface waters into a frightening wave turbulence with flying spray and foam.

Some idea of the weather conditions was gained from a report by Sir James Clark Ross who, in 1840, spent 68 days in Christmas Harbour during the winter months. Gale-force winds blew on 45 days and only three days were free from snow and rain. The Challenger Expedition of 1874 spent 26 days at the island in the month of January when gale-force winds prevailed for 16 days.

An early visitor to Kerguelen Island was Captain James Cook who, in 1774, sailed into Christmas Harbour two years after the island was discovered by Kerguelen-Tremarec. He found the bottle containing that navigator's declaration claiming the land for France. Cook again visited Christmas Harbour in 1776 on his third voyage to Antarctica, to replenish the ship's fresh-water supply.

From the year 1776 to 1873, Kerguelen Island was continually visited by sealing and whaling vessels. Fur seals and sea elephants were slaughtered until in time their numbers were decimated and in 1893 the island was virtually abandoned as far as the sealing industry was concerned.

In 1893, the French Government leased Kerguelen Island to

William Bossiere for a term of 50 years. He introduced a number of sheep in 1908, without success. Between the years 1911 to 1913 several hundred sheep were landed but the rather ill-conceived project was finally abandoned as the animals would not breed.

Early this century, an adventurous surveyor named Raillier du Batty, fascinated by glowing reports of the island, decided to make a close acquaintance with it. A small ketch was purchased and with several companions, all inexperienced sailors and navigators, he set out from France to reach Kerguelen Island. Their navigation could not have been that bad for they reached the island without once sighting land.

The party spent several years on the island surveying and charting the many waterways and harbours. Late one evening a member of the party stumbled into a sea elephant wallow and could not extricate himself. Loudly calling for help, he was almost submerged before du Batty answered his cries and rescued him. Du Batty's excuse for the delay was that he thought his companion was singing.

To assist in paying expenses, du Batty's ketch had been filled with as many barrels of sea elephant oil as it would hold. Unfortunately, on the return voyage most of the barrels had to be jettisoned when they fought gale after gale in the Roaring Forties.

However, to return to the *Discovery* at Port Jeanne d'Arc. The whaling company of Irvine and Johnston at Cape Town had agreed to transport 400 tonnes of coal briquettes to Kerguelen Island for the expedition. We were relieved to find the coal had arrived and was stacked on shore near the end of the wharf jetty.

Early next morning, Sir Douglas, Campbell, Ingram and I began rearranging cases in various holds to provide space for the stowage of coal. In the afternoon Falla, MacKenzie and I went ashore to collect bird specimens, also pintail duck and rabbits for the larder. Rabbits were introduced to the island about a century ago as a food supply for shipwrecked mariners. Since then they had increased enormously in numbers, upsetting the natural plant balance and destroying many of the succulents. The rabbits possessed fine coats of fur, giving them a plump appearance; their bodies, however, were tough and stringy when cooked and eaten. But it was a welcome change of diet, so no complaints were heard.

During our visit a constant watch was kept for savage wild dogs we had been told roamed the island in packs. Du Batty wrote of "large white animals with long flowing hair which run with the swiftness of wind." The dogs are descendants of several Samoyed sledging dogs which escaped from the Gauss Antarctic Expedition when it established a base on the island in 1902 to observe the transit of Venus. Sledging dogs were landed for a spell on shore before the expedition left for the Antarctic.

The escapees, now feral dogs, revelling in the cold conditions and an inexhaustible food supply, increased in number over the years. On one occasion while collecting I realised two Samoyed dogs were following in my tracks. They made no move to come near. When I stopped they stopped. I finally walked towards them, calling and whistling in a way that I thought would assure them of my good intentions. But it was to no avail. They finally turned and slowly scampered away. So much for the savage dogs of Kerguelen.

Walking back to the ship along a high cliff fronting the Buenos Aires Channel, I accidentally came across a wooden cross overgrown by thick undergrowth. Attached to the cross was a beautiful bronze crucifix. At its base a sealed bottle contained a message pressed against the clear glass. It read in English and French:

> The Gratitude and favours given us by Divine Providence during our voyage and our stay in Kerguelen. We have built this Calvary, which we put under the safeguard and recommend to Pious cases all those coming here under us.

Port Jeanne d'Arc.
Le 6 Mars 1924.

Etienne Peau

Chargé de Mission scientifique à Kerguelen, par le Ministre de l'Instruction Publique et le Muséum National de la France.

Lionel Peau
Son fils et son aide dans Cette Mission.

At first sight of the crucifix I found my thoughts drifting back a century or more, before realising it had been erected only five years before our arrival. Over the years I have frequently wondered if the crucifix still stands facing the distant entrance to Royal Sound — a haven of rest from the tempestuous seas of the Southern Ocean.

Returning to the ship late in the afternoon, I found that several strong cables had been added to the mooring lines of the Discovery as a precaution against expected strong winds. The crew had also started coaling the ship, 20 tonnes having been carried on board and dumped into the port and starboard bunkers.

November 14 and 15 were spent in the holds rearranging and moving cases from one hold to another. Sir Douglas, Campbell, Marr and I carried out this task resulting in a forward hold and the sail locker being freed for coal storage. The crew brought 30 tonnes of coal on board during the two days.

Captain Davis, worried about the safety of the ship, was anxious to finalise coaling as soon as possible. He had visions of a strong gust of wind either blowing the ship away from the wharf or carrying away the wharf with the ship still attached to it. To ease his mind it was decided that from the next day the crew would continue coaling through the day while scientists and ship's officers would carry out "volunteer" coaling from 6.15 P.M. to 9.30 P.M.

The next morning was sunny with a light breeze. The good weather was exceptional and unexpected. Falla and I set out to collect birds and visit nesting colonies to observe variations in breeding times. The birds showed no fear; even when sitting on their nests, they allowed us to approach closely. Others would walk or hop over to inspect us and at times follow us around the rookeries.

Although the island is mainly mountainous there are large areas of boggy marshes and peat bogs. Walking was slow and tedious. Vegetation includes grasses, herbaceous plants and ferns, thickly covering the areas. Most universally distributed plants are Kerguelen cabbage and a shrub-like type known as *Acaena*, occasionally used by the sealers for tea making. The predominant plant is *Azorella*, a moss-like type growing in large, rounded, cushioned masses.

Kerguelen cabbage, (*Pringlea antiscorbutica*), was found and named by a surgeon and naturalist, William Anderson, who accompanied Captain James Cook on his voyages to the Antarctic. The cabbage is readily digestible and is of great value as an antiscorbutic. Early navigators to the southern seas frequently called at the island for quantities of the fleshy leaves to alleviate the suffering of vitamin-starved sailors, stricken with scurvy. The cabbage is found growing in abundance from sea level to heights of 600 metres.

Towards evening, scientists began wandering back to the ship from their various activities. Sir Douglas, Campbell and Hurley arrived back from climbing the nearby Red Dome Mountain. Geological specimens were collected and Hurley was enraptured with the scenery he had photographed. Johnston with great patience spent the day collecting small insects and spiders from vegetation.

At 6.15 P.M., scientists began coaling. Coal piled at the end of a long jetty had to be transported to the ship by means of a flat-topped trolley. Loaded by three men stationed at the dump the trolley was then pushed by three other men along rails, slightly uphill, to the ship's side. There, it was unloaded by a team, carried on board and stowed in a forward hold.

On return journeys the "pushers" sat on the trolley. Gaining speed as it descended downhill, it had to negotiate a slight curve — the scene of several derailments — before coming to an abrupt stop against stacked coal. On a number of occasions the trolley arrived minus a passenger or two, thrown off en route. Order of the day was speed, which led to many cheerfully accepted bruises and lacerations.

During coal operations Captain Davis decided to come ashore

and innocently accepted a ride on a returning trolley. As it gained speed the skipper crouched on hands and knees hanging on as best he could. Marr, standing alongside the track, noticed a crouching figure and gave the behind a resounding smack as it sped by. Recognising the cry of anguish, Babe melted into the darkness. He returned later expecting to be placed in irons but the incident was taken in good part, even though it was noticed the skipper was still rubbing his behind for some time afterwards.

At the conclusion of the evening's coaling, all hands retired to the whaling company's quarters for a very much needed clean-up. Laughing over the many amusing incidents we also congratulated ourselves — mainly the trolley pushers — on still having unbroken legs and arms. We were pleased to hear that in the two and half hours 20 tonnes of coal had been stowed on board, considerably more than the crew's daily efforts.

November 17 saw a marked change in the weather. Wind had veered from the east to the south-east, a quarter from which strong winds can be expected. Snow had fallen through the night and persistent rain had set in.

Coaling the ship continued for the next three days — the crew working through the day, scientists in the evenings. At midday, the Kilfinora arrived from the Crozet Islands and, unable to berth at the wharf, anchored nearby. Sir Douglas was informed by her skipper that his ship must tie up no later than the evening of the 19th as fresh water was urgently required.

At our rate of coaling this was impossible. Sir Douglas asked if the crew of the Kilfinora could assist in coaling during the day. His request was granted and both crews worked together for two days with scientists carrying and stacking briquettes into every conceivable space, including the decks and aft winch house. We still coaled during the evenings, but not with the same zeal as on the first occasion. As a reward, Sir Douglas produced two bottles of port, a gesture which was very much appreciated. Its effects were very noticeable. After our issue of two glasses, voices rose higher and higher as one vied with the other to be heard. Repartee ran riot.

On the morning of the 19th, one month after leaving Cape Town, Sir Douglas selected a party to accompany him on a two-day field trip to investigate the upper reaches of the Bras d' Bossiere, a north-easterly extension of the Buenos Aires Channel in which the ship was berthed. The men chosen were Hurley, Ingram, Johnston, Falla, Eric Douglas and myself.

Coaling was still in progress but would be completed during the day. Scientists leaving on the field trip were told to be ready to set out at 10 o'clock next morning. As we ceased coaling we were informed that the scientific staff had moved 54 tonnes during the evening.

At the stipulated time, the motor boat, heavily laden with equipment and seven men, left the ship. Freeboard was almost non-existent. On our way we pulled in alongside the *Kilfinora* and presented the captain with a case of whisky and two cases of oranges; an acknowledgement of his agreement to assist us in coaling.

The weather was perfect as we moved slowly down the channel. Landings were made on two small islands near the entrance to the Bras d' Bossiere where hurried collecting was carried out. Dense, luxuriant growth of vegetation covered the island and burrows of the dove or Antarctic prion were in abundance. This species is the most plentiful bird on Kerguelen Island and must breed there in colossal numbers. Nesting had not started and each burrow contained only a male bird. Females were away feeding at sea.

While we were on shore, Sir Douglas and Eric Douglas made several short hauls with a small rectangular dredge in a little more than three metres. The mass of kelp caught in the dredge was found to be the abode of an amazing variety of small marine life. Professor Johnston spent hours transferring specimens, with a pair of forceps, from the kelp into glass tubes containing preservative.

Continuing our way upstream, we had difficulty negotiating a tidal rip between two small islets at the narrow entrance to the Bras d' Bossiere. Finally entering the arm we found ourselves traversing a magnificent fjord with sides 450 to 600 metres high with a sheer drop of about 300 metres from the summit to the start of its talus slope. The cliff face presented a beautiful example of columnar basalt, standing out in relief as if carved by a giant hand.

As we moved upstream, each turn brought into view U-shaped and hanging valleys, formed by centuries of large-scale glacial action. Rounding one of the headlands, a dense cloud of spray, at first thought to be smoke, was noticed rising high in the air, but still some distance away. Moving closer, the roar of falling water indicated a waterfall of considerable size.

Shallowing water was now impeding our progress with the motor boat frequently running aground. Running inshore the boat was tied up securely and the party proceeded on foot. Shortly after landing we were savagely attacked by a skua gull, obviously protecting a nearby nest. On the alert, ready to duck as the skua dived at our heads, we searched for its nest. It was occupied by a female sitting on two eggs. By this time the male skua had given up his attack and was standing at the nest ready to defend his mate. Hurley took several photographs and cine-film of the nest and its occupants.

Following the shoreline for about a kilometre, we rounded a headland to be confronted with a full view of the waterfall. It was a magnificent spectacle. Vast volumes of water, falling from a height of about 50 metres, crashed onto a terrace of sloping rock before spilling into the channel. The noise was deafening and spray rose in dense clouds.

Time passed quickly and we returned to the boat much later than planned and found it high and dry, left by the falling tide. Tents were pitched and we settled in for the night.

At 4.30 A.M. all hands were busy stowing camp equipment on the boat in readiness for a quick dash upstream. Tide was high but beginning to fall. The sun was rising and there was little or no wind; all signs leading to a pleasant day.

Passing the waterfall, we were deluged by falling spray. After continuing for about a kilometre with the boat frequently scraping against submerged rocks, further progress was blocked by large boulders spread across the channel. The scenery was exceptionally beautiful and Hurley was busy with his cameras.

On the return journey we stopped for lunch alongside several large mussel banks exposed by the falling tide. The Bras d' Bossiere is literally crowded with mussel shells. These appear to be the staple diet of black-backed gulls, who have developed a unique method of opening them. During lunch, my attention was drawn to the strange behaviour of several gulls. Each bird was seen to lift a mussel shell from the bank in its beak, then flying aloft to a fair height, hovered momentarily as if taking aim and then dropped it on to a flat-topped rock. The impact was sufficient to break the shell. The gull then dived down and with the aid of its beak extracted the fleshy interior. Hurley and I walked across a mussel bank, ankle deep in shells, to reach one of the "anvil" rocks. It was completely surrounded by shell fragments which had accumulated to a considerable depth. Hurley was keen on filming this unique food-gathering procedure but there was not enough time because of the falling tide.

A further dredging downstream in 3.5 metres produced a net full of mussels embedded in a vile smelling mud. Near the entrance of the Bras d' Bossiere a landing was made on a small island for shore collecting. Professor Johnston and I engaged ourselves in turning over boulders in between tide marks, each exposing a mixed bag of marine life. Another dredging was carried out by Sir Douglas alongside a mussel bank, exposed by the tide for at least a kilometre. The catch included quantities of kelp, also specimens consisting mainly of heart-urchins, starfish and marine worms of unusually large size. Falla found many prion burrows and a number of South Georgian diving petrel burrows. The latter contained birds sitting on eggs, their incubation fairly well advanced.

Late in the afternoon a strong wind developed from the west with intermittent heavy falls of snow. A nasty short choppy sea on the channel made our return journey to the *Discovery* unpleasant and wet. In our absence the ship had moved from the wharf to an anchorage in midstream to allow the *Kilfinora* to berth in order to take on water and coal. Difficulties had been experienced in moving the *Discovery*. Her mooring cables had become entangled with anchor chains and she had not been moved to an anchorage until late in the evening of the previous day.

We were informed next morning that we were to remain at anchor and would not leave until early next morning. This delay was necessary to ensure that coal briquettes, stacked high on deck, were securely battened down to prevent movement in the heavy seas that were expected on our voyage to Heard Island.

Scientists also gained another day for shore collecting. Sir Douglas and Marr visited a coal seam located by Moyes while we were away on our two days' field trip. It was exposed in Waterfall Gully, a short distance west of Port Jeanne d'Arc. It consists of a narrow band of inferior coal, about 60 centimetres thick, heavily impregnated by volcanic ash and small water-worn pebbles. Similar coal deposits have been recorded on the island at Christmas Harbour and Cumberland Bay. Microfossils found in the coal — spores and pollen grains — indicate that in the past conifer and other trees flourished on the island.

Falla and I, in our search for nesting birds, climbed several high points. Panoramic views were breathtaking. Always in the vicinity of nesting colonies were numerous paddy-birds, friendly and inquisitive birds also seen on the Crozet Islands. The Kerguelen paddy-bird, or sheathbill, is a distinct species and has a habit of standing on one leg with the other tucked away under a wing. A number of nesting colonies visited included two of the Kerguelen cormorant. Situated on narrow ledges of a cliff face, the birds were observed from some distance away. Nest building was in progress and pairs of birds were indulging in courtship ceremonies. In this procedure the female stood on the nest or nesting site, while the male, standing close in front, started the ceremony by swaying its neck from side to side. The female then responded by stretching her neck and inclining it towards the male. He then placed his neck alongside and together they continued to sway in unison, finally stopping with their stretched necks pressed close together, remaining immobile for some time.

Returning to the *Discovery*, we found most of the scientists busily engaged writing letters. The *Kilfinora* was leaving for Cape Town and her captain had agreed to carry our mail. His ship, now a sealing vessel, was originally one of the mystery "Q" ships built by the British government during the war to combat German submarine activities.

She was then fitted with a bridge fore and aft to make her steaming direction uncertain from a distance. Her appearance was that of a slow cargo vessel, but she was capable of attaining up to 17 knots. When challenged by a surfaced U-boat, concealed guns could swing into action within minutes.

We also learned from crew members of the *Kilfinora* that the feral Samoyed dogs we had expected to find in large numbers had left the Port Jeanne d'Arc area and now occupied the island around Christmas Bay Harbour.

While the *Discovery* was berthed at the wharf, the ship's sole remaining lifeboat was taken ashore and stored at the whaling station until our return the following year. Its space on the ship was needed to stow the seaplane when assembled later on the voyage.

Heavy snow fell during the early hours of the 22nd. At 7 A.M., anchors were weighed and the ship steamed slowly down the Buenos Aires Channel, through the spectacular Davis Strait and into Royal Sound. Anchors were dropped in Island Harbour near the entrance to the Sound at 12.30 P.M. The weather was perfect; a light breeze, sunshine and a flat, calm sea. A rising barometer indicated fair weather would continue and a decision was made to sail for Heard Island at 11 o'clock the next morning. Moderate weather was hoped for as the ship's decks were stacked high with briquettes, resulting in a slight list to starboard.

Our anchorage was close to the ruins of an early French whaling station and almost alongside a sealing vessel with a broken keel and damaged rudder post. Abandoned, she had remained at anchor for many years and although weather-worn was still bravely floating as if ready to proceed to sea.

Early in the afternoon I joined a shore party which landed on nearby Grave Island. The island received its name from the presence of about 20 graves near the water's edge. Each is marked with a plain white wooden cross on which is carved the deceased's name, age and the ship on which he served. Erosion of the timber has made the writing almost indecipherable, but it seems the majority had been crew members of a ship called the *Isaac Hicks*, while on a voyage from New London, South Africa, in 1873. They had contracted scurvy, the dreaded sailors' disease of those days.

Grave Island was crowded with nesting birds of many species and the ground was riddled with burrows of prions. By some means, rabbits had reached the island and vegetation was close cropped, providing little cover for ground-nesting birds. Skua gulls were nesting in the vicinity and members of the party had to be continually on the alert to evade their diving attacks. They dive at high speed and, being fairly heavy birds, could cause head injuries if they made contact.

Picked up later by the motor boat, we learned from Sir Douglas that he and Eric Douglas had made three hauls with the small dredge in about 3.5 metres. The net on each occasion was filled with red and brown algae with little marine life.

Falla and I resumed skinning and filling out bird skins on our return to the ship. Johnston and Marr, almost submerged in accumulated specimens, continued sorting and preserving. We planned to complete this work before reaching Heard Island where further collections were to be made.

The barometer had dropped rather alarmingly during the night and early morning. A hasty decision was made to remain at anchor for another 24 hours in case the weather deteriorated. The ship's anchorage in Island Harbour was safe with good protection afforded by the surrounding Hog, Grave and Cat Islands.

After breakfast Sir Douglas and a party left to visit North Island further out in Royal Sound, and do more dredging. Zoologists remained on board to carry on with their work. Simmers was busy on deck filling a meteorological balloon with hydrogen gas before sending it aloft to check upper air currents. Suddenly the gauge swung to an alarmingly high pressure. Simmers, moving with great alacrity, was just in time to escape as the balloon burst with a loud report. All hands dashed to what sounded like a disaster area. Occupants of the laboratory, about five metres away, startled by the loud report, rushed out to find that no damage had been done except to Simmers's reputation. These balloons were regularly released when the sky was free of clouds, on several occasions reaching a height of 15,000 metres.

The North Island party returned at midday having seen a variety of birds, including Gentoo penguins and a large number of pintail ducks. Doc Ingram had been detailed to shoot as many as possible for the larder. His tally was 20 ducks. Two tow nettings from the motor boat produced good results and Sir Douglas proudly presented Johnston with two buckets filled with sea water and still-swimming organisms. Snow had been steadily falling all morning, otherwise weather conditions were perfect.

In the afternoon, Sir Douglas, Simmers, Falla and I left to visit a small unnamed island several kilometres north-west of North Island. A small rookery of about 30 rockhopper penguins was found, the first we had seen on Kerguelen Island. Simmers had accompanied us to increase our duck supply, but with no success for only a few were seen. A dredging off the island resulted in a poor catch.

Snow was falling and the sky was overcast as we returned to the ship. However, the barometer was high and steady and good weather was forecast.

Enforced Stay on Heard Island

E ARLY ON THE MORNING of the 24th, the weather was fine except for falling snow and heavy clouds. Anchors were weighed at 9 A.M. with scientists manning the capstan. Chief Officer MacKenzie suggested we should conform with tradition and sing a shanty, a sailors' working song which supposedly makes light of heavy work. Not knowing any we complied by singing "Here we go round the Mulberry Bush", much to MacKenzie's disgust.

With anchors firmly secured, the *Discovery* moved out from her anchorage into the open water of Royal Sound, heading towards the northern headland of the entrance called the Prince of Wales Foreland. Back in its natural environment, the ship, true to form, rolled heavily as she met a moderately large swell coming in from the south-east. Doc Ingram immediately showed early signs of seasickness.

At midday only the high mountains of Kerguelen Island could be seen. A southerly course was set for Heard Island, a distance of 243 miles.

The ship had been rolling in a heavy swell through the night, but later the next morning the sea had subsided to an almost flat calm. A light wind from the north-west swung to the south-west in the afternoon, coinciding with a falling barometer which indicated a drastic change in the weather. The crew hurriedly secured anything on deck that could come adrift in the event of strong winds.

Good progress had been made since leaving Kerguelen Island. At midday, 124 miles were logged for the 24 hours' run, reaching a position of 51°24'S, 71°31'E. We had left the Roaring Forties and entered the Shrieking Fifties. At our present speed it was estimated the ship would arrive off Heard Island early next morning in the hours of darkness. Engines were reduced to half speed. Light snow falling most of the day limited visibility and the crew stood watches on the forecastle head on the lookout for icebergs. We were now well within the range of isolated bergs.

Zoologists worked continuously in the laboratory in an attempt to clear up collections before reaching Heard Island but so much outstanding material made this impossible. Bird skinning is meticulous work and we found our daily tally averaged about 10 birds. Larger birds, particularly penguins, took much longer to prepare as thick layers of fat had to be thoroughly removed from the skin before a preservative could be applied and the specimen filled out to its original shape. It was becoming increasingly cold in the deck laboratory and in no time our feet and hands were half frozen. Feeling was renewed in our hands by submerging them in a bucket of sea water placed nearby.

It had been hoped that after leaving Kerguelen Island a start would be made on our programme of complete oceanographic stations, involving the operation of vertical and oblique nets, water sampling bottles and temperatures from various specified depths to as great as 3600 metres. Running a station, however, was impossible as the winch house and decks were stacked with coal briquettes. These were being gradually transferred to the bunkers as coal was consumed.

The anticipated storm did not eventuate although in the early hours of the 26th a wind from the west increased to about 30 kilometres an hour with stronger gusts. At dawn it dropped to a light breeze. Seas had moderated and conditions were ideal for a landing on the island. This was contrary to expectations. We had been advised several times, finally by the captain of the *Kilfinora*, that landings could only be made on rare occasions. The general story of Heard Island is one of continual gale-force winds with its coast lashed by terrific seas.

In bright sunshine, the *Discovery* steamed slowly past Shag Islets, seven miles north of the island. In the distance, Big Ben Mountain, originally named Kaiser Wilhelm Peak, came into view. It was a magnificent sight, rising to a height of 2700 metres with steep, rugged slopes, heavily crevassed with glaciers descending directly into the sea.

Steaming closer inshore, we passed close to a fantastic needle-shaped rock standing alone and rising to a height of about 30 metres. Laurens Peninsula, forming the north-western end of the island, was then identified. Skirting the coast we passed the entrance to Atlas Cove and shortly afterwards entered Corinthian Bay. Anchors were lowered at 9.15 A.M. in 18 metres.

Sir Douglas had already selected a shore party consisting of Doc Ingram, Eric Douglas, Moyes, Johnston, Hurley, Falla, Marr and myself. Much to his disappointment, Campbell was asked to stay on board to overhaul the echo sounder which had been malfunctioning. Simmers and Howard also remained on board to continue with their duties. Equipment and food for two nights' stay on shore had been stowed in the motor boat; it was swung over the side and we were ready to move off.

Heard Island is one of Britain's most isolated possessions. It was discovered in 1853 by Captain J. Heard, in command of the barque *Oriental*, while on a voyage between Melbourne and Boston. The island, somewhat crescent-shaped, is 40 kilometres long and about 16 kilometres at its greatest width. There are no safe anchorages in the few bays, and skippers must be ready to up anchor and head their ships to the safety of the open sea in threatening weather. Atlas Cove, separated from Corinthian Bay by Rogers Head, is well protected, but its shallow water precludes the entrance of ships of any size. In the past, landings by sealers were made on beaches through a surf which, even in calm weather, is usually heavy.

When the position of this newly discovered island was made known various sealing companies, mainly from the United States, lost no time in sending vessels to exploit the untouched fur seal and sea elephant populations. In 1853, Captain Rogers, in command of the American sealing vessel *Corinthian*, accompanied by four tenders, was the first to arrive at the island where they reaped a rich harvest. It is recorded that in one day's work 500 barrels of oil were taken, representing the slaughter of approximately 150 sea elephants.

The first scientific party to land on Heard Island were members of the famous Challenger Expedition which arrived there in February 1879. The ship anchored in Corinthian Bay and a party including two geologists went ashore in a ship's boat. Assistance through the surf was given by sealers who had been left on the island. While on shore they recorded evidence of a recent lava flow emitted from a volcanic vent at Rogers Head. The party was later signalled back to the ship because a steadily increasing wind threatened her safety.

Forced to leave her anchorage and put to sea, the *Challenger* cruised for several days around the island carrying out marine investigations. As a second landing seemed impossible for some time, because of the stormy conditions, the ship left.

At the time of the *Challenger*'s visit sealing operations were in full swing. At least 40 sealers were distributed in parties on the low-lying areas of the island. Sealing vessels usually visited the island late in October and if possible remained at anchor until December. Vessels were provided with heavy anchors and chains enabling them to ride out most of the gales. During their stay, barrels of seal oil — blubber boiled down on shore — were continually rafted through the surf to the ships. It was a hazardous procedure resulting in the loss of lives.

Another method of operation was for a sealing vessel to land men on shore to accumulate barrels of oil, while the ship returned to port. Months later, the ship would return to relieve them and take off the stored seal oil. In the meantime, the spartans left on shore lived in rough, semi-underground dugouts, working under the most appalling conditions. Occasionally, ships missed a relief voyage and the sealers were marooned for another year. Food was plentiful. Fresh meat was derived from penguins and seals and their blubber provided oil for cooking and lamps. Eggs were available during the penguins' breeding season. Sealers, surprisingly, survived the terrible winter months and usually had large quantities of oil and seal pelts ready for transhipment to the relief vessel when it finally arrived.

The history of the very lucrative fur-seal industry is a tragic story of slaughter which went on for almost a century until the species virtually became extinct. In the 1800–01 season, American sealers from Long Island ports sailed south and returned from subantarctic islands with 112,000 seal pelts. This incredible rate of catch continued until their numbers had become so decimated that hunting them became uneconomical. During the BANZARE voyages, only occasional seals were sighted, usually occupying inaccessible areas. Finally protected by law, seals have increased in numbers and will again flourish.

Back on the *Discovery* in Corinthian Bay, the shore party was ready to attempt a landing. Sir Douglas was hoping the party, while ashore for two days, would occupy a shipwrecked mariners' hut situated near the shore of Atlas Cove. To reach the hut a run of about 6 miles in the motor boat was necessary and two trips had to be made.

The first party set out with the boat heavily laden with equipment and occupants. Sir Douglas was at the tiller and Eric Douglas was ready for any emergency in case of engine trouble. A moderate swell was running, with a calm sea. Nearing Rogers Head we passed inshore of a reef of partly submerged rocks over which the swell was breaking. Soon after entering Atlas Cove a landing was made on a beach of black volcanic sand. Innumerable sea elephants, including many pups, crowded the beach. Equipment and food was quickly unloaded and Sir Douglas and Eric Douglas left on their return journey to bring ashore the remainder of the party.

The hut was located on a nearby rise and found to be in reasonably good condition. It was originally built in Norway and was brought to the island in sections and erected by sealers at the expense of the British Government.

The six-sided hut was fitted with upper and lower bunks around the inner walls and a stove in the centre for heating. There was very little room to move but in our eyes it was a mansion. A small shed attached at the rear was stacked with cases of tinned fish, beef, and large casks of bread rusks. Hurley, Moyes and I began a general clean up. We removed a thick covering of ice from the floor and before long it was made habitable.

Assistance was then given to the rest of the party which had been carrying gear from the beach. It was heavy work because a passage had to be forced through the closely packed sea elephants, and at the same time we had to negotiate soft masses of *Azorella*, tussocks of pea grass and soft sand. After a good deal of trial and error, our gear was finally arranged in some semblance of order within the hut.

Early in the afternoon the motor boat arrived after an uneventful trip with the remainder of the shore party. A few additional items were unloaded, the boat anchored offshore and the dinghy hauled high and dry on the beach. The newcomers admired their quarters, but we were faced with a dilemma. There were only eight bunks and nine of us in the party. Four sides of the hexagon-shaped hut, each two metres long, were occupied by two bunks one above the other. The remaining two sides were taken up with a window and a door. To decide the allocation of bunks, names of the party were placed in a hat and as a name appeared a bunk was selected. I finished up with a top bunk with very little headroom while Falla, last name out, had the doubtful honour of sleeping on the floor.

For the rest of the day, members of the party set out in different directions in pursuit of their various interests.

The area between Atlas Cove and Big Ben Mountain is covered by a low-lying plain composed of dark volcanic sand. It extends from West Bay on the west coast to Corinthian Bay on the east coast, a distance of about three kilometres. Immediately to the south, Big Ben Mountain forms a barrier across the island with glaciers descending its slopes, for the most part directly into the sea. They terminate in ice-cliffs, about 30 metres in height, against which waves pound unceasingly, resulting in undermining which causes falls of immense masses of ice.

Big Ben is a towering volcanic peak assumed to be inactive. However, in 1910, Captain H. Seymour of the ship *Wakefield*, while making an unsuccessful attempt to land on the island, reported seeing clouds of smoke rising from its summit. His report was accepted with some doubt for it was generally thought it was cloud vapour he had seen. The summit is usually obscured by cloud and rarely seen. However, in 1978, a party of scientists spent several weeks on the island and on a number of occasions smoke was definitely seen issuing from the crater. There can be no doubt the volcano is still active.

Rounding Rogers Head in the motor boat, I had noticed three strangely shaped conical masses of rock, one rising to a height of approximately 75 metres. Falla and I decided to walk there for a close examination. They proved to be remnants of a large volcanic crater, already recorded by a geologist of the Challenger Expedition in 1879. The sides of the crater had mostly been demolished by centuries of weathering. Against the spectacular high side of the crater, facing the sea and standing as a colossal monument, talus slopes of rock debris are piled to heights of 45 metres. On these slopes of about 45 degrees, about 10,000 macaroni penguins were nesting or preparing to nest. A large number were each sitting on a single egg while others still courting would soon be breeding.

Nests were precariously situated in between boulders, on narrow ledges or on flat surfaces ringed by small pebbles laboriously gathered by the occupants. Sitting birds vary their position on the nest. Some stand almost erect, others crouch or lie prone, but the egg always rests on top of the feet, completely covered by a fold of skin.

Scrambling through the rookery, we were deafened by the cacophony. Penguins never live in harmony. Quarrelling incessantly and squawking loudly, they peck at their neighbours, or stray penguins as they force their way through the rookery. Nests are closely packed together, possibly for warmth and against the depredations of sheath-bills. Pairs of these birds were active in the rookery, standing together and no doubt deciding which penguin they would harass and rob of its egg.

The outer surface of the high standing crater wall, protected from prevailing winds, is covered by laminations of lava as it welled out from the crater during eruption and later hardened. The whole headland is almost covered by lava with a most irregular, rough surface, honeycombed with caverns which are connected with one another underground. Rockhopper penguins had accepted the caverns as nesting places which are well protected from the bitterly cold winds. We watched with amusement as their heads continually popped up with enquiring looks as if to identify the intruders walking overhead.

On our return to the hut, we found that Hurley had prepared a meal and had the stove working at full pressure, giving out a terrific heat. Hurley was a most unusual person. Requiring only a few hours' sleep each night, he was completely tireless. Gifted with an energy without bounds, he walked many kilometres, weighted with usually three cameras and a heavy tripod, in search of photographic and cinematograph shots. His cheerfulness never faltered, even under the most trying circumstances.

Eating meals in the limited space of the hut was an interesting experience. We had to eat in our bunks with very little headroom; only a few centimetres separated the plates from our mouths. Within a short time the stove, fed with seal blubber, became so heated it glowed a dull red. Heat and fumes finally became so oppressive that we were continually vacating our bunks and heading outside to get a breath of fresh air but we were soon driven back by the severe cold. Little sleep was possible until the stove had cooled down in the early hours of the morning. Falla had an unpleasant night on the floor with many interruptions.

The morning of November 27 broke with a complete change in the weather. A fairly light breeze from the south veered to the south-west, increasing in violence and bringing with it continuous rain and heavy falls of snow. Ignoring the conditions, Falla and I, accompanied by Hurley, revisited Rogers Head for further observations on the bird life. Hurley was interested in photographing the rookeries and spectacular features of the headland where the scenery is magnificent.

Rockhopper penguin nests built in the innumerable small lava caves were lined with grass and in almost every case contained two eggs. We were surrounded by hundreds of birds as they followed us around. Showing no fear they exhibited displeasure at our presence in their usual way by fluffing their feathers and raising their beautiful bright yellow crests. Others kept popping their heads out of innumerable holes, jack-in-the-box fashion, and adding to the general commotion by loudly squawking.

Rogers Head is also a favourite nesting place of skua gulls. We counted more than a hundred nests generally built on hummocks of grass, all occupied by a bird sitting on two eggs. Skuas were in great numbers and because of the nesting were particularly pugnacious. Time and time again they dived at us in their attacks and we had to duck as a swish of air heralded their close approach. On one occasion, as Hurley ducked, he instinctively raised his camera tripod to protect his head. The skua made no attempt to swerve and hit the tripod, breaking two of the instrument's legs and breaking its own neck in the process.

There appeared to be a definite distinction between breeding and non-breeding skuas; the plumage of the latter indicating they were less mature birds. There was also a difference in their habits. Non-breeders spent most of their time feeding and quarrelling amongst themselves on sea elephant carcasses. Breeding skuas limited themselves to nesting areas; males and females remaining generally at their nests. Nearing dusk one or the other would fly aloft and await the arrival of prions as they returned from their day's feeding at sea.

Large flocks of prions flying back to their burrows were forced to run the gauntlet of hostile attacks from the hovering skua gulls. Diving amongst them, skuas killed dozens of prions in midair. After the prions had reached the safety of their burrows, the skuas landed and fed on the bodies of their fallen prey. The ground in the Rogers Bay area was matted with disembowelled prion pelts, all in a perfect state of preservation because of the intense cold. The abundance of prion skins was of great value to Falla because comparative measurement of the bills is one of the main methods of determining specific rank.

Returning from the sea at dusk, individual prions flew unerringly to their respective burrows, usually under clumps of the ubiquitous *Azorella*. Alighting at the entrance, the bird called to its mate in a low guttural tone before entering. On one occasion we removed a prion from its burrow for our collection and returned that evening to watch the behaviour of its mate on its homecoming. Landing at the entrance, its call was unanswered. The prion became very agitated, looked around in all directions, and after pecking at the ground finally entered the empty burrow. We revisited the burrow next evening to find the bird dazed and almost paralysed. Obviously, it had not left the nest and had been lamenting the loss of its mate.

Heavy falls of snow finally drove us back to the hut. In our absence Sir Douglas had shot a young sea leopard. Three female sea elephants were also shot and later skinned; one as a museum skin and two as commercial skins. The two skins were for the Hudson Bay Company who wished to experiment in a process which would soften the coarse hair and thus be of some commercial value. Working on the skinning in falling snow and cold strong wind was decidedly unpleasant.

During the morning, Sir Douglas, Marr and Eric Douglas, dredged in Atlas Cove. Rough seas finally drove them back on shore. Later in the day Sir Douglas and Ingram roamed the foreshores in search of fur seals, but without success.

All the party had returned to the hut before dusk, temporarily revelling in the heat and fug. The door of the hut was always left partly open at night to allow the entrance of fresh air. Those with bunks near the door were envied by back and top benchers. In the early hours of the morning, a large bull sea elephant attempted to push its way into the warmth of the hut but became firmly wedged in the doorway. Professor Johnston, occupying a lower bunk near the doorway, was awakened to find himself face to face with a snorting and snuffling intruder. Jumping from his bunk, he made valiant but ineffectual attempts to make the sea elephant back out by waving his arms and making shooing noises as if it was a cat.

Everyone was now wide awake watching the proceedings. In the midst of the commotion the sea elephant violently sneezed, startling Professor Johnston to such an extent that he jumped backwards, fell over Falla in his sleeping bag, and finished up flat on his back. Advice from bunk inmates was freely given, some valid, some humanly impossible. Moyes almost fell out of his top bunk rolling with laughter while Doc, waking to see the play going on, asked in a pleading voice, "Am I dreaming or am I in a bloody lunatic asylum?"

Finally, several of us debunked and managed in time to push our unwelcome guest back out of the doorway, a proceeding he resented if his grunts and groans were any criteria. Peace reigned again and Falla moved his sleeping bag to the rear of the hut.

Original plans were that the shore party would return to the *Discovery* next morning. This was impossible for during the night the wind had steadily increased and was now blowing at gale force. Most of the party made their way to Rogers Head to see how the *Discovery* was standing up to the wild conditions. Huge seas rolling in were breaking from the offshore reef to Rogers Head, a distance of about a kilometre. Through the fog and mist, the *Discovery* could be seen rolling heavily, and tugging at her anchors as waves raced past her and crashed on

Corinthian beach. Sir Douglas and Eric Douglas walked to the beach and signalled the ship, "Propose to remain ashore another day." The message was acknowledged.

For the rest of the day Falla and I continued skinning the sea leopard and sea elephant carcasses. Annoying visitors were hundreds of cape pigeons; showing no fear, they settled on our arms and shoulders picking at pieces of blubber as they were pared from the skin. Catching them in our hands, we threw them aside, but they still persisted in a wild scramble for food. In desperation to get rid of them I got my gun and fired a shot over their heads. A bird was wounded accidentally, whereupon it was immediately torn to pieces by other cape pigeons and devoured.

Cape pigeons have a wide distribution. Occurring in large flocks they nest on subantarctic islands and the Antarctic continent. Cheeky, attractive birds they are easily recognised by their black-brown head and shoulders; the rest of their upper parts is mottled, white with black spots. They were almost daily visitors to the ship on our voyage from Cape Town.

Completing our task of flensing, Falla and I returned to the warmth of the hut, but it was some time before we regained any feeling in our half-frozen fingers.

One of the drawbacks to the hut's position was its lack of fresh water. Ample fresh water was present in depressions nearby but was undrinkable, having been fouled by sea elephant and penguin movements. As a result, our freshwater requirements had to be brought from several springs at least a kilometre away across the sandy plain.

Water was needed so I set out with a large kettle and an open container. It was a continual fight to make progress against the wind, and to make matters worse heavy falls of snow at times blotted out all visibility. Regaining the hut, I found the open container of water, no light weight, covered with sand and unusable.

Provisions brought ashore were by this time depleted, but there was no shortage of food. Hurley had already utilised penguin eggs in preparing omelettes and he was applauded as the equal of any world-famous chef. Norwegian fish cakes and bread rusks were being steadily consumed. Several meals of penguin steaks had been particularly appetising.

There was no improvement in the weather overnight and in the morning gale-force winds, coming in from the west, showed no signs of lessening. Falling snow persisted and conditions became even worse during the day. Seas had increased and terrific waves were pounding on both Corinthian and West Bay beaches. The Discovery was still at anchor, rolling and pitching wildly. We expected Captain Davis to leave for the open sea at any moment. A signal to the ship intimated it would be impossible to leave the island under present weather conditions. In reply, Captain Davis said he would raise a flag when he thought it would be safe to return.

Early in the afternoon, a number of us, braving the elements, set out to visit West Bay on the weather side of the island, a distance of more than a kilometre. Walking in the teeth of the gale-force wind was arduous and progress was slow. Arriving at the beach, we were amazed at the size of the waves rolling in and crashing on the beach. Occasional mountainous waves swept across the beach, surging inland over the plain surface for considerable distances. Caught unawares by the first king-sized wave, several of the party, although standing well back from the beach, were drenched to the waist and very nearly thrown off their feet as it surged past them.

For some distance inland the sandy plain surface was covered with debris, including broken ship's spars, two massive mahogany logs, several trees with branches still intact and numerous pieces of driftwood of all descriptions. The power of the waves to hurl the logs, weighing at least three tonnes, to their present position must have been tremendous. Certainly, they would have dwarfed those we were now watching.

Sir Douglas and Ingram walked to a glacier front at the base of Big Ben Mountain. To reach it they crossed several old moraine ridges deposited in past years by the gradually retreating glacier. Interesting rock specimens were collected. Sir Douglas was impressed by the large size of many boulders dislodged from the mountainside by glacial action. One, he estimated, would weigh at least 18,000 tonnes.

Sea elephants were plentiful on this side of the island where the beaches in two smaller bays were literally covered with them. An over-all count was approximately 1300. Several rookeries of macaroni and rockhopper penguins were seen on rocky slopes, but time did not permit a closer inspection.

Returning across the sandy plain, we were more than gently assisted on our way by the strong westerly wind, which, if anything, was increasing in velocity. Several of the party experimented by lying back against the wind. Amazing angles were achieved without falling, except during slight lulls when experimenters fell flat on their backs. By the time we reached the hut we were all covered with black sand, blown up in clouds by the wind.

We found Hurley had been busy again. The stove was roaring its head off and dinner was ready to be served. Before retiring, Falla,

Mawson at the tiller of the motor boat as it heads towards Heard Island.
(Photo: S. Campbell.)

adhering to the draw result, refused to accept any offer of a bunk and bedded down on the floor. Our night's rest was again interrupted at about midnight by a large sea elephant pushing against the half open door of the hut. Closing it and then resting against it, the sea elephant promptly dropped off to sleep. In no time the temperature in the hut had reached suffocation point and attempts were made to dislodge our unwelcome visitor. Pushing the door, which opened outwards, produced a narrow opening through which repeated jabs and pokes had no effect on the slumbering animal. It was a stalemate until a sharp pointed tripod leg was brought into play. After several hefty jabs he began to realise he was unwanted and shuffled off with many grunts and belches. With the door half open again, heat in the hut became bearable and all hands settled down to complete their night's rest. We appreciated that on this occasion Doc had made no mention of "lunatic asylums".

There were no signs of improvement in the weather the next morning. Gale-force winds had seemingly increased in force rather than lessened. Later in the morning the wind veered slightly to the north, but with no noticeable difference in strength. Heavy falls of snow overnight covered the landscape with a thick mantle of white; very picturesque, but a hindrance to our activities.

A return to the ship was out of the question. Sir Douglas was beginning to worry about our enforced stay and was naturally anxious to sail south and carry on with our programme of work in Antarctica. Furthermore, our valuable supply of coal was being slowly consumed. Although at anchor, a good head of steam had to be maintained on the *Discovery*. Each day's stay at Heard Island meant one less spent in the south.

Immediately after breakfast, Sir Douglas with some of the party set out for Corinthian Bay. The fury of the sea was at its worst. Never before had I witnessed such mountainous seas; the noise was deafening as the waves crashed high on the beach. We were just in time to see the *Discovery* steaming out to sea. Rolling to her gunwales, she slowly made her way past Rogers Head on a north-easterly course where she disappeared from sight in the fog and mist. We were now really marooned.

Despite shocking weather conditions, the shore party endeavoured to continue with their various pursuits. Johnston spent most of his time collecting marine life from the foreshores of Atlas Cove; searching for parasites in sea elephant carcasses and netting freshwater pools for their contained life. He also devoted time to securing a collection of the meagre insect fauna. These consisted mainly of wingless flies found sheltering amongst Kerguelen cabbage leaves, several species of moths and a species of beetle frequenting roots of *Azorella*.

About midday, Falla, Ingram, Marr and I left the hut to walk to Erratic Point where Sir Douglas had seen the large 18,000-tonne boulder the previous day. It was found resting in a precarious position, almost balanced on a ledge about 30 metres above rocks over which waves were pounding.

Immediately below the boulder, an extensive cave had been formed with its entrance facing the sea. Reaching the cave was a hazardous procedure. Marr made a successful attempt by crawling along a narrow ledge covered with soft soil. Falla and I followed by sitting on the ledge and, with legs dangling over the edge, wriggled our way across. Doc Ingram, coming on the scene later, plunged across without hesitation with one leg on the ledge and the other ploughing its soft edge. The drop was about 24 metres.

Our entrance into the cave, which extended back for quite a distance with a steeply sloping floor, caused a minor panic among the macaroni and rockhopper penguin inhabitants. Feathers and the residue of many moults covered the floor and lined the nests which were simply hollows in the feather carpet. It was the first time we had seen two species intermingling and sharing the one rookery. Macaroni penguins greatly outnumbered rockhoppers. Both species were nesting with each bird sitting on two eggs.

There was a great commotion as we entered their domain, with penguins rushing in all directions, squawking madly and becoming gloriously mixed up in the confined space. Many birds left their nests, others remained and pecked at birds rushing past, all of which led to a state of utter confusion. Finally, the penguins quietened down and to some extent sorted themselves out, but it was obvious many were not sitting on their original nests.

Outside the cave entrance a sloping rock surface extended about a hundred metres to the sea. Although crowded with penguins, none of them appeared to have any great desire to brave the huge, wildly breaking waves, sending spray flying high in the air, and feed in the open sea.

Great care was necessary in returning across the narrow ledge which had been broken away in places by Doc's earlier headlong dash. Sitting down, we cautiously moved around the cliff face. The walk back to the hut was tiring, through flying sand, hustled by the wind, and the ground deep in snow. We all realised our good fortune in having a warm hut to return to instead of tents, which would not have stood up to the unceasing strong winds.

December 1 dawned with little likelihood of any improvement in the weather. The *Discovery* was still at sea, but appeared in sight later in the afternoon. She did not come inshore and continued on a course down the east coast.

Braving the shocking conditions, the whole party set out on a three-kilometre walk to Gravel Bay, a small indentation around the northern headland of West Bay. Hurley had visited the beach several days before and was so impressed by the large number of sea elephants that he was hopeful, despite the weather, of securing a film sequence of two bulls fighting. Numerous families were scattered over the beach, each jealously guarded by a battle-scarred bull.

Hurley was lucky. No sooner had he set up his cinecamera than an unattached bull lumbered out from the surf. Slowly undulating towards a family group, obviously with the purpose of taking it over, he was met and challenged by the guarding bull. They attacked, roaring savagely, and with tremendous force thumped their bodies together, at the same time slashing at each other with deadly strokes of their tusks. The roaring of the contestants and noise of the combat was deafening. After an hour's fighting it was obvious the younger and more agile newcomer was wearing down his older opponent whose body blows were weakening. Suddenly, he turned, and with blood streaming from his chest, sluggishly made his way to the water and disappeared out to sea. The victor moved in amongst his new family of 15 cows, some with newly born pups, and settled down to recover from the fight. During the combat, the ladies of the harem slept soundly, quite unconcerned as to its outcome.

Hurley could hardly believe his good fortune in having such a good contest virtually stage-managed for him. He was estatic. He had filmed it from beginning to end. Although conditions were not ideal for photography, the results later proved to be excellent. A sequence of the combat was included in the expedition's official film, *The Siege of the South*. It was presented with an excited, improvised, running ringside commentary, with the bout divided into rounds.

Leaving the overwhelming cacophony of the beach arena, Falla, Doc and I made our way to a nearby headland. We came across two large rookeries of rockhopper penguins, a nesting colony of cape pigeons and a nest of a light-mantled sooty albatrosses. The nest was located on a steep cliff face and was inaccessible.

Sooty albatrosses have a spectacular and graceful flight; usually in pairs, side by side. Now and again they simultaneously sweep into a series of complex movements, then, diving to sea level and skimming low over the wave-tops, they suddenly rise in a steep climb. Never, during the flight evolutions, thought to be part of their courtship routine, do the birds deviate from their side-by-side position. On one occasion, while watching a sooty albatross nest through binoculars, a bird took to the air leaving its mate sitting on the nest. It put on a wonderful performance of aerobatics, flying high in a strong wind, as if displaying its prowess, before returning to its nest.

A solitary king penguin in brilliant fresh plumage was found wandering in a nesting colony of macaroni penguins on a hillside near West Bay. He seemed perfectly at home as he shuffled along with great solemnity between the nests, at times stopping to inspect some of them more closely. His presence in the rookery was accepted by the macaroni penguins with complete indifference, and even with a certain amount of homage. A group of macaronis followed close by in his footsteps as if forming a guard of honour.

Nesting colonies of king penguins were not seen by us on the island, but I understand several large colonies are located at Spit Bay on the other end of the island. King penguins are regal-looking birds with a dignified manner and stately walk. They breed only on subantarctic islands. Always standing erect with beaks usually pointed upward, they are almost 90 centimetres in height. Their attractive appearance is enhanced by a bright orange ear patch extending to a yellow band around the throat.

During our absence, a king penguin, wandering past the hut, was captured and tethered to await Falla's return. It had resigned itself philosophically to its fate and became quite tame, although refusing to eat scraps of meat and tinned fish. Falla decided to take it alive on board the *Discovery*, a decision not well received by other members of the party.

Weather conditions had slightly improved the following day. The wind had moderated but huge seas were still rolling in and creating a heavy surf on Corinthian Bay beach. Waves were white-capped at sea. The *Discovery* was not at her anchorage, but at about midday she appeared in sight, heading towards the entrance to Atlas Cove. Hurriedly loading the motor boat, Sir Douglas, Marr, Eric Douglas and Johnston set out for the entrance. Arriving there they encountered terrific seas and, seeing no sign of the *Discovery*, returned to learn that the ship had run into Corinthian Bay and anchored.

Walking to the bay, messages were semaphored to the ship, finishing with a message from Captain Davis to come off the island. Hurrying back to Atlas Cove, Sir Douglas and the same party again set out, this time to reach the ship at anchor. Those left behind moved around to Rogers Head to watch the motor boat's progress. It finally appeared in sight rounding the headland, but well out to sea, battling against what Sir Douglas later described as "short, big, troubled waves in which, on several occasions, we nearly capsized". Tracing their course for more than a mile, we were relieved to see the boat range alongside the ship with its occupants safely on board. The boat was hauled up on its davits and swung inboard. There was a general feeling of relief that a second trip had been abandoned.

In the afternoon, Falla, Doc and I left to visit the cliff face of an immense glacier, which, descending from Big Ben Mountain, formed a barrier across the southern end of Corinthian Bay. On our way we passed a number of excavations, originally hut sites of early sealers. Built practically underground, all that remains of the huts are broken-down timbers, a few uprights and some galvanised iron sheets.

The remains of huge iron cauldrons, used for boiling down blubber, were partly covered in the black volcanic sand. How these were brought ashore in ship's boats through a heavy surf was beyond our comprehension.

Arriving at the glacier we found it descended directly into the sea, forming a coast of vertical ice-cliffs about 45 metres high which extended south for several kilometres. Waves pounded unceasingly against the ice front.

At beach level, a narrow cleft led into a large cavern in the solid ice mass. Entering it was an eerie experience. We found ourselves in an enormous ice-cave with a ceiling about nine metres high. Walls of clear ice faded in depth through varying hues of green and blue to total darkness. Entombed in the ice, and clearly visible, were rocks of varying size weighing up to half a tonne or more. These rocks, known as erratics, had been torn from the mountainside by the slowly descending glacier until they had reached their present position. Moving imperceptibly, the erratics would, in time, reach ground level, and as the ice melted would be deposited to form a rock formation known as a moraine. Moraines attain considerable size as this process continues.

Our stay in the cavern, although awe-inspiring, came to a hasty end. A sudden convulsive movement of the glacier, together with a loud grating noise, accompanied by shuddering movements underfoot, was more than sufficient for us to make a hurried retreat to the safety of the open beach.

While on the island we had frequently heard distant thunderous noises caused by avalanches crashing on the ice-covered slopes of Big Ben Mountain. A similar noise was reproduced while standing on the beach, caused by the fall of a large mass of ice, about the size of a small cottage, from the top of the glacier front into the sea. I was fortunate to witness the whole incident, which gave me the impression that it was happening in slow motion because the fall of the ice mass seemed to take an incredibly long time. On its impact with the sea and becoming submerged in a mass of foam, a large crater formed and then slowly filled. From its centre a column of water arose to what appeared an amazing height; it remained suspended as if by some invisible force before collapsing back into the sea. In the meantime, the ice mass had surfaced and was floating out to sea. It is recorded that in the early sealing days a boat's crew rowing from Atlas Cove to Spit Bay, keeping too close to the glacier front, were all drowned when their boat was engulfed by falling ice.

Walking back along the beach, we noticed a small flock of terns flying to and fro over the line of breakers. Their flight was swift and erratic. A lucky shot brought one down, but instead of being washed ashore it began to drift out to sea. Several skua gulls dived to investigate the floating bird, but they were not interested. It was left to a black-backed gull to make determined efforts to lift it in its claws and bring it ashore where it could be devoured. Our hopes that it would be successful were not fulfilled. Its weight was too much and after several attempts the tern was abandoned and drifted out to sea.

Terns of the subantarctic islands belong to an interesting group and Falla was keen on examining as many birds as possible. However, they were hard to come by. There was always the possibility of securing Arctic tern stragglers which may have deviated from their usual migratory routes in their remarkable journeys of 14,500 kilometres each way, from the Arctic to the Antarctic and back. Although some doubts are still raised by ornithologists, it is generally accepted that this migration does take place and terns found in the northern and southern hemispheres are the one species.

Terns have been captured, banded and liberated while nesting in the Arctic regions. Four birds with identity bands still attached have been recorded from the coast of Western Australia, New South Wales and South Australia. Another record is from New Zealand. These birds had deviated from their usual migration routes which appear to be down the east coast of South Africa and the east coasts of North and South America.

The Arctic terns' year is by no means a restful one. After nesting in the Arctic regions they fly south to the Antarctic to enjoy its summer months. Towards the close of the southern summer they fly back to the Arctic to breed. They therefore enjoy two summers in each year. Following an examination of Arctic terns collected later in Antarctic waters, Falla was also of the opinion that they are migratory birds of the Arctic species.

Unpleasant weather conditions had persisted throughout the day and we were grateful to have a warm hut to return to, made more comfortable with four less occupants. Falla, for the first time, had the pleasure of sleeping in a bunk. Before we retired the wind rapidly increased in violence and prospects of returning to the ship next day seemed hopeless. Hurley in an optimistic mood suggested the strengthening wind was a good sign — a prelude to quieter conditions. We were by no means convinced but all heartily agreed.

Heavy snow was falling next morning with little visibility. Wind had certainly eased, but the distant roar of surf on the beach at Corinthian Bay seemed a good indication that heavy seas would prevent the motor boat making its journey to the island to take us off.

After breakfast we all walked around to the beach. The *Discovery* was still at anchor wallowing in the big seas. When our presence was noticed by those on board they began signalling. With the absence of Eric Douglas I was the only one left with any idea of semaphoring, which I had learnt at school. My scant knowledge was insufficient to read the message. Later, I read the following entry in Simmers's diary: "After the ship signalled a message, a figure we presumed to be 'Cherub' [Fletcher] dropped to the ground where we decided he was deciphering the message. Again he would rise, walk to the most awkward place for us to read and would send repeat." The nickname of Cherub was given to me when I appeared dressed as a cherub at a fancy dress ball on the *Nestor* during our voyage to Cape Town to join the *Discovery*.

Later in the morning, Falla walked to the beach at Atlas Cove to check our gear, already packed and covered by a large tarpaulin. Suddenly, we heard his excited cry: "Here they come, rounding the headland." Hurrying to the beach with the rest of our gear we saw the boat coming towards us with its detachable half-cabin removed.

Sir Douglas, standing at the tiller, covered with snow and drenched by spray, called for us to get everything on board quickly because they were leaving immediately. Gear was soon stowed, taking up the forward half of the boat. A covering tarpaulin was then fastened to the gunwales; it extended back to almost cover the cockpit. In the meantime, three cases of tinned food, brought ashore by Sir Douglas, were placed in the hut to replenish what we had used.

Finally, with all hands sitting on the cockpit floor and Sir Douglas at the tiller, we set out for the *Discovery*. We had been so busy getting away that we had had no time for conversation, but now Sir Douglas regaled us with a description of their exciting trip from the ship.

Early in the morning, as the wind lessened, Captain Davis suggested an attempt should be made to bring off those on shore as all signs indicated the weather would worsen through the day. Sir Douglas agreed and Eric Douglas when asked what he thought of the decision said, "I'll give it a go." The motor boat with great difficulty was swung over the side.

Sir Douglas told us that after leaving the ship they encountered heavy seas and had difficulty making headway. Visibility was limited because of flying spray and a fairly thick fog. Keeping well out to sea, they rounded the offshore reef over which waves were crashing and headed in the direction of Rogers Head. When the boat was a short distance from it the engine began to miss and it finally stopped. With no headway, the boat wallowed in the wave troughs and was in danger of being swamped. Eric Douglas, checking the engine, decided a blockage had cut off the petrol supply. He immediately began to uncouple the fuel pipe from the tank and in the process the connecting nut slipped from his fingers and rolled under the floor boards. The anchor was thrown out but it did not reach the bottom as the attached rope was too short. A dredging line was then tied on and the anchor reached bottom and held. Spasmodic movements of the boat made work almost impossible but Eric eventually cleared the blocked fuel pipe; floor boards were lifted, the nut found and repairs completed. To their great relief the engine started.

While this adventure was being related we left the partly protected waters of Atlas Cove and met the full force of wind and waves. A heavy fall of snow completely obliterated all landmarks. On our starboard side waves could be heard crashing on the reef, so we headed out to sea for at least a mile before it was considered safe to turn and steer for the *Discovery*.

Huge waves swung the boat in all directions as it dived into the troughs, and at the tiller Sir Douglas had a hard task steering a straight course. Water sweeping over the bow, shed by the tarpaulin, was a constant worry and cause of anxiety. Heavy snow, still falling, restricted visibility. Navigation was by the sound of breaking waves away to our starboard. It was an eerie experience, as if relegated to a very small, tempestuous world of our own. No one talked. I'm sure, like me, they listened to every beat of the engine. A stoppage at this stage would have been disastrous. Doc Ingram was seasick.

Wind-driven snow spicules caused painful discomfort and we were forced to cover our faces from the continual blast. Eric Douglas replaced Sir Douglas at the tiller as his face and eyes were too painful to continue.

It was now almost two hours since we set out from Atlas Cove and we were more or less in a position where the *Discovery* should be anchored. The sound of waves breaking on the Corinthian Bay beach gave us some idea of our distance from shore. Visibility was virtually nil as we cruised blindly in various directions. Finally, after almost giving up hope of finding the ship she appeared in sight, pitching and rolling to an alarming extent. It was obvious that boarding her would be a nerve-racking exercise.

As expected, disembarking was a wild experience. After the gear was hauled on board, each occupant of the boat, one at a time, jumped to the shrouds as the boat levelled on its rise and fall with the waves. No mishaps occurred. All were safe on deck including Falla's king penguin, which, by some means, he had been permitted to bring with him. I was later told by a ship's officer that Doc Ingram being ill over the boat's side had caused him some worry. However, what he thought was blood was the tomato sauce Doc had put on his fish cakes at breakfast to make them more palatable.

By midday the *Discovery* was ready to sail. Anchors were weighed and the ship steamed out of Corinthian Bay to meet the force of a full gale. The island was almost immediately lost to sight.

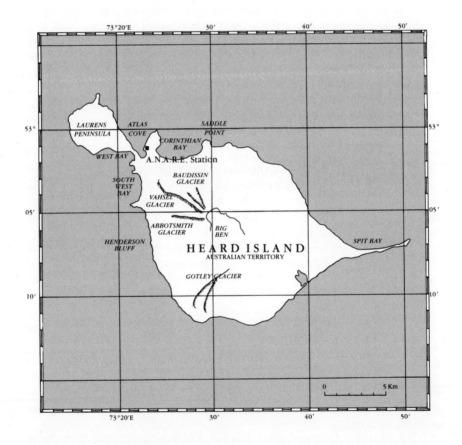

A recent map of Heard Island.
(By courtesy of the Antarctic Division.)

A Fairyland World of Ice

F ROM HEARD ISLAND a south-south-east course was set,
with the object of reaching the Antarctic coast near Gaussberg,
about 100 miles west of Haswell Island. Gaussberg Mountain is an
extinct volcano, about 425 metres high, and is connected to the
continental ice-cap by an ice causeway 180 metres in height.

Gale-force winds, experienced since we left Heard Island, lessened
in the early hours of the following morning, December 4. Seas had
moderated although a heavy swell was running in from the west. The
barometer was rising and we expected a spell of good weather.

During the previous night, the last members of the shore party to
leave the island had complained of a stomach disorder and a feeling of
nausea. Doc Ingram, also suffering, diagnosed food poisoning, no doubt
due to a tainted tin of fish cakes. Fortunately its effects were not lasting
and we soon recovered.

During the night, deck duties had been allocated to members of
the scientific staff, if required. Although not feeling the best I was
detailed to assist the helmsman between 3 and 4 A.M. but my services
were not required owing to an improvement in the weather. The lifting
of the ship's rounded and overhanging stern, particularly in heavy
following seas, had a strong tendency to swing her off course. Steering
was manual and it took the brute strength of the man at the helm to
keep the ship head on and prevent broaching. In big seas two men were
necessary at the helm.

It was good to be at sea again, even though the ship was rolling
her gunwales under. The laboratory was a scene of great activity although more time was taken up with holding on than getting any work
done. Johnston and Marr were endeavouring to sort and preserve the
large collections they had made on Heard Island. They were assisted by
Ingram, meticulously sorting small organisms dredged from shallow
waters of Atlas Cove. Falla and I, in our corner, had started skinning
and filling out birds. Several of them, remaining from the Kerguelen
Island collection, were completed and we began work on the large series
from Heard Island. Many days of this task were ahead of us. Before a
bird is skinned it is routine to record the colour of its eyes and any soft
parts, and take measurements of wing length, tail, various leg structures
and bill. Many well-prepared bird skins, housed in museum study
collections, and properly cared for, are more than a hundred years old

and still in good condition, so we knew that a careful job would be worthwhile.

The wind, instead of decreasing in force through the day as expected, veered to the south-west and increased in violence. With sails down to a minimum, the ship's progress was reasonable — 120 miles being logged at midday. Falling snow persisted, reducing visibility. We were now far enough south to encounter occasional northerly drifting icebergs and all hands were on the alert to sight our first bergs.

Sir Douglas explained we were following a course to gain echo sounding readings of depths which would prove that the Kerguelen–Heard Island submarine ridge, or bank, continued to the Antarctic coast, near Gaussberg. Extension of the bank to the south had been suggested by the earlier Challenger and Gauss expeditions, but without any direct evidence.

Today, 50 years later, the Kerguelen–Gaussberg submarine ridge is recognised as one of the world's major oceanographic features. It extends from Kerguelen Island for a distance of 1500 kilometres to the Antarctic coast, some distance west of Gaussberg. West and east of the ridge the ocean floor is comparatively level with depths of 4200 metres. The ridge itself rises from the sea floor in the form of a great mountain range up to heights of at least 4000 metres.

Soundings, taken every two hours through the day, ranged from 1240 to 1650 metres. Our echo sounder was one of the first made in England under licence from the Admiralty. The equipment consisted of a pneumatic hammer fitted in the hull of the ship, aft on the starboard side of the keel, and a receiving microphone situated forward on the port side of the keel. The depth recording part of the installation was housed in the chart room.

The use of fresh water was rationed as the supply was limited and had to be conserved. A little over half a litre, issued daily to each person, had to fill our needs for drinking, washing, teeth-cleaning and shaving. The latter chore was unnecessary as all hands had grown beards — some bushy, others patchy or almost non-existent. An early morning wash was a simple task of wiping one's hands and face with a dampened face towel. Late in the evening, however, a sudden decision found me in the engine room begging a small tub of hot water from Chief Engineer Griggs so I could have a bath. My request was reluctantly granted with a warning not to make a habit of it.

On my way along the deck to the engine room, with a towel over my shoulder, I met Sir Douglas who later told those in the wardroom that Cherub Fletcher had gone mad. Apparently Professor Johnston became quite agitated until informed that my insanity was due to my craving for a bath. The extreme cold really made bathing unnecessary.

Early the next morning I continued bird skinning. The wind had fallen to a light breeze, but a heavy swell kept the ship continually rolling. At breakfast Babe Marr, who usually had little to say, related a strange dream he had during the night. He dreamt he was eating flannel cakes and when he awoke he had found half his blanket missing.

An overcast sky and a falling barometer indicated the calm conditions would be of short duration. Temperature on deck was almost minus 2°C. At noon, sails were taken in and we continued under steam, averaging about four knots. Decks and rigging were covered with a thick mantle of snow while icicles, suspended from the rigging, proved a hazard as they dropped on the deck.

Our position at midday was 55°43'S, 77°56'E. Soundings were again taken every two hours; depths being slightly deeper than the previous day. They ranged from 1830 to 2380 metres. It was evident we were still following the submarine ridge with much deeper waters to the west and east.

Early on the morning of December 6, scientists and ship's officers gathered outside the cabin of Eric Douglas and serenaded him on the occasion of his birthday; we then moved forward to Doc Ingram's cabin to repeat the performance. It was a double birthday.

Calm conditions persisted during the morning with occasional bursts of sunshine. Early in the afternoon the light breeze from the southeast increased in force with rising seas. The ship began plunging headlong into huge rollers; tonnes of water swept over the forecastle head and cascaded along the decks and finally poured through the scuppers back to sea. Violent movements of the ship, as she rolled heavily, made work impossible and most of us retired to our cabins. The wind increased to gale force. In an effort to steady the ship, her course was slightly altered and speed reduced until we were just making headway.

Simmers was endeavouring to write up his meteorological reports in his cabin. During the voyage he had earned an unenvied reputation for his uncanny ability and skill in creating minor personal disasters. His list of mishaps was added to when an extra heavy movement of the ship catapulted him over the back of his cabin chair, breaking its back, and at the same time spilling a bottle of ink over his books and reports. Hearing the commotion I rushed into his cabin as he came to his feet smiling, revealing a gap in his front teeth where he had broken a tooth off a partial denture.

Five depth readings were taken during the day. At 4 A.M., depth of the sea floor was 2490 metres, rising to 2023 metres at 8 P.M. A higher ridge, 1835 metres, was recorded at midday.

Before retiring, Hurley and Moyes, with great ceremony, produced two bottles of port and the birthday boys were toasted until the supply gave out. Doc Ingram was obviously not enjoying his birthday celebrations overmuch for he was again suffering from the pangs of seasickness. Usually a mirth-provoking subject, particularly from those who have never suffered from it, we had the greatest admiration for Doc's stoicism. Never losing his sense of humour, he simply retired to a quiet spot until he recovered.

The wind had decreased the next day and the sea was relatively calm, although a heavy swell from the south-east did nothing to ease the ship's rolling. Work in the laboratory continued with little rest, but seemingly with little reduction in the size of the collections. There were many interruptions as we were frequently called upon to assist in other duties.

Sir Douglas was anxious to have the large steam winch, situated at the ship's stern, overhauled in readiness for deep-sea dredging and the towing of plankton nets; it was also considered necessary to rewind and check the steel cable on the drum. Before this could be done, coal briquettes stacked in the winch house had to be removed. A chain of six scientists was formed along the deck and about three tonnes of briquettes were thrown from one to the other and dumped into empty bunkers until they filled. Work was then suspended until the next day.

Late in the afternoon a number of icebergs were sighted in the distance. Light snow had been falling most of the day and visibility was limited.

Depth soundings of the sea floor showed a marked shallowing. At 8 A.M., a depth of 1654 metres was recorded, gradually rising to only 641 metres at 6 P.M. A sudden drop of almost 730 metres then took place in the next two hours. This spectacular rise of the sea floor was named the Banzare Rise. Sir Douglas suggested the possibility of an uncharted island, either to the east or west of the shallow area, but time prevented any deviation from our course to investigate.

December 8 broke fine and clear. An overcast sky was clearing with the sun making valiant efforts to break through; the barometer was rising.

There was great excitement on board as the ship was now passing many large icebergs. These huge masses of floating ice, nine times greater in bulk underwater than visible above sea level, rose to a height of 30 metres or more. The majority were tabular in shape, flat-topped with steep sides. Others, which had suffered denudation, or because of underwater erosion, had capsized, revealing an upper surface composed of spires and fanciful shapes similar to turrets and ramparts, reminiscent of forts and mediaeval castles.

Scattered amongst the large icebergs were smaller, and shapeless, old, weather-worn bergs. Also floating low in the water were remnants of bergs, known as "growlers". These are difficult to see and avoid. My introduction to this new and strange environment could not have been under more superb conditions. Bright sunshine showed up the dazzling white of the bergs as they floated on a deep blue calm sea under a cloudless light blue sky. It was a fascinating sight.

I was called upon to assist Sir Douglas, Campbell and Ingram in removing the remainder of the coal from the winch house. Bunkers were soon topped up and the rest were stacked on deck. The task of letting out and rewinding the steel cable on the winch drum was now taken in hand. A check of the cable was essential as it had been loosely wound on the drum from the dock in London. The cable, 9000 metres in length, had a maximum circumference of 4.7 centimetres and a breaking strain of ten tonnes. It gradually tapered to 3.5 centimetres at the free end with a breaking strain of seven tonnes.

The cable was paid out with the ship steaming slowly ahead. Depth of the sea floor was 2375 metres, so that allowing for warp, at least 550 metres was trailing along the bottom.

Checking of the cable proved a wise precaution as the end of it was found to be insecurely fastened to the drum. While rewinding, the cable was greased, and guided on the revolving drum to fit snugly together row by row, finishing up with 36 layers. This long and tedious task was successfully completed at 9.30 P.M.

The weather continued fine next morning but with an overcast sky, intermittent falls of snow and a deck temperature of almost minus 2°C. Icebergs were greater in number than the previous day. They were a strange and wonderful sight, the varied frozen architecture of individual bergs being a continual source of wonderment.

Sightings of whales had gradually increased during the past few days. When spouting in the distance, only a feathery, momentary puff of vapour could be seen. Later, as two whales swam close to the ship, it was noticed that the spouting — as a whale exhales — consisted of a sizeable jet, rising straight upwards with a shape and direction that is a characteristic of blue whales. These colossal warm-blooded mammals — the largest of all living creatures — grow to a length of 36 metres. A blue whale of that size has a body circumference of 15 metres and a weight of approximately 100 tonnes or more. Its 26.5 tonnes of blubber would yield almost 14 tonnes of oil.

Daylight had been increasing as we steamed south and we were now experiencing 23 hours each day. At noon, after a distance run of only 70 miles, our position was 61°36'S, 77°59'E. Three soundings during the day gave depth readings of the sea floor ranging from 2560 to 2310 metres. We were still traversing the Kerguelen–Gaussberg submarine ridge.

At 8 P.M., a start was made to run our first plankton and hydrographic station with Babe Marr instructing and supervising operations. This was the first of many similar stations embracing a standard series of observations including water samples, water temperatures and a knowledge of the plankton life from various depth zones to the surface, on this occasion from depths, in metres, of 2000–1500, 1500–1000, 1000–800, 800–600, and in 100-metre depths to the surface.

Three steam donkey engines were used to lower and raise the steel-encased reversible water bottles and vertical plankton nets. Each engine had attached to it a winding drum on which was wound 3500 metres of wire with a breaking strain of one tonne. Wire from the drum passed overhead around a grooved pulley wheel which was fastened to a davit. This was swung outboard sufficiently to prevent the wire from fouling the ship's side. A dial indicated the depths of the water bottles or nets.

An engine on the forecastle head was used for lowering and raising Eckman water bottles from depths below 600 metres. A second donkey engine, situated amidship, was used to gain water samples with Nansen Pettersen bottles from 13 determined zones to a depth of 600 metres. Each water bottle had a built-in thermometer which gave temperatures of the water in each particular zone.

To obtain a water sample, say between 1000 and 800 metres, the bottle was lowered to 1000 metres and then raised at a metre a second. When the dial reading showed the bottle was at 940 metres a brass messenger was released which slid down the wire and hit the bottle when it rose to 800 metres. It then activated a mechanism which caused the bottle to capsize, effectively sealing it and preventing the entry of any further water on its haul to the surface. At the same time the thermometer thread was broken, thus allowing no change in the water temperature reading of that zone. Times of releasing the messenger at various depths were known; they reached water bottles or nets, spot on, at required depths.

Water samples for salinity and routine analyses were dealt with by· Alf Howard in his small laboratory situated off the wardroom. He also recorded the temperature readings.

A third donkey engine, situated further aft, was used for lowering and raising the vertical plankton nets. During the running of this particular station, catches were obtained from depths of 1000–750, 750–500, 500–250, 250–100, 100–50 metres and 50 metres to the surface. Attached to the net opening was an encircling cord bridle with a mechanism which, when activated by the descending messenger, effectively closed the net so that further plankton life could not enter on its haul to the surface.

To operate the nets, one of the team stood on a small platform which, when lowered from the ship's side, was immediately below the swung-out davit. His duties were to fasten the net to the wire, adjust the closing bridle, lower the net below the sea surface and move the hand of the depth dial to zero. His position was an unenviable one. He was partly submerged in the water because of the rolling of the ship, and he also had to contend with the platform being forced up on its hinges against the ship's side.

Containers with plankton samples, when removed from the nets, were attended to by Marr and Johnston in the deck laboratory. Catches from the vertical nets were generally small, consisting mainly of tiny organisms. When the net was surfaced, the operator on the platform washed down the sides of the net so that any clinging organisms were swept down into the container attached to the end of the net. This was then removed and taken to the laboratory. The amount of water in the container was reduced by passing the contents through a sieve of the same mesh as that of the net. The plankton residue was then placed in a glass jar with a 10 per cent solution of formalin and labelled with the station number and depth obtained. The latitude and longitude of the station was recorded so that its exact position was known.

While the station was in progress, engines were stopped and the ship drifted. To complete the station programme, oblique tow nettings were made from the ship's stern. A Kelvin tube in a brass case was attached to the end of a wire cable operated by the main winch. Lowered to the surface, a silk tow net with a mouth ring 70 centimetres in diameter was then fastened to the cable, followed shortly afterwards by a second tow net with a mouth ring of a metre. Engines were started and the nets paid out for 200 metres. Hauling in began immediately at a speed of two knots for about a kilometre, by which time the nets had surfaced. The maximum depth of fishing was indicated by the Kelvin tube. Good catches generally resulted from the tow nettings. The time involved in running the station was five hours.

At the conclusion of the station, Sir Douglas, Ingram and I moved six tonnes of coal briquettes, stacked on the deck, into an empty bunker. The decks were now free of coal and our total remaining stock was 300 tonnes.

In the evening, strangely enough, another double birthday was celebrated — Professor Johnston and Babe Marr. In the absence of any liquor, toasts were out, but they were each presented with a cake. One was saved for Christmas Day. The other quickly disappeared with the able assistance of their well-wishing colleagues.

I arrived on deck the next morning to find the sea strewn with icebergs in all directions. We had also entered the northern fringe of drifting pack-ice, remnants of the previous winter freezing of the sea. Early in the summer months it had started to break up and was floating north in flat expanses, some of considerable extent, but only a metre in height.

Loosely packed, it proved no hindrance to the ship as she pushed her way through on a south-easterly course. Light falling snow gave a final touch to my feelings that the ship and her company had been transferred to a fairyland world. All hands were soon on deck, clambering into the rigging for good vantage points from which to record, with their cameras, our first sight of a sea almost completely covered with ice.

The *Discovery* continued her way through the floe-ice with engines turning over slowly, following at times the long, winding leads opening into large ice-free areas, but all the time steadily moving south. Sir Douglas, surprised at such formidable ice so far north, was convinced we had come south in a season of severe ice conditions; not very reassuring since we were still about 300 miles from the Antarctic coast.

During the day we were thrilled with our first sight of emperor penguins. Mostly solitary birds, they were standing on rafts of floe-ice and showed no signs of alarm as the ship glided close by. Remaining calm and dignified they made no effort to take to the water.

Restricted to the Antarctic, these penguins are handsome birds; their appearance enhanced by bright orange patches on both sides of the head and a band encircling the throat. The largest of all penguins, they grow to a height of 120 centimetres with a body girth of the same measurement, and a weight of about 40 kilograms.

Adélie penguins now began to appear and within the next few days became a common sight; usually standing on floes in groups of varying numbers or swimming and porpoising in patches of open water. These attractive birds, about 45 centimetres high, have a glossy bluish-black back and a white front, reminding one of little gentlemen dressed in immaculate evening clothes.

Work in the laboratory had almost come to an end. Johnston and Marr had completed preserving the plankton and tow net catches, and Falla and I were nearing the end of skinning the Heard Island collection of birds.

At midday our position was 62°36'S, 78°22'E. Soundings of the sea floor were deeper than usual, ranging from 3540 to 3612 metres. Low dark clouds had been gathering during the morning, but as the barometer remained high and steady we hoped the fine weather would continue. At 2 P.M., two tow nettings were carried out from the stern. The nets were towed at a depth of 100 metres at a speed of two knots for about a kilometre. A good catch resulted, mainly diatoms and small free-swimming crustacea (copepods).

Since leaving Heard Island I had been suffering from toothache, a filling having dropped out of a cavity while chewing solid chocolate. Doc Ingram decided to replace the filling. Producing his dentist's equipment and carefully following instructions, he prepared a mixture, filled the cavity and advised me not to bite on it for several hours. It was a great relief. Later in the evening I received an almost professional haircut and beard trim from Morton Moyes. According to Campbell, it effectively changed my appearance from Henry VIII to Sir Francis Drake.

The ship made steady but slow progress through the night. In the morning the sea was more open although there was still an abundance of scattered icebergs and occasional stretches of compacted pack-ice through which the ship bumped her way with only a slight slackening of speed. The sky was still overcast, but now and again the sun broke through to dispel the greyness and bring out the glistening whiteness and beauty of the bergs.

Seals were now becoming numerous, generally crab-eaters, stretched out fast asleep on the floes. This is a common species in southern waters and is a more agile and larger species than the less common Ross and Weddell seals. We were also meeting up with Antarctic breeding birds; flying species which rarely leave pack-ice limits. These included snow, Antarctic and silver-grey petrels. Cape pigeons, which also nest on the continent, were also in considerable numbers. Most were feeding in the open waters in which food was plentiful.

Adélie penguins were now in abundance. In the summer months they nest in vast rookeries on the continent, moving north to the pack-ice edge early in the winter. This pilgrimage is essential as they feed mainly on krill, a small shrimp-like crustacean that crowds the sea and is the staple diet of most Antarctic life, including whales. Adélies were a never-ending source of interest and amusement.

As the ship approached close to a floe on which a group of Adélie penguins were standing, the majority of them remained unconcerned, while others became agitated and dived from the floe and swam at incredible speeds under water to adjacent floes. On reaching them, they shot out of the water and with unerring judgment landed feet first on the surfaces, which were a metre above sea level. Now and again a bad landing was made and the bird, sliding over the ice on its back, squawked loudly as if admonishing itself for its stupidity.

The ship had been out of wireless communication with Australia for the past few days, but contact was made again after slight adjustments. First message received was for "Birdie" Falla, informing him he was the father of a beautiful daughter, Elaine Margaret. Later in the evening, Hurley and Moyes each produced a bottle of South African wine, which they had been keeping for an extra special occasion. They guaranteed it of good vintage, the grapes having been grown on the sunny side of a hill. Congratulations and the health of the parents and Elaine continued until the bottles ran dry.

The Discovery trapped in heavy pack-ice off Princess Elizabeth Land. (By courtesy of the Mawson Institute. Photo: F. Hurley.)

I arrived on deck the next day to learn that the ship had been hove to since 4 A.M., by order of Captain Davis, as he required rest. He had been on the bridge most of the night navigating the ship through heavy pack-ice. The ship's officers were not overpleased at this seeming lack of confidence in their ability to continue on course.

Later in the morning, determined efforts were made to break through the ice. It had become very thick and consolidated. To make progress it was necessary to charge the ship at large, unbroken masses of floe-ice on to which the iron-clad bow would override before recoiling from the impact. This process was repeated until the floe broke apart to form a lead into which the ship forced her way. Progress was very slow.

Finally, the ship was forced to a halt by impenetrable pack. Sightings from the crow's nest showed unbroken ice to the south and no signs of any open water. Furthermore, there was a definite "ice-blink" away to the south — a white reflection on the low clouds — indicating nothing but ice ahead for many miles. On the other hand, the sighting of dark shadows is a sure sign of navigable open water.

Our position at midday was 65°18′S, 80°12′E. Soundings ranged from 3345 to 3270 metres, so we were in relatively deep water and about 80 or 90 miles from Gaussberg.

Captain Davis was reluctant to make any attempt to push the ship south, stressing the possibility of her becoming trapped in the ice and frozen in. Sir Douglas agreed and in the early afternoon a course was set to the south-west. Later, it was changed to the west and we entered open, ice-free water. In the meantime, the heavy clouds had dispersed, the sky was completely free of clouds and the sun was shining in all its glory, transforming the surroundings into a scene of splendour.

Taking advantage of the open water, oblique nets were towed astern at a depth of 100 metres. A course was then set to the south-west and good progress was made until thick compact pack-ice was again met with and the ship was stopped. Indications were that the pack was closing in to the west and north-west making progress in those directions open to doubt.

An easterly course appeared to be the most promising to extricate the ship from the cul-de-sac she had entered. Sir Douglas finally decided to sail east, keeping to the southerly fringe of pack-ice, and if suitable conditions persisted, we would make an attempt to reach Haswell Island in longitude 93° east, off the coast of Queen Mary Land where a base had been established during his 1911-14 expedition. This would involve a journey of about 400 miles east from our present position. If fortunate enough to reach there, Sir Douglas planned to have the aeroplane assembled, make several flights and raise the flag on the continent. The ship was headed east and later turned to the north-west.

Hurley, who had been spending a good deal of time in the crow's nest, reported seeing signs of land on the distant southern horizon. Sir Douglas after an inspection through binoculars was of the opinion that Hurley had seen several ice-built islands or grounded bergs. He estimated their height to be about 150 to 180 metres.

Antarctic nesting birds were in large numbers, generally flying in flocks and feeding in open expanses of water. Snow petrels, with their pure white plumage, are most attractive birds. They rarely, if ever, leave the limits of pack-ice. Flocks resting on floes or bergs were unnoticed until disturbed, when, as if by magic, they suddenly rose and took off in a low, swift flight.

Wilson storm petrels, also known as Mother Carey's chickens, are a fascinating and intriguing species. They are a common species at Kerguelen Island where large flocks were observed in Royal Sound and now, here in Antarctic waters, they were just as abundant. Storm petrels have a wide range extending from the Antarctic to northern waters of the Indian and Pacific Oceans. Large numbers frequent the Australian coast. They are small birds with an overall dark plumage except for a relatively wide white patch on the rump.

The petrels' swift, erratic, fluttering flight has earned for them the soubriquet of "Butterflies of the Seas". Never at rest, they flutter over the sea or pack-ice almost as if they were in a state of panic, occasionally diving to pick up floating organisms, but never alighting on the surface. Early seafarers believed their presence foreshadowed stormy weather and they were not looked upon with favour.

In the past it was believed that storm petrels laid their eggs while flying at sea by manipulating the egg under a wing until it hatched. The young were then supposed to float on the sea until capable of flying. It seemed there was no other way these restless birds — never seen other than on the wing — could breed. Another interesting theory was that storm petrels possessed an instinct to leave for a common area when about to die. This belief was recorded when vast areas of their tiny bones were found on shifting sands on the Cape Verde Islands.

Ritchie Simmers, taking advantage of the almost cloudless afternoon, sent aloft one of his balloons to record upper air currents. It was observed until it reached a height of 850 metres and became obscured by light cloud.

At 11.30 P.M. I climbed to the crow's nest, 34 metres above deck level, to witness the sunset. Conditions were ideal for a spectacular display: bright sunshine and a gathering of clouds low on the horizon. It was close to midnight as the sun sank below the horizon; sky and clouds were covered by a golden glow until the sun reappeared about 20 minutes later. While it was below the horizon the atmosphere was suffused by a mauve radiance.

As the sun emerged, its bright golden glow was diffused by irregularities in bergs and pack-ice into tints of pale green, blue and lilac.

Incredibly long shadows were thrown by scattered icebergs on to the millpond surface of the deep-blue sea, and an eerie silence completed an experience I will never forget. Carried away by this feast of nature, I was suddenly brought back to reality by the thought of having to regain the deck. After several nerve-racking moments, while vacating the barrel of the crow's nest, my descent down the mainmast was successfully achieved.

Throughout the night and early hours of the next day, the ship had been bumping a passage through dense pack-ice until brought to a halt at about 10 A.M. Further progress east was impossible. In all directions ice-blink indicated compact ice conditions. The perfect weather of the previous day had deteriorated. A falling barometer, a slowly strengthening south-east wind and the gathering of dark clouds gave promise of a blizzard eventuating at any moment.

The ship, with engines stopped, was drifting in a fairly large pool of open water. It was decided to remain there and await the expected blizzard. Our position at midday was only slightly different from that of the previous day as a good deal of backtracking had been done. It was an unlucky day — Friday the 13th.

Arctic terns were now becoming numerous; flocks of 30 to 40 birds were continually flying around the ship with others resting, head to wind, on floe-ice. Falla, inspecting them through binoculars, said they all appeared to be in winter (non-breeding) plumage. He was keen to secure specimens for a close examination to enable him to compare their characteristics with those of the northern Arctic tern. Birds could have been shot from the deck, but recovery of their bodies would have been a hopeless task.

McCormick's skua gulls, a distinct species from the subantarctic skuas, were recorded for the first time. In the summer months their range is only to the limits of the pack-ice; their activities in the dark winter months are largely unknown.

As we were settling down for the evening, Sir Douglas suggested a full plankton station. Babe Marr demurred to some extent, having experienced the difficulties involved with drifting ice, but being a man of few words he went ahead with preparations. Station No. 26 was commenced at 7 P.M.

To begin with, a plankton net was lowered to 1500 metres, according to the depth indicator, but this was approximate because the hauling wire had been carried off the vertical by a drifting floe. The messenger was then released to close the net at 1000 metres. In the meantime, the wire had cut its way into the side of a floe and prevented the messenger from descending. Campbell and I, with two crowbars, climbed down a rope ladder on to the floe-ice. We reached the wire after crossing several bridging pieces of ice. The wire was freed after some difficulty, allowing the messenger to continue on its journey. Later, while the net was being hauled to the surface, it became caught under an ice-floe. Descending again on to the broken pack we manoeuvred the net, undamaged, between two floes and it was successfully hoisted to the ship's side. Apart from these incidents the station was completely without further trouble, terminating at 11.30 P.M.

The pack had closed in the next morning and the ship was held fast with little possibility of breaking through in any direction. Captain Davis made several visits to the crow's nest but made no comment on regaining the deck. Water skies were visible to the north, south-east and south-west, indicating large stretches of ice-free water, 40 miles distant.

As the ship was jammed in amongst high ice-floes, a decision was made to "water ship", that is, to replenish our supply of fresh water. This task was undertaken by the scientific staff with a great deal of enthusiasm. Campbell, Simmers and I climbed over the ship's side on to solid ice-floe, complete with shovels and crowbars. Our job was to fill large cane baskets with hardened snow, hacked from the floe surface. When filled, the baskets were dragged to the ship's side, hauled on board by block and tackle and their contents then emptied into two long tanks situated on deck level alongside and above the engine room. The tanks were fitted with steam coils which, when heated, quickly converted the ice into fresh water.

It was hard work filling the baskets, but zest was introduced by occasional snowball fights — fillers against receivers. Men on the floe with the greatest amount of ammunition were usually the victors, but they deplored the fact that the deck gang retaliated with hard snow which had been strenuously shovelled into the baskets beforehand. In the space of two hours, 2000 litres of water had been added to the ship's diminishing supply.

At midday our position was virtually the same as the previous day. The wind from the south-east had strengthened, but not to the extent expected and did not help in opening up the pack. Several large icebergs, about half a square kilometre in area, were noticeably forcing their way through the heavy pack in a slow northerly drift. They appeared to be on a collision course with the ship. Although we were not making any headway, coal was being consumed and our limited supply was down to 275 tonnes.

Following a discussion with Captain Davis, Sir Douglas agreed to abandon further attempts to reach Gaussberg and Queen Mary Land as it was now obvious we had met with a season of heavy and extended pack-ice. When conditions improved the ship was to be headed west towards our main objective — Enderby Land.

Later in the afternoon an attempt was made to force the ship through the pack to the north-west, but after a mile of charging and battering through compacted floes, she again came up against impenetrable ice. Further progress was out of the question and the engines were stopped. Falla had shot several snow and Antarctic petrels during the day and their bodies were easily recovered by walking across the ice. We were busy skinning and filling them out for the rest of the day. They were an important addition to the collection.

The ship was still held up in heavy pack the next morning; no progress was made through the night. A change of wind had driven ice in from the north and, to some extent, had broken up the compacted masses of ice. The ship remained stationary during the morning with engines silent. The lowest of two readings by the echo sounder gave the depth of the sea floor as 3065 metres. We were still in deep water and well north of the Antarctic coast.

The ship drifted into an area of broken ice later in the afternoon and Captain Davis decided to force a passage to the north. The attempt proved unsuccessful. When charged by the ship, the ice, instead of splitting, just crunched, gradually building into a mass of soft ice into which the ship's bow jammed. Continual reversing and charging made little impression and after three and a half hours, with a gain of only two miles, the attempt was abandoned. Engines were again stopped.

Southing had been made through the night, but once again the ship was stationary, held up in thick pack. Our latitude at midday was 65°41' south, the farthest south so far attained. We were still north of the Antarctic Circle.

At 9 A.M., Sir Douglas, worried at our enforced delays, gave instructions that determined efforts must be made to force a passage to the west. Full speed was signalled to the engine room and for the first time large floes were charged at a speed other than slow. Usually, the ship's impact and overriding of the bow was sufficient to split the floe, allowing the ship to shoulder her way in and thrust aside the two large masses of ice. These, scraping along the planking, created a rather unpleasant sound.

All rafts of floe-ice have a depth of about six metres below sea level. In time, this "keel" is eroded by water action, leaving long, downward projecting solid spikes. As the floes swing with the passing of the ship, the spikes strike against the planking creating loud, nerve-racking, cracking reports. It was on these occasions that we were comforted with the knowledge of the ship's stout planking.

The pack began to open to the north-west at about midday and the ship was headed in that direction. Taking advantage of every favourable lead, forcing our way towards ice-free pools and veering away from heavy pack, we began to make better progress.

All thoughts of an impending blizzard had gone. It was a perfect day; the sun was shining and there was a light breeze.

Besides the profusion of bird life, seals were plentiful, generally asleep and at peace on their icy beds. Two crab-eater seals were shot and hauled on board. Falla and I began the task of skinning them.

Earlier in the morning, while on the forecastle head, watching the ship's bow ploughing through the ice-floes, I was excited at seeing the huge head of a blue whale emerge from an ice-free pool about 50 metres away. It immediately spouted, ejecting a sizeable jet of water and vapour, straight and narrow, into the air. It was accompanied by a report, reminiscent of a railway steam engine on its first movement from a station.

Following its spouting and without any cessation of movement the whale began to dive, its long body gracefully curving as it submerged. An appreciable amount of time elapsed before the dorsal fin appeared and a further wait, until with a final flick of its tremendous tail, it disappeared from sight. I had watched at least 30 metres of whale, as if in slow motion, appear and disappear at a short distance. It was a memorable sight to watch one of the world's largest creatures. At least five blue whales had been sighted in close proximity to the ship. It seems unbelievable that these giant mammals are just as much at home in seas covered by broken pack-ice as they are in the open oceans.

At last, Campbell and Eric Douglas were directed to assemble the de Havilland Moth seaplane. The fuselage rested on a grating above deck level, usually occupied by the ship's lifeboat, while various sections and parts were still in their original packing cases. The two airmen began assembling the plane in readiness for flight when conditions were favourable. Reconnaissance from the air would give valuable information regarding pack-ice distribution and location of land.

The ship was still making slow progress to the north and northwest as the pack permitted. In all directions south there was an unbroken ice-blink, but a water sky indicated open water in the direction in which we were headed.

Late in the evening we steamed past an iceberg estimated to be about six kilometres long, three kilometres wide and a height of 45 metres. Hurley took still and cinematograph shots of this immense berg.

Fifty years later, interested scientists gathered together at an International Conference on Iceberg Utilization in the USA. Its main business was to discuss the possibility of towing large bergs to arid regions of the world to provide fresh water. At the conference, a plan was considered to select a relatively small iceberg of a million tonnes in Antarctic waters, cover it in sailcloth and plastic to slow its melting, and with the aid of five powerful tugs, tow it to the Arabian Peninsula. It was estimated the journey would take eight months with a loss of 20 per cent expected. The enormous cost would be well recouped by the sale of resultant fresh water. A project such as this appears to be fraught with overwhelming difficulties, but no doubt they were well debated. One cannot be too negative on such a proposal, as today seemingly impossible ventures are being successfully carried out.

Before retiring, Falla and I had removed the skins from two crab-eater seals. The task of carefully removing all vestiges of blubber from the skins still remained. Campbell and Eric Douglas unpacked the aeroplane parts until midnight. They were keen to get the plane assembled and ready to fly.

The ship made slow progress on a northerly course through the night. The pack became more open and navigable by morning and the ship was headed west. Good progress was made for several hours, even with a little southing, but once again we encountered thick pack-ice which was impossible to penetrate. The ship was turned with some difficulty and retreated to the north. The perfect weather of the previous day continued.

Hurley spent the greater part of the day perched in the rigging, with his cinecamera. He exposed 120 metres of film on highlights of the ship's battle to make headway through the heavy pack. Following his example, many scientists also took to the rigging with their cameras to photograph the unrivalled panoramic scenes.

Arctic terns were numerous; at least 12 to 15 flocks of 30 to 40 birds flew past the ship during the day. Our first sighting of a sea leopard was one seen slumbering on a raft of floe. He was left undisturbed.

Our position was further north at midday than it was the previous day, but distance to the west had been gained. Late in the evening the ship entered a large pool of ice-free water in the lee of a large berg. The opportunity was taken to lower a tow net with a two-metre-diameter ring opening over the stern. About 1500 metres of cable was paid out and the net was then towed at a depth of approximately 1000 metres for two hours at two knots. The net, hauled in at midnight, contained a remarkably good catch. It included 15 fish, fascinating medusae (jellyfish), cuttlefish, worms and krill.

At the conclusion of the tow netting, engines were stopped with the idea of allowing the ship to drift until early next morning.

The good weather of the past few days was now replaced by heavy snowfalls, bitterly cold sleet and a thick fog. At 9.30 A.M., engines were started up and, steaming around our sheltering iceberg, a course was set to the west through loose scattered rafts of floe-ice. Later, as conditions improved, the ship was moving more freely and our course was altered to the south-west. There was little change in our position from that of the day before.

Marr and Johnston continued sorting and preserving the previous day's netting catch. It was much more interesting than originally thought and they estimated that at least 140 species of macroscopic life were collected. The seaplane was now beginning to take shape as the airmen continued assembling it. Falla and I had almost completed the greasy task of flensing the seal skins. Before retiring, Doc Ingram reminded us that we had only five shopping days left before Christmas.

It was December 19. Two months had passed since we set out on this expedition. We were continuing on our southerly course at a slow speed but making fairly good progress. Many diversions were necessary to avoid icebergs and compacted pack. The pack became more scattered with long leads later in the morning. However, ice-blink to the south and south-west held no promise that these conditions would continue.

Snow, which had been falling almost continuously the previous day and through the night, had ceased, leaving the ship completely enveloped in a thick white mantle. At midday, after a run of 70 miles, our position was 65°39′S, 74°08′E. Sir Douglas promised a celebration when we crossed the Antarctic Circle, which, if our present rate of progress continued, would be late in the evening. No doubt, several bottles of Yalumba port would be produced. Later, heavy snow squalls limited visibility and the ship's speed was reduced.

At 8 P.M., the ship entered an extensive pool of open water and Captain Davis suggested stopping the ship to run a complete plankton station. He also remarked it would give him an opportunity to catch up on some much needed rest. The station, No. 29, was duly run from 9 P.M. to shortly after midnight. Depth of the sea floor was 2574 metres. At the conclusion of the oblique tow nettings the ship's engines were stopped and she was allowed to drift.

Campbell and Eric Douglas had finally assembled the seaplane. Its position was most vulnerable to winds from any direction, and fearing for its safety in case of a strong blow, Campbell decided to lash it securely to the deck grating. He approached MacKenzie for the loan of several long lengths of rope, which he was given, with strict instructions not to cut them. When lashing down was completed there appeared to be more rope than plane. MacKenzie had an obsession that scientists requiring a small length of rope would, without hesitation, cut pieces from the shrouds. If we had a knife in view, his eyes never left us, as he walked around the deck.

Six soundings during the day showed a marked decrease in depth of the sea floor, ranging from 2980 to 2329 metres. Sir Douglas estimated we were about 75 miles from the coast. At midnight the clouds had cleared on the western and southern horizons and I enjoyed the spectacle of another magnificent sunset.

Early the next morning Hurley reported loose scattered pack to the south from his vantage point in the crow's nest. Sir Douglas decided to continue south with some westing if possible. Captain Davis, after a visit to the crow's nest, was reluctant to proceed as the pack consisted largely of heavy masses of pressure ice. Nevertheless, engines were started and the ship headed south.

Campbell, still worrying about the safety of the aeroplane in strong winds, decided that after each flight the floats would have to be removed, thereby lowering the height of the plane and lessening wind resistance. This procedure would also allow the plane to be fastened down by bolts extending through the grating planks. He did not want to contend with having to lash it down with ropes after each flight.

Sir Douglas was anxious for the plane to become airworthy as he was keen to observe from the air the extent and distribution of the pack in which the ship had been more or less imprisoned for the past seven or eight days. Campbell told him the plane would not be ready to take to the air for at least two days as the engine had to be checked and tested. In any case, in our present position there was little chance of finding sufficient open water for the plane to take off.

Johnston and Marr completed sorting the catch from the previous night's oceanographic station. Results from the oblique nettings were most disappointing and not nearly as interesting as those obtained from previous stations.

After some days of unsuccessful attempts to contact Australian wireless stations, Sparks Williams managed to communicate with Flinders base in Victoria. Reception was good and delayed messages were being received and sent.

Following open leads and avoiding dense pack, the ship was able to keep to a course slightly west of south for most of the day. At midday we had logged only 45 miles for the day's run and that was not always in the right direction. Heavy pack was again encountered at 8 P.M. and the ship had to charge large floes repeatedly to break her way through. By 11 P.M. we had battled our way to latitude 66°31' south, our southernmost position so far and only a few miles north of the Antarctic Circle. The lowest of seven readings from the echo sounder gave the depth of the sea floor as 1970 metres.

Captain Davis was awakened at 4 A.M. when the ship struck a large mass of floe-ice and swinging away heavily, heeled over. He lost no time in reaching the bridge where he found that Colbeck and Child, during their early morning watches, had been quietly edging the ship south in an attempt to make a few miles and cross the Antarctic Circle.

Confronted by heavy pack-ice the captain ordered the ship about and to retreat back on our course. At this point we must have been very

Expedition members relax as they begin their long voyage south.
(Photo: S. Campbell.)

close to the Circle. Moyes, in plotting our course, said we had crossed, but by Colbeck's reckoning we were a mile or two north of it. The conflict of opinion was purely academic as we were now steaming north.

Although Sir Douglas was anxious to force our way west, Captain Davis was of the opinion we should continue retreating to the north. Finally, a course to the west was settled on. However, heavy pack-ice very soon forced the ship to head north-west where large stretches of open water were met with. A good speed was maintained until 11.30 A.M., when fog and snow reduced visibility to such an extent that the ship was stopped. Pack-ice had also closed in and further passage to the north was effectively blocked. The ship was hemmed in and we could only move back along the track we had made coming in.

Our position at midday, although we had again travelled 45 miles for the day's run, was only a few miles north of the previous day's position. Soundings showed little difference from those recorded the previous day.

Visibility improved late in the afternoon and the ship was headed back on our track, but soon afterwards thick ice had closed in and the ship was again stopped. She had made her way into a long stretch of open water, formed by the protection of a line of large bergs about three kilometres long, and 30 metres in height.

Efforts were speeded up to get the plane into the air. Conditions were ideal for flying with light wind, sunshine and calm open water. Final adjustments had been practically completed when the wind suddenly increased in strength, suggesting a possible blizzard. Campbell immediately set to work to remove the floats and fasten the fuselage to the grating. Wind-driven floes began to drift into the open water and very soon the ship was surrounded by ice.

I spent most of the afternoon salting the seal skins and packing them in containers. Sparks had again lost wireless communication with Australia.

The expected blizzard did not eventuate and the next morning broke fine and sunny with only a few scattered clouds. The ship was still trapped in the pool of water which had been cleared of ice during the night and it was sufficient to allow the plane to take off with a fair margin of safety when it was ready to fly.

The airmen had been working on the plane since early morning and Sir Douglas was advised it would be ready for a flight immediately after lunch. The ship was still drifting with her engines turning over occasionally to maintain position. All eyes anxiously watched the open water as floe-ice was again beginning to drift in.

At 2 P.M., the motor boat was lowered over the ship's side in readiness to tow the plane to a take-off position. However, trouble intervened; the plane's engine refused to start. Constant swinging of the propeller produced no response except occasional spasmodic backfires. The trouble was thought to be dampness in the twin magnetos. These were removed and placed in the galley oven to dry out, but at this stage all thoughts of a flight that day were abandoned.

As the motor boat was in the water, Sir Douglas, Hurley, Falla and I cruised around the edge of the pool to collect birds. Altogether, we secured five snow petrels, a silver-grey petrel, two cape pigeons and an emperor penguin. The penguin was to provide fresh meat for dinner on Christmas Day; more than five kilograms of dark-coloured flesh was later taken from the breast by the ship's cook. The bird itself weighed almost 30 kilograms. Before returning to the ship, Hurley climbed on to a large raft of floe-ice and photographed the Discovery with a background of large bergs, dense floe-ice and pressure ice. Back on the ship Falla and I got to work immediately on skinning the birds we had collected.

During the past 24 hours the ship had hardly moved from her position of the previous day. A thick mist developed with an increasing very cold southerly wind later in the afternoon. Sir Douglas was of the opinion it was an offshore wind and land could not be a great distance away. The floor was also shallowing and our last recorded depth was 1910 metres at 8.10 P.M.

Several blue whales spouting close to the ship were a challenge to try our skill at whale marking. The gun was produced and attempts made to fire information discs into the whale's body. Volunteer marksmen soon retired, as the gun kicked like a mule when fired, leaving the shoulders bruised and sore for days. The arrow-like wooden rods with barbed discs attached never once kept a straight course when fired. They darted right and left, high and low, veering away in an erratic flight, but never close to the giant target.

Late in the evening, Frank Hurley, from the crow's nest, reported large areas of open water to the south-west, from which a thick mist very similar to smoke was rising, no doubt caused by the offshore cold wind. It appeared that the pack was opening up into a series of long, open leads. However, as visibility was poor a decision was made to remain in our present position until the mist lifted.

The overnight fog and mist had thickened early next morning and visibility was down to less than a hundred metres. The airmen were already replacing the magnetos which had completely dried out. The engine still refused to start. Campbell felt sure the intense cold (minus 2°C) was the main reason for its reluctance to fire. In an attempt to heat the engine, Doc Ingram's petrol primus was borrowed and placed in a tin tray below the engine.

While we were at breakfast, an unexpected roll of the ship capsized the primus and it crashed on the deck, exploded and burst into flame. The dreaded cry of "fire", shouted from the bridge, caused a rush of all hands on deck to find the flames had been subdued with a fire extinguisher. Doc's primus, part of his bacteriological equipment, was an unrecognisable mass of twisted iron.

Less dangerous efforts were made to warm the engine by heating bags in the fiddley and placing them over the engine but it still refused to start. Campbell and Eric Douglas were quite nonplussed. Both were still of the opinion the trouble was fuel not vaporising in the induction pipe.

Late in the evening visibility had improved sufficiently to allow Captain Davis to force the ship through heavy pack to the south. After travelling about three miles we entered a large stretch of ice-free water. Engines were stopped and the ship allowed to drift. A freshening wind from the south-east began to drive heavy pack-ice to the north and it also drifted into the open water. Engines were started and kept slowly turning over to keep the ship in the shelter of several large bergs. Simmers predicted the possibility of a blizzard threatening to develop at any time. The sky was becoming covered with dark, rapidly moving clouds and the barometer was falling.

Sir Douglas informed the scientists he had discussed our situation with Captain Davis in an endeavour to determine the best course to take in extricating the ship from her present position in order to proceed west. His suggestion was to force our way to the north-east in the hope of meeting navigable pack and then change course. Captain Davis disagreed. He was anxious to work to the south-west towards the coast. The final decision was to remain where we were, watch pack movements, then, if possible, push our way west.

As the wind increased during the afternoon, work on starting the plane's engine was suspended and the floats removed. Campbell and Eric Douglas were quite certain they would have the engine functioning in the morning as they had thought of an ingenious device for heating it. A funnel of canvas over four metres long was made with one end arranged to fit over the engine, while the other end was fastened against the ship's funnel within the fiddley. An electric fan was placed at that end to force hot air through the canvas funnel to the engine. The funnel heat was over 40°C and was 32°C when it reached the engine. They also proposed heating the engine oil on the galley stove before transferring it to the engine. The airmen were keen to try out the experiment when the weather improved. Temperature on deck was minus 6°C and less than 2°C in the wardroom.

Falla and I spent the day skinning and filling out birds collected from our excursion in the motor boat. The task was completed before retiring at 11.30 P.M. Leaving the deck, I noticed that a strong southerly wind had blown most of the surrounding pack away to the north leaving the two large icebergs isolated in open water with leads extending to the west. Low on the horizon the midnight sun glowed like a ball of fire, bathing the sky and clouds with unbelievable varying colours of blue and gold.

In the early hours of Christmas Eve, the blizzard struck with winds of 72 kilometres per hour and visibility was reduced to almost zero by driven snow. Apparently, a belated attempt had been made during the night to sail west, but as the wind increased the ship was turned back to shelter in the lee of the two large bergs. The blizzard raged all day with heavy falls of snow. The ship steamed up and down in the protected open water with engines turning over slowly.

Professor Johnston had been working through the intestine of the emperor penguin in search of parasites. In great excitement he informed us the intestine was nine metres long and from it he had collected more than 500 tapeworms; a discovery which made his day.

Christmas Day came in with a slight lessening in the wind. It was bitterly cold with thick falling snow and was the coldest I had experienced. At 6 A.M. I was awakened by Father Christmas — Campbell well disguised. He wished me a Merry Christmas and presented me with a bag of biscuits on which was written, "A man cannot live on bread alone".

Later, the airmen decided to try out the engine of the seaplane. The previous night they had placed the canvas funnel in position and warm air had been circulating around the engine all night. Heated oil was then poured into the sump. Apparently appreciating the kind and generous treatment the engine roared into life with the first swing of the propeller. After running for some time the engine was stopped and was closely covered to maintain as much warmth as possible until conditions were suitable for flying. It was obvious a flight would be impossible during the day.

All hands assisted in decorating the wardroom until it had a festive appearance. In the centre of the table was a large Christmas cake presented by a well-known caterer in Adelaide. It was guarded at each corner by a bottle of Yalumba port.

At midday all hands, except those on watch, gathered in the wardroom. The cake was cut by Sir Douglas, glasses charged and toasts drunk to the King, and success of the expedition. Captain Davis was in a very cheery mood and read wireless messages from Lord Passfield, the Antarctic Committee in London, and Mr Scullin, Prime Minister of Australia.

First sitting of Christmas Dinner was at 12.45 P.M. A beautifully prepared souvenir menu was presented to each member as he was seated.

Commander Moyes, dressed in full commissionaire's uniform complete with medals — one for each year of undetected crime —

assisted with drinks and smokes, and was a tremendous success. He also acted as conductor of the orchestra played on the gramophone. Presents, from pupils of the Woodlands Church of England Girls' Grammar School of Adelaide, were addressed specifically to expedition members and distributed by Sir Douglas. In no time, the wardroom resembled a jumble sale as we rummaged through parcels containing tin whistles, bottles of sweets, books and all types of novelties. It was a wonderful and very much appreciated thought of the pupils.

The second sitting was a more free and easy, hilarious one. I stayed on and joined in the singing of songs and impromptu cabaret turns; one by Falla who took the part of a forward young lady of low ideas.

The dinner was a great success. Our main course — baked emperor penguin breast — approached rather timidly by the fastidious, was generally voted as equal to any game bird. Doc said it was very reminiscent of grouse.

Feeling a little the worse for wear, particularly after smoking my second cigar, I retired to my bunk, but I was soon called on deck to assist in our first attempt at dredging with the large Monegasque dredge. At 3.30 P.M. the dredge was lowered over the stern and about 2000 metres of cable was paid out until the dredge rested on the bottom. This dredge had a heavy steel rectangular frame with an opening about two metres long and 85 centimetres wide. The long, attached net had a 25-millimetre mesh of strong cordage.

Steaming slowly ahead, the dredge was dragged over the bottom for 30 minutes. The ship was then stopped and the dredge hauled in by the large steam winch at about 30 metres a minute. When swung inboard by block and tackle, it was found to be full of rocks, some 60 centimetres in diameter and stained with manganese. Later, as mud was washed from the catch, it was found to contain a remarkably good series of echinoderms (sea-urchins, brittle-stars, starfish, sea cucumbers), and other interesting forms.

The wind had dropped to a light breeze and the open, ice-free pools were again flat calm. Low, dark clouds reflected on the surface gave the water an ominous black appearance on which the vivid whiteness of bergs and large floe-ice stood out in marked relief.

Most of the pack-ice had been driven north by the blizzard, leaving open water to the west and south-west. Scattered icebergs were still numerous. The ship was headed west and good progress maintained. For several days we had sighted what appeared to be an ice island in the distance and we were now on a course towards it. We finally passed it some distance to the north. Sir Douglas studied it from the crow's nest with strong binoculars and estimated its height to be at least 90 metres, bounded by cliffs about 20 metres high and a length of five kilometres in a south-easterly direction. Shortly afterwards the ship's course was altered to the south.

For the past three days we had been steaming over relatively shallow waters. Depths of the sea floor had ranged from 1822 to 727 metres in the past two days. At this rate of shallowing, land could not be far to the south.

Chief Steward Dungey reported sick to Doc Ingram, complaining of symptoms that suggested appendicitis. He had been observed quaffing sly nips of port and whisky through the day, so he was ordered to bed with a further diagnosis to follow an examination next morning.

Slow progress to the south was made during the night, but the next day saw further movement of the ship barred by solid unbroken pack-ice, extending away to the south-west. During the early hours, several large rafts of floe were hit; one with sufficient force to hurl me out of my bunk. Two or three others suffered the same fate.

The ship was now steaming backwards and forwards along the pack-ice edge while a decision was reached regarding our further movements. Progress was possible to the south-east and Captain Davis agreed to force the ship in that direction.

Visibility was poor. A light south-easterly wind showed signs of increasing in strength. Snow had ceased falling; a fact which appeared to intensify the severe cold, even though there was no appreciable drop in thermometer readings.

At midday, 61 miles had been logged for our daily run, largely backing and filling, but we had at last crossed the Antarctic Circle. Our position was 66°57′S, 71°51′E. There was little cause for a celebration; time was passing, coal diminishing and we were well behind in our exploratory programme.

Slow progress was made during the afternoon on what was now an easterly course until about 8 P.M., when the ship was again halted by a barrier of thick compacted floe-ice extending away to the east and south.

The southern horizon was clear and Sir Douglas, from the crow's nest, thought he could see what appeared to be land — rising ice slopes at an approximate distance of between 20 to 30 miles. Opinions differed regarding the actual presence of land, but Captain Davis apparently had no misgivings and charted coast at latitude 67°30′ south.

Wind from the south-east, backing to the east, began to strengthen, bringing with it heavy falls of snow. At this stage our underlying thoughts were how essential it was to find sufficient open water to permit a survey flight of the plane. This would immediately determine the position of the Antarctic coast and also a way of escape for the ship from the seemingly vast area of ice in which she was trapped.

Sir Douglas decided that when an opportunity arose we would proceed on a northerly course until reaching the edge of the pack-ice and open sea; then proceed on a westerly course, unimpeded by pack-ice, to Enderby Land, one of our main objectives. If ice conditions improved, we would make southing whenever possible.

Close to midnight we saw a remarkable sight. The sun was setting in a flood of gold and mauve on the southern horizon. Intervening miles of compacted floe-ice, forced up by pressure, had formed innumerable pinnacles up to six metres in height. It was brought into relief by the low, setting sun, and further accentuated by the casting of long shadows. It was an amazing scene. Sir Douglas said it reminded him of a miniature model of a big city. Before retiring he informed us that a complete plankton station would be worked first thing next morning. The ship drifted in a relatively small pool of open water for the rest of the night.

I was awakened at 6 A.M. to assist in running the station. Depth of the sea floor was 475 metres. It was a dull morning and bitterly cold with low-lying dark clouds and a light breeze from the south-east.

Our early start on the station was delayed owing to the freezing of the three donkey engines, used for hauling and lowering nets and plankton nets. Blow lamps were used and they were soon functioning once again. There were several mishaps while working the vertical plankton nets. On one of the deeper hauls, the messenger was released too soon, thereby closing the net before reaching its specified depth. The net then had to be brought to the surface, its closing mechanism reset and the net lowered again for a rerun. Later, the operator controlling the donkey engine allowed it to overrun, pulling the net and fittings through the overhanging pulley.

Oblique nets were later towed astern at a depth of 160 metres, resulting in a surprisingly good catch. Finally, the large Monegasque dredge was lowered over the stern, and with the ship steaming slowly ahead, more than 900 metres of cable was paid out until the dredge rested on the sea floor. The ship was then stopped and allowed to drift with the dredge dragging over the bottom. After 20 minutes, the winch, under a heavy strain, brought the dredge to the surface. Its six-metres-long net was bulging with material.

Because of its extreme weight, a special block and tackle was attached to a boom from the mizzen mast and after some difficulty the dredge was swung inboard over the gunwale. While it was temporarily suspended, Johnston rushed towards it to secure organisms attached to the net. A dozen voices called to him to come back, but it was too late; the boom broke away from the mast under the heavy weight and crashed to the deck. The boom passed so close to Johnston's head that it removed his balaclava from his head. It was a miraculous escape from certain death.

The dredge net had been badly torn and a good deal of the catch was lost. The remaining material consisted of a rich variety of specimens, including squid, octopi, starfish, sea-urchins, bivalve shells, worms and sponges. Most numerous were brittle-stars and a pink coral. A single fish was in the catch. The zoologists immediately began sorting the mass of material, assisted by Sir Douglas and Doc Ingram.

Conditions were still impossible for the plane to take to the air. It was disappointing that we had to leave the area before a further investigation could be made of the distant ice slopes, sighted the previous day. However, in the clearer light of the day the slopes were not visible, so that it was more than possible that what had been seen was a mirage.

When dredging had been completed, the ship was headed on an easterly course and at midday we were still below the Antarctic Circle in latitude 66°48′ south. The lowest depth of the sea floor during the day was 504 metres. Much later, it was proved by the Norwegians that the depths recorded by us throughout the past few days were not a shallowing towards the coast, but a definite ridge. They named it the Fram Bank.

During the night our course was altered to the north and the ship recrossed the Antarctic Circle. Later in the morning her course was altered to the west. We were travelling at half speed and making a good passage through scattered loose pack-ice.

Throughout the day, Sir Douglas, Ingram and I were kept busy sorting the large quantity of dredged material. It was a cold but interesting task as exciting specimens came to light. A surprising number of small cephalopods (octopi and squid) were in this catch. These creatures play an important part in the food of sperm whales, seals, sea elephants and birds. They usually spend their days at considerable depths in the sea. Great hordes of squid rise vertically at night to swim near the ocean surface. Cephalopods possess sucker-studded tentacles surrounding the mouth which are used for seizing and holding creatures as they feed.

Fragments of octopus tentacles, as thick as a man's arm, have been found washed up on the coast of Japan, indicating a body of at least two metres in length with tentacles of an incredible length. Regardless of these, so far unauthenticated, monsters, octopi are still the largest of all invertebrate animals. In early seafaring days, legends were rife of giant octopi seizing vessels with their long tentacles and dragging them down into the ocean depths.

A moderately light wind from the south-east had been blowing for most of the day. Later in the evening it began to strengthen to half gale force. The ship was steaming west at half speed and making good progress through widely scattered floes. Icebergs of varying sizes were plentiful, the ship's course being continually altered to pass between them. Most of the bergs had a bewildering diversity of caverns, arches and grottos, formed by wave action at sea level. The calm water we had been experiencing was now a disturbed sea, and waves rolling into the various berg caverns created loud booming noises which continued through the night.

In the evening, a dartboard was produced in the wardroom and a number of us tried our skill at dart throwing. I won several chocolate issues from some of the players, including Doc Ingram. He then produced a large tin of toffee, challenging me to a match — winner take all. To everyone's surprise, including his own, he threw his first dart into the narrow circle followed by two in the bull's eyes. He retained his toffee and also my chocolate winnings.

Through the night we had made good progress to the south-west, but early in the morning we met heavy pack-ice and the ship was headed north. It was an unpleasant day with snow falling and the wind from the south-east having increased to gale force. Waves, somewhat subdued by heavy ice, were short and steep with deep troughs, the surface almost obscured by spray whipped from the wave crests.

At midday, after a 24-hour run of 125 miles, we had reached the position of 65°06′S, 67°53′E. In that time we had retreated some distance to the north, but some westing had been achieved. The submarine bank had been left behind, depths of the sea floor ranged from 2390 to 3365 metres during the day.

Despite the windy conditions, Sir Douglas, Ingram and I completed sorting the material dredged several days ago. The specimens had been preserved and stored and work in the laboratory had temporarily ended.

Late in the evening, while steaming west along a wide open lead, the ship was gradually forced north towards a line of heavy pack-ice. To prevent the northerly drift, the ship was swung around to head into the south-easterly wind. We maintained our position with engines turning over slowly.

December 30 broke with the wind blowing a full gale. The weather began to improve late in the morning and the ship was headed south-east through fairly heavy floe-ice, heaped with overriding ice forced up by pressure exerted by strong winds. Progress was slow and the ship had to battle almost every inch of the way.

It was bitterly cold and Sir Douglas, Campbell, Doc Ingram and I revelled in the task of transferring four tonnes of coal from a stack near the galley to one of the bunkers.

Stormy conditions of the past two days had kept most of the bird life sheltering, wherever possible, on floes and bergs. Groups of Adélie penguins were huddled together on low floe rafts while occasional solitary emperors stood upright with shoulders hunched, leaning towards the wind to retain balance, and looking very disconsolate. Whales were regularly being sighted together with numerous crab-eater seals.

Late in the evening, although little distance had been made through the day, we had gained some mileage to the south.

Campbell and Douglas return from their flight after sighting Mac Robertson Land. (By courtesy of the Mawson Institute. Photo: F. Hurley.)

New Year's Eve Party

THERE WAS a remarkable change in the weather the following morning. It was a perfect day with bright sunshine and a cloudless sky; the wind had completely dropped. I was immediately struck by the quietness. After days of becoming conditioned to the unceasing noise of 80 kilometre-an-hour winds shrieking through the rigging, the silence was beyond belief.

The ship had entered a large area of open water as calm as a millpond, and was drifting with engines stopped. Further progress south was barred by a line of unbroken hummocky floe-ice extending south, east and west. The opportunity was taken to run a complete plankton station; depth of sea floor was 4950 metres. It was commenced at 10 A.M. and successfully concluded at 2 P.M.

Conditions were ideal for the plane to be taken up on its first flight. During the running of the plankton station, Campbell and Eric Douglas had checked the plane and all was in readiness. Immediately after lunch the plane, with both airmen, was hoisted outboard and lowered by a block and tackle attached to a derrick swung out from the mizzen mast. Great care was necessary in swinging the plane outboard and lowering it from its position on a section of grating above deck level. Limited space, because of the ship's shrouds, made the operation difficult in preventing possible damage to the plane's wings. With the ship on an even keel in calm water there was no cause for worry, but with the ship rolling it was a hazardous procedure. As the plane settled on its floats, the lowering rope was unhooked, the engine started with a first swing of the propeller and, with cheers from all hands on deck, it taxied out into open water.

After taxiing for some time to warm the engine, speed was increased and the plane took to the air. It then set off in a southerly direction after circling the ship several times and was soon lost to sight.

In the meantime, the motor boat, with Falla and I on board, was lowered over the ship's side to patrol and render assistance in the event of the plane having to make a forced landing. Unfortunately, Chief Engineer Griggs had filled the tank with sea water instead of petrol — the height of optimism — and the engine came to a sudden stop after running for a few minutes. The cause was soon located and I drained the tank to the best of my ability and filled it with our reserve supply of fuel. The carburettor was then cleaned out and after several attempts the engine fired and we got under way.

While waiting for the plane's return, Falla succeeded in shooting six birds, including two of the elusive, swift-flying Wilson storm petrels. The plane was later seen coming in to land. We headed towards it but the engine again stopped because of water in the petrol.

The plane taxied to the ship under its own power and Sir Douglas was asked if he wanted to take the place of Eric Douglas on another flight. It was now late in the afternoon and he declined. Meanwhile we were having trouble with the motor boat. By continually draining the carburettor, I managed to get the engine running in short bursts until it finally gave up near the ship and refused to start. Somewhat abashed, we completed the journey by rowing. The plane by this time had been hoisted inboard and fastened down.

Discussing their flight later with Sir Douglas, the airmen stated that beyond the unbroken heavy pack, which, they estimated, from a height of 1500 metres, extended south for 45 miles, was open water about 10 miles across. Following this was the appearance of low, undulating, ice-covered land. Their observation of distances could be open to some doubt as they had received instructions not to fly beyond gliding distance of the open pool in case of engine failure.

The airmen also reported that during their flight of more than an hour they sighted black-topped peaks projecting through thick pack-ice to the south-west, about 45 miles from the ship. These islets were placed at 66°40'S, 64°30'E, a position found to be in error when we visited them on our next voyage. Sir Douglas named them the Douglas Islands after Rear-Admiral E. F. Douglas, C.M.G., hydrographer of the Royal Navy. Sir Douglas was certain that land had been sighted by the airmen and he named it Mac Robertson Land after Mr (later Sir) Macpherson Robertson of Melbourne. This new land, now defined as lying between 73rd and 60th degrees of east longitude, was visited again on our second voyage when landings were made on a magnificent stretch of rocky coast.

Taking advantage of the perfect conditions, Simmers sent up two balloons, one reaching a height of 15,300 metres. Its flight was recorded for 26 minutes before it became lost to sight.

At the conclusion of a special New Year's Eve dinner, Sir Douglas produced a bottle of rum and toasts were drunk to all and sundry. An announcement was then made that the Antarctic Circle Concert Party would have pleasure in entertaining members of the wardroom. The programme and some of the items were as follows:

NEW YEAR PARTY
S. Y. *Discovery* — Antarctica

FOR GENTLEMEN ONLY
SONG . . . "On the *Discovery*"
SKETCH . . . "Hawaiian Islands"
SONG . . . "The Intrepid Antarctic Explorer"
HAKA . . . "New Zealand Dance" by Falla, Doc, Eric Douglas,
Campbell and Fletcher
SONG . . . "The Captain's Lament"
SKETCH . . . "Shooting a Trawl"
All songs rendered by the Antarctic Circle Choir by Falla, Campbell,
Fletcher, Ingram and Simmers.

ITEM I "On the *Discovery*"
(Tune — "Vive la Compagnie")

Oh, this is the song of the BANZARE
On the *Discovery*.

The Antarctic coastline seems totally fled
On the *Discovery*.

Bay ice and bergs and penguins galore
But no bloody sign of the mythical shore.
But it's Christmas today
So let us all say
Here's to discovery.

Sir Douglas, our leader, has been down before,
Making discovery.

He's taking us now to Enderby's shore,
On the *Discovery*.

His hobby is knocking off big lumps of rock
And issuing cardigans, singlets and socks,
Cursing the slow
But making it go,
On the *Discovery*.

Moyes, our commander, who puffs at his pipe
On the *Discovery*;

In stars and Antarctic experience ripe,
On the *Discovery*.

144

Round his feet in the Fiddley we all sit and learn
While the ash bucket top marks a ring on his stern,
    No wonder he's blue,
    Afflicted with Stu,
    On the *Discovery*.

Ingram, our Doctor, is well known to some
    On the *Discovery*.

Pooshes bars and cases and says "they must come",
    On the *Discovery*.

With his tales of adventure he's filling a book
And at his Swiss socks it's a pleasure to look;
    Treating our sores,
    Wearing plus fours,
    On the *Discovery*.

Frank Hurley, the man with the camera, you know,
    On the *Discovery*.

He takes pretty pictures on fast plates and slow,
    On the *Discovery*.

He makes gimbal tables and fish traps and fun,
Shoots more with his camera than Doc with a gun;
    Crowing at dawn,
    Hailing the morn,
    On the *Discovery*.

There is a Professor of parasite fame
    On the *Discovery*;

He spies on sea elephants, spoiling their game,
    On the *Discovery*.

Tapeworms and bugs and their organs of sex,
What in the hell will he bring to us next?
    Trawls full of rocks
    And elephants' cocks,
    On the *Discovery*.

The man with the smile and the Teddy Bear beard,
    On the *Discovery*,

Is Cherub, from Sydney Museum we've heard,
    On the *Discovery*.

He sleeps on a sofa near Harvey's cold feet,
He gets up when he hears that there's something to eat,

Skins birds between meals,
Scrapes blubber off seals,
On the *Discovery*.

Our meteorologist, Simmers by name,
On the *Discovery*.

From the land of the fern and the kiwi he came,
On the *Discovery*.

His instruments delicate, those he ain't bust,
Are all over the ship from the keel to the must.
Talks all day
With nothing to say,
On the *Discovery*.

We've not sung the song of the officers yet,
On the *Discovery*.

For reaching the Circle we're much in their debt,
On the *Discovery*.

For Chiefy and Welchy keep warm down below
While mates three in number stand up in the snow
And J.K.'s the skip
Of this sturdy old ship
S. Y. *Discovery*.

ENCORE
We carried an aeroplane down all the way
On the *Discovery*.

And two jolly airmen on Government pay
On the *Discovery*.

They work winches and launches and hammer and screw,
For the Moth she was stubborn and prospects looked blue,
But now it's New Year
They've been in the air
On the *Discovery*.

ITEM 3 "The Intrepid Antarctic Explorer"
(Tune — "The Old Tarpaulin Jacket")

The intrepid explorer lay dying,
And as in his cabin he lay,
To the friends who were gathered around him
These last dying words he did say:

146

NEW YEAR'S EVE PARTY

Chorus

Wrap me up in my Whybrows and Burberry,
My Jaeger scarf wound round my mouth,
And with three Cardiff briquettes please bury me
The day we find land to the south.

The *Discovery* sailed off in the evening,
She steamed all that night back and forth,
But Moyes' first sight in the morning
Made her thirty-nine miles to the north.

They put out the tow nets for plankton
And took echo soundings all day
But Griggsy threw on some more blubber,
They made no more southing that day.

And once when they thought they were winning,
The spirit of ice in its wrath
Blew the fast pack under their bowsprit
And they drifted away to the north.

To stop drift they put out big dredges,
They buggered up nets by the score,
But at dinner J.K. told Sir Douglas
They were still further north than before.

The intrepid explorer still dying
And wearied of shifting about,
To the other intrepid explorers
These last dying words he did shout.

Final Chorus

Put me down on the first bit of pack-ice
With Yalumba uncorked near my mouth,
And leave me to die unmolested
For I see now we'll never get south.

ITEM 5 "The Captain's Lament"
(Tune — "Down in the Cane Break")

Once I went exploring in the old *Discovery*,
We had one bloody scientist and seamen 53,
We didn't have an aeroplane or echo sounder then,
We didn't have long-haired sheep in a wooden pen.

Chorus

The sea we sailed like Captain Cook,
Our stars we knew like a ruddy book,
We ate salt-horse and liked it very well,
In forty years things have gone to hell.

We didn't have Yalumba or Tomargo squash,
We didn't have hot water and we never had a wash,
We didn't play with plankton nets or shoot the otter trawl,
We didn't dredge with Monegasque and make an utter balls.

We didn't have an engine to help us on our way,
We didn't let the scientists have stations every day,
We didn't count the dust motes or let balloons go free,
We only sailed like Captain Cook upon the wide blue sea.

But now these days are over and seamen six have we,
Thirteen bloody scientists who do not know the sea,
They say all sorts of stupid things which pain me in the head,
So now I think I'll leave the bridge and make my way to bed.

The sketches were well received; participating members hurriedly left, but later decided there was no menace in the audience suddenly rising to give them a standing ovation. Sir Douglas, carried away by the excitement, produced two bottles of Yalumba port to finalise proceedings.

Festivities came to a sudden end at 9 P.M. when Sir Douglas announced we would carry out a tow netting. A net with a two-metre diameter ring opening was towed for 90 minutes at a depth of 165 metres. To permit this, 1800 metres of cable was paid out. A good catch included four fish.

Nearing midnight, Campbell, Doc and I climbed the mainmast to admire the midnight sun and welcome in the New Year. We heard 16 bells struck on the navigating bridge and knew we had entered into another year. It was an awe-inspiring spectacle. The sun, a fiery ball of gold, bathed the landscape in an unbelievable variety of all colours of the spectrum. To complete this memorable New Year's Eve I read part of a pamphlet by the light of the midnight sun.

New Year's Day came in with the sky obscured by dark clouds and light falls of snow. Unbroken pack prevented further progress to the south. At 3 A.M., engines were stopped and the ship drifted in fairly open water. Sir Douglas had a long discussion with Captain Davis regarding future movements of the ship, apparently with little or no agreement. Finally, at 2 P.M., Sir Douglas decided some move had to be made and we headed north-west with the object of making westing whenever possible.

At midday our position was only a few miles north-west of our previous day's position. Sir Douglas was becoming alarmed at our enforced slow progress and said we would have to make concerted efforts to reach open water and steam directly to Enderby Land. Accordingly, our course was altered more to the north with the ship following open leads through heavy packs of pressure ice. Throughout the afternoon and night a slow passage was kept to the north.

To celebrate New Year's Day the cook and steward, as a surprise to members of the wardroom, put on a special dinner which was very much appreciated. The steward, completely recovered from his suspected attack of appendicitis, proved Doc's diagnosis of an overdose of cooking sherry to be correct.

The next morning the ship was still battling her way north along leads through wide expanses of thick floe-ice. From the crow's nest the sea was covered, as far as the eye could see, with flat-topped ice about six metres above sea level. The leads we were following, with a little imagination, resembled roads extending away in all directions. The officer on watch had the unenviable task of selecting the right lead to follow so as not to end up in a blind alley. On these occasions the ship would batter her way through the impeding ice into an adjoining lead.

At midday we had logged 56 miles since our noon position of the previous day and had reached 65°22'S, 64°45'E. A light wind was blowing from the north with almost continual falling snow.

The ship had now entered an area of broken, scattered pack and was heading west, but shortly afterwards changed course to the south-west and made steady progress.

Towards evening the wind swung to the north-west and began to increase in force. Simmers forecast a severe blow. Campbell removed the floats from the plane and secured the fuselage to the deck grating.

Falling snow had enveloped the ship and rigging with an eight to ten centimetre thick covering. Doc and I had an interesting experience examining, with the aid of a magnifying lens, the feathery masses of individual snowflakes as they came to rest. Each was composed of minute crystals arranged in delicate, intricate designs of great beauty. It is believed that, like human fingerprints, no two snowflakes are alike in design. Once again, Nature works her miracles.

Slow, but steady progress to the south-west continued until, nearing midnight, open leads ceased and the ship was confronted with thick, unbroken pack-ice. From the crow's nest it appeared our only way of escape was to keep on our course by battering the ship through heavy pack.

During the night a passage was forced by constant ramming of the ice and at about 2 A.M., the ship was again negotiating open leads. By now I took little notice of the severe shocks and bumps as we charged large masses of ice, and I slept peacefully through the night.

Good progress had been made to the south by morning; the pack was becoming open again, and at midday we had reached 66°01'S, 62°30'E, so that we had made good southing and also gained distance to the west. Our distance run of 24 hours was 59 miles.

The ship was now lying in a wide stretch of open water with scattered small fragments of floe. A light swell from the west indicated only light pack in that direction, so we continued on our south-westerly course. Later, as conditions improved, this was altered to south, and with little hindrance the ship continued on her way at half speed. At about 9 A.M. we crossed the Antarctic Circle, but afterwards, near midnight, we entered a cul-de-sac with heavy pack to the south and west. The ship was allowed to drift while our situation was considered and a decision made as to further movement.

Since leaving the Fram Bank we had been travelling over reasonably deep water. During the day soundings had recorded a rise in the sea floor from 3448 metres at 1 A.M., to 2252 metres at 8 P.M. Three hours later it had shallowed to 1009 metres, suggesting a close approach to land.

Later, in the wardroom, Sir Douglas informed us that he had received a wireless message from Major Casey (later Lord Casey) advising him that the Norwegians had discovered and claimed land between Coates and Enderby Lands. This new land was well west of the planned and recognised limit of our activities, which were to the 45th, but not exceeding the 40th degree of east longitude. The message was an added incentive to Sir Douglas to waste no time in reaching Enderby Land and laying claim to that area for the British Crown.

Snow, which had been falling all day, continued the next day but later ceased; clouds cleared and for the rest of the day we enjoyed brilliant sunshine. During the night the ship had been drifting in a large ice-free pool and Captain Davis was reluctant to proceed further until the pack had broken up. The pool's only exit was the one we had used coming in; elsewhere it was impenetrable ice. A wind from the south was beginning to freshen.

Before breakfast, Frank Hurley, always crazy with surplus energy, had climbed to the crow's nest and later reported he had sighted land away to the south. Visibility was not the best and he admitted he could be mistaken. However, at 9.30 A.M., Second Officer Child said he had seen without any doubt several peaks (nunataks) projecting through a sloping land surface. After taking observations of its position, he made an entry in the ship's log that land had been sighted.

Sir Douglas, after a visit to the crow's nest, clearly saw two volcanic peaks to the west-south-west. He estimated one to be 15 miles distant and the other 30 miles. However, as distances are so deceptive in the clear Antarctic air, they could have been underestimated.

During the morning slight progress had been made by forcing the ship through heavy pack to the west, our midday position being 66°35'S, 61°17'E. We had crossed the Antarctic Circle, but it was re-crossed later as our course was altered to the north-west to escape thick compacted pack-ice. Depth soundings of the sea floor were 1620 metres at 11 A.M., increasing to 2162 metres at 9 P.M., as we moved north-west. The southerly wind which had showed signs of rising had subsided to a dead calm.

Hurley, again from the crow's nest, sighted a number of islets in much the same position as those recorded by the airmen on their previous flight. Visibility was perfect, and later Sir Douglas clearly saw the rising ice plateau of the mainland with many projecting mountain peaks. He estimated the ice-cliffs of the coast to be no more than 30 miles away. He was also convinced the islets sighted in the morning were actually mountain peaks on the plateau.

To validate his conclusions, Sir Douglas told the airmen to have the plane ready for a flight early next morning. In the meantime, a tow netting was planned at 7 P.M. The large net was towed for two miles at a depth of about 685 metres. After an hour the 1370 metres of paid out cable was winched in and the net hauled on deck. The catch included the largest haul of krill so far caught in a single netting, together with medusae of several types and eight fish.

Perfect weather continued through the night and at 4 A.M. I was called to assist Campbell and Eric Douglas to prepare the plane for a reconnaissance flight. As this was proceeding, the freshening wind from the south-east was sufficient to raise slight choppy waves on the pool surface. The pool was also decreasing in size by loose ice drifting in. It was decided to postpone the flight until later in the day.

While waiting for the weather to improve a complete plankton station was run in a depth of 2010 metres. Commencing at 11 A.M., it was completed without incident at 2 P.M.

The wind had now lessened to some extent, although the pool still had a disturbed surface together with a slight swell. Campbell agreed to attempt a take-off and the plane was swung over the side. With Sir Douglas as observer, it was taxied out to the extreme limit of the pool where, after warming the engine, Campbell gave it full throttle. It skimmed over the surface in a flurry of spray and finally took to the air after a long run.

Once in the air and gaining altitude, the plane headed south and soon disappeared from sight. The time of take-off was 2.30 P.M. from a

position 66°30'S, 61°06'E. Forty-five minutes later, the plane was back circling the ship, dipped its wings several times, and then flew in a westerly direction. Returning, Campbell brought the plane down in a perfect landing and taxied to the ship. The plane was hoisted to its position on the upper deck grating and its floats were left attached since a further flight was planned next day.

Colbeck, who was on watch when the plane returned, took bearings of the direction it had taken after dipping its wings. He had assumed correctly that this was Campbell's way of indicating the direction of open pack-ice.

Later, in the wardroom, Sir Douglas described what he and Campbell had observed on their flight. Ascending to 4000 feet, they had flown south and then east and west. He said that from the air, the newly discovered Mac Robertson Land presented a magnificent spectacle. Well defined ice-cliffs of the coast were in longitude 61° east and extended along approximately latitude 67°. They saw traces of its outline for 50 miles to the east and about 80 miles to the west towards Kemp Land. Away to the south, ice-slopes of the land, studded with isolated peaks of varying heights, could be seen rising rapidly to a height of about 1000 metres until lost to sight in the distance.

To the south-east, running back from the coast, were high ranges of black rocky mountains. Rocky outcrops on the coast were also sighted. The pack-ice between the ship and the coast, about 15 miles, was fairly heavy but scattered. Sir Douglas thought the ship could force a passage through it. However, beyond that were several miles of solid ice still attached to the coast.

Open water, in which the ship was drifting, was fast closing in and a course was set to the west towards the open water seen from the plane. Good progress was made until reaching a large pool when it was decided to carry out a tow netting. The large net was towed for two-thirds of a mile at an approximate depth of 100 metres. The echo sounder was temporarily out of order and only two readings were possible during the day; one at 10 A.M., recording 2113 metres, and the other at midnight of 1892 metres which indicated a rise in the sea floor.

A feature of the tow netting catch was an abundance of krill. Within the past few years a rough, but discerning, guess is that Antarctic life, including most whales, feed on at least 200 million tonnes of krill each year. The indiscriminate slaughter of whales and seals over the past half century, since the advent of whaling factory ships, has led to a marked change in the ecological balance. Krill, to some extent un-checked, are crowding southern waters to an alarming degree.

An idea of the drastic depletion of whales is realised when the

Full sail helped to steady the rolling of the Discovery.

catches of only four seasons are quoted. The combined whaling fleets during the two seasons 1927–28 and 1928–29, killed 72,000 whales with an oil yield of more than a million tonnes. A decade later, in the 1937–38 season, between December 8 and March 7, the catch was 46,000 whales, representing 500,000 tonnes of oil. The following season, 38,321 whales were caught, consisting of 14,059 blue whales, 20,788 fins, 2591 sperms and other species 883. Operations that season included 34 factory ships, two shore stations and 281 chasers. Seven nations were engaged with a total personnel of 12,795. With such forces against them, and continuing over the years, it is no wonder that most of the whale population has diminished almost to the point of extinction. This depletion has led to a disproportionate increase in the amount of krill.

Thoughts were then turned to the possibility of utilising these small creatures, which are rich in protein, as a basic food supply for the starving populations of many impoverished countries. In 1977, Russia harvested 200,000 tonnes of krill from Antarctic waters and the Japanese 20,000 tonnes for experimental purposes. It is generally accepted that the vast supply of krill could be used as a source of food, but under strict supervision so that the unique life of Antarctica will not be jeopardised.

But let us return to the *Discovery* and the year 1930. At the conclusion of our tow netting, Sir Douglas decided against pushing further south through heavy pack towards the coast. At 8 P.M. the ship was headed west and entered an area of scattered pack allowing good progress to the south. Meeting solid pack again, we turned to the west, making slow but steady headway.

Late in the evening, two high mountain peaks, clearly visible on the land ice-slopes, presented an interesting mirage which, with a good imagination, looked like a volcano in eruption. It was a superb, sunny evening but Simmers, whose weather predictions were rarely astray, warned us that developing conditions indicated a forthcoming blizzard.

As we continued our passage to the west, an ocean swell coming in from the north-west suggested open ocean in that direction. The swell, passing under large areas of low flat-topped pack, caused it to rise and fall as if a giant "looper" caterpillar was making its way below the ice.

I was awakened at 6 o'clock the next morning by the ship rolling and pitching and the howl of wind as it swept through the rigging from the east. Hurrying on deck I was greeted by a full hurricane; the wind was averaging about 80 kilometres an hour with gusts of up to 110 kilometres an hour. Four hours earlier, heavy snow had started to fall. Fortunately, the ship had changed course and headed north with the opening gusts. By the time the hurricane had reached its peak the ship had left the pack behind and was in open ocean except for occasional growlers and icebergs.

The ship was now heading into the full force of the wind, but with the engines turning over at full speed we were practically stationary and not making steerage way. Great difficulty was experienced by the two helmsmen and it was only their herculean efforts that kept the bow head on into the huge waves as they raced by.

Fearing for the safety of the plane, the officer on watch had called Campbell at 4.30 A.M. It was fully exposed to the fierce wind and it was then too late to detach its floats. Assisted by Eric Douglas and Marr, extra lashings were attached. Nothing further could be done and the two airmen then stood by as the plane strained at its fastenings. If they broke, nothing could save it from going straight overboard.

Throughout the day, which seemed without end, the ship went berserk in its fight against waves of frightening size. Pitching, lurching, rolling and wallowing, the bow rarely above water, the ship was almost completely submerged as waves swept over the forecastle head and went crashing over the gunwales, covering the decks with at least 30 centimetres of surging water. Perishing cold and falling snow, driven almost horizontally, added to our discomfort.

In the afternoon, selecting a favourable opportunity, the ship was turned and with engines slowly turning over, proceeded on a north-westerly course with a following wind. Visibility was at a minimum which was a source of worry to the ship's officers as there were many icebergs in the area. On one occasion two large bergs, close together, suddenly loomed up ahead; the ship was steered between them with little to spare on either side.

The wind showed no signs of lessening as evening approached, and seas, if anything, had increased in size, but with a shorter distance between wave crests. This resulted in extraordinary spasmodic movements of the ship, as if she was endeavouring to emulate the convolutions of a corkscrew. Doc Ingram had long before retired to his bunk. Enquiring if I could do anything for him, I was told to go away and let him die in peace.

Hurricane-force wind continued through the night until it suddenly dropped to a moderate breeze at 4 o'clock the next morning. Big seas were still causing the ship to plunge about in most disconcerting and unpleasant movements. Heavy snow had been falling almost continuously and the ship was a picturesque sight, her rigging and furled sails covered with snow and long icicles which were beginning to drop from the rigging. Campbell was worried about possible damage to the seaplane's wings. Hessian bags tied down over the fabric wings did not protect them, for the dagger-shaped icicles penetrated both the hessian and wing fabric. A long mat commandeered from the chartroom, while being placed in position over a wing, was blown overboard by a sudden gust of wind, almost taking Campbell and Marr with it. Its loss was not regarded too favourably by the ship's officers. Despite all efforts the wings were badly holed, but Campbell said the tears could be patched when conditions improved.

Our course had continued to the west with a little southing during the morning. At midday our position was 66°24'S, 59°07'E, which was not far short of the Antarctic Circle. Two days previously, we had been below it but much further to the east.

At midday there was a remarkable rise in the sea floor, more than 1500 metres in 90 minutes' slow travel of the ship. At 10.30 A.M. a sounding registered a depth of 2153 metres; at midday, only 510 metres. Shallow readings then continued through the day.

Good progress continued in the open sea, well north of the pack-ice edge. At 1.30 P.M. the ship was stopped while tow nettings and a dredging were carried out. Conditions were not very suitable because of the disturbed sea but even so, excellent catches resulted. Dredged material included a number of continental rocks (erratics) which had to some extent damaged the more fragile specimens of marine life. The net was also torn while being dragged over the rocky sea floor. The depth was 713 metres.

Later, two tow nettings, paid out with more than 600 metres of cable, were towed at a depth of about 350 metres, the catch consisting almost entirely of krill. The dredged material, when sorted, revealed a rich representative series of echinoderms, pycnogonids (sea spiders), univalve and bivalve shells, sponges and polychaete worms. It was a remarkably good catch.

As visibility improved it was possible to make out, at a short distance, the northerly edge of the pack-ice. A north-easterly wind had forced the floe-ice back to form a definite line of demarcation between the open sea and compacted pack-ice. It stretched from the south-east to the north-west as far as the eye could see. Waves pounding on the outer edge were throwing spray high in the air and causing adjoining rafts of floe to swing and grind together, presenting an ominous barrier.

January 8 saw little or no change in the weather. Heavy snow was still falling and the seas were still rough. The barometer, which had been falling, was now rising steadily and there was every prospect of a return to better conditions. For the past 12 hours the ship had been steaming backwards and forwards along the pack-ice edge, waiting for visibility to improve.

Taking advantage of the slight improvement in weather conditions, Campbell had detached the floats from the plane and securely bolted it in position. It was a difficult and hazardous task but it was safely accomplished and there were no further worries of the plane being blown overboard or damaged. It was miraculous that the plane had survived the hurricane wind of the previous day.

At midday we had reached the position 66°13'S, 58°13'E; good progress had been made to the west during the past 24 hours. Wind had again increased from the south-east and snow was still falling heavily with no signs of the weather moderating. Deck temperature was well below freezing point. Because of poor visibility the ship was headed north away from the ice and later due east.

Late in the evening, while making a visit to the deck, I met MacKenzie who, rather surprisingly, challenged me to a wrestling bout. I reluctantly accepted his challenge although I was puzzled at its timing. The rolling of the ship, falling snow and a howling wind did not appear to me to be ideal conditions for wrestling. Evenly matched, the contest continued for some minutes when suddenly Sir Douglas arrived to witness what to him must have appeared a life and death struggle. He angrily demanded to know what was going on and we explained it was a friendly wrestling match. He dubiously accepted our explanation and reprimanded us. Rather chastened, we disappeared below decks.

The next morning brought no change in the weather, except the wind had veered to the north-east, but had not lessened in strength. Visibility was still at a minimum because of falling snow. The ship was making slow progress to the east into the seas.

We were informed by Sir Douglas that he had received a wireless message from Dr Henderson, Department of External Affairs, notifying him of a correction in the message received on New Year's Day. Land discovered by the Norwegians was not between Coates and Enderby Lands, but was between Kemp and Enderby Lands. The coast claimed by them, about 96 kilometres in extent, was almost immediately south of our present position. This news of the Norwegians' claim was very disheartening. Sir Douglas believed there was a tacit understanding that the Norwegians' activities would be restricted to the west of Enderby Land.

The edge of the pack-ice along which we were traversing to the west began to show signs of breaking up with leads of open water extending south. However, Captain Davis was reluctant to enter the pack under the existing weather conditions. It was then decided to carry out a tow netting. A net, with a ring opening of about two metres diameter, was lowered over the stern and about 1800 metres of cable was paid out with the ship steaming at one and a half knots. The depth of fishing was about 1400 metres. After being towed for two miles, the net was winched in and hoisted on deck. The catch was disappointing, possibly because the net was not fishing correctly at the slow speed of tow. The catch included a great deal of krill and four fish.

After the tow netting, Sir Douglas, Campbell, Doc and I moved five tonnes of coal briquettes from the sail locker to an empty starboard bunker, which we completed in 40 minutes. Our decreasing coal supply was rapidly reaching a critical stage and becoming a constant worry. Captain Davis stated he would have to return to Kerguelen Island when the coal stock was down to 100 tonnes.

The ship was still skirting the pack-ice edge the next morning. About midday, our course was altered almost due east and we made good progress in loose, scattered pack. Snow was still falling, but visibility was improving.

Wireless communication with Australia had again been lost; on this occasion, according to Sparks, due to a faulty aerial. It had been joined in several places and he proposed erecting a new aerial when the weather improved.

At about 3 P.M., the ship turned south following the pack-ice edge. Later, our course was altered to the east again. Late in the afternoon, the easterly wind swung to the north-east, veered east again and suddenly increased in force to a full gale. Protected to some extent by a line of pack, the ship remained in moderately calm water.

The gale had blown itself out during the night and there was only a light breeze the next morning. The weather was clearing with the promise of a fine day. We crossed the Antarctic Circle before midday and were in the same position as we were six days earlier.

The possibility of reaching land in this area appeared remote and Sir Douglas decided we should turn west, following the pack-ice edge, and hope for openings which would lead to the coast. In any case, we were on our way to Enderby Land.

Swinging the ship on her westerly course she collided with a large raft of floe-ice on which six emperor penguins and about 20 Adélie penguins were watching the ship, furiously waving their flippers as if to warn us off. Cameras were rapidly produced and photographs taken, particularly of the emperors. Hurley managed to film the penguins before they dropped on to their stomachs, tobogganed to the floe edge and dived into the sea with barely a splash. The Adélies were in a state of panic, rushing backwards and forwards, some diving into the water, but almost immediately popping out back onto the floe.

Bird life had been plentiful during the past few days and Falla was kept busy identifying and recording the various species. These included many large flocks of Arctic terns, each containing 200–300 birds. Two Ross seals were sighted, the remainder being crab-eaters.

The ship continued to make good progress to the north-west and began to roll as she met a light swell running in from the north, indicating open sea in that direction. Campbell and Eric Douglas spent all day repairing the holes and tears in the fabric of the seaplane wings.

Soundings of the sea floor depths through the day were interesting. At midday the depth was recorded as 2225 metres; at 2 P.M. it had risen to 1010 metres. Shallow conditions continued until nearing midnight the sea floor had descended again to 2248 metres. During the day we must have been in close proximity to land, which could not be seen because of poor visibility.

Flag Raised on Proclamation
Island

D URING THE NIGHT the ship had steamed along to the north-
west at its full speed of five knots. I arrived on deck the next
morning to find the ship skirting the pack-ice edge by no more than her
length. The line of demarcation between heavy unbroken ice and open
sea was very pronounced except for light brash ice through which the
ship passed without any difficulty.

At about midday we were approaching a number of large tabular
bergs, some a kilometre long and all with heights ranging from 30 to 40
metres. They were obviously grounded and Moyes was busily engaged
in determining depths of the sea floor. During the day he took 30
readings which proved most interesting. At 4 A.M., an echo sounding
registered a depth of 2310 metres, decreasing to 263 metres at midday.
Shallow readings continued until a minimum depth of 208 metres was
recorded at 8.09 P.M.. The bottom was very undulating with rises and
falls of 180 metres or more over short distances.

At midday, visibility had increased to such an extent that the
officer on watch, "Bonus" Child, was able to report an extensive stretch
of land to the south. At this point our position was 66°03'S, 57°43'E.

Later in the afternoon, I climbed to the maintop and, with the aid
of binoculars, could clearly see the ice-slopes of the sighted land, rising
to about 6000 metres before disappearing from view in the distance. The
coastline was formed of ice-cliffs, at least 30 metres high. They were
continuous with no signs of rock outcrops. No attempt was made to
reach the coast because it was fronted by two miles of compacted ice.

Approaching the western boundary of Kemp Land, a wide
embayment in the coastline, in about 66°17'S, 56°20'E, was named
Magnet Bay. Some distance inland and south-west of the bay, a series of
rocky peaks rising to heights of about 900 metres in approximately
longitude 55°30' east, was named the Nicholas Range.

Continuing west, the ship entered water free of floe-ice but
crowded with icebergs, the majority of them grounded. A heavy swell
coming in from the north made the ship slowly roll from side to side. All
hands were seething with excitement. At last we were in close contact
with the continent and confident that a landing would be possible early
next morning.

It was a fascinating experience as the ship was manoeuvred through the closely scattered bergs. Our course was continually altered to pass around them; at times we almost brushed against their steep vertical sides, which were higher than the mast-tops.

At 4 P.M. it was estimated we were about 70 miles from Enderby Land and still making good progress. It was now possible to take the ship closer to the coast, which could have been reached at any time. Our objective was to look for exposed rock outcrops where a landing could be made, raise the flag, and claim the territory for Great Britain.

As one would expect, the bird life was prolific in an area of rocky outcrops suitable for nesting sites and penguin rookeries. Flying birds were in abundance, circling the ship in large flocks, while numerous Adélie penguins either rested on pieces of floe or sported in the water. It was obvious their rookery was not a great distance away. Through the day a good many whales had been sighted — far more than usual — and also a pack of about 50 killer whales.

A high black-coloured island was sighted in the distance ahead at about 10 P.M., and shortly afterwards a series of small islets were also seen. Sir Douglas informed the scientists a landing would be attempted at 2 A.M.

The ship steamed past a cape which later proved to be the most northerly extension of Enderby Land. It was named Cape Batterbee. My rest was longer than expected, as it was not until 5.30 A.M. that I was awakened by Sir Douglas shouting, "Rise and shine, the shore party leaves in thirty minutes." In no time, scientists with their necessary equipment arrived on deck, waiting with excitement for their first steps on the Antarctic Continent. Good fortune seemed to be favouring us at last. It was a superb day with bright sunshine and a light breeze.

The rocky island lay a short distance away, separated from the ship by unbroken pack. After unsuccessfully manoeuvring the ship between bergs to reach an open lead, an approach was made from the west where the ship finally entered a large pool fairly close to the island. Disembarkation of the landing party was delayed an hour or more while attempts were made to anchor the ship, without finding a suitable holding bottom. During this time the ship's yards brushed against the side of a large grounded berg. The ship was then allowed to drift while the motor boat was lowered over the side. Scientists clambered on board and we set off for the shore.

Shortly after leaving the ship the old trouble of water in the carburettor caused the engine to miss badly and it finally stopped. Oars were unshipped and we began to row, but the engine was soon running again and we continued on our way, dodging rafts of floe and bergs. We made fast against a low shelf of ice, and then we all stood aside while Sir Douglas stepped ashore.

Sir Douglas, who had studied the island from the ship with bino-culars, said we would climb to the summit, about 260 metres, where the flag would be raised. On landing, the party received a noisy welcome from thousands of Adélie penguins. We had arrived at the front of an enormous rookery, occupying a rocky slope and rising back for a con-siderable distance. The whole area was covered with nesting birds and the cacophony from the penguins was deafening as we moved through the rookery.

Simmers and Howard, finding a suitable spot, immediately began setting up their instrument for magnetic observations while the remainder of the party started their climb to the summit. Hurley and I chose the shortest route, straight up a fairly steep side. It was an unfor-tunate decision as stretches of ice higher up had to be negotiated by cutting footholes. A slip would have had unpleasant results. Hurley climbed off in a different direction while I continued up the rock face. I finally reached the summit to find Marr already there. Sir Douglas, Ingram, Falla, Johnston and Moyes arrived shortly afterwards, having followed an easier, but longer, ascent.

After waiting some time for Hurley to appear, Marr and I set out to find him. We found him in an awkward position, unable to move in any direction. He had no further trouble when relieved of his heavy camera equipment and we all arrived back on the summit.

A start had already been made to build a cairn from the many rocks scattered over the limited surface. By midday, the cairn, quite large and well constructed, was completed, with a flagpole firmly secured through its centre. A square of hardwood was then attached to the pole, on which Hurley had beautifully carved, "The British Flag was hoisted and British Sovereignty asserted on 13th Jan., 1930".

The ceremony of claiming land according to official instructions then commenced. A hollow square was formed by the party, the Union Jack raised, and Sir Douglas prepared to read the Proclamation. Un-fortunately, it had been unthinkingly sealed in a canister, now buried deep in the cairn. However, with recourse to his memory and promptings from Moyes and Hurley, he was almost word perfect as he repeated the Proclamation:

In the name of His Majesty King George the Fifth of
Great Britain, Ireland and the British Dominions beyond the
Seas, Emperor of India.
Whereas I have in command from His Majesty King
George the Fifth to assert the sovereign rights of His Majesty
over British land discoveries met with in Antarctica.
Now, therefore, I Sir Douglas Mawson do hereby proclaim
and declare of all men that, from and after the date of these

presents, the full sovereignty of the territory of Enderby Land, Kemp Land, Mac Robertson Land, together with off-lying islands as located in our charts constituting a sector of the Antarctic Regions lying between Longitudes 73° East of Greenwich and 47° East of Greenwich and South of Latitude 65°, vests in His Majesty King George the Fifth, His Heirs and successors for ever. Given under my hand on board the Exploring vessel "Discovery" now lying off the coast of this annexed land, in Latitude 65°50'S. Longitude 53°30'E. The Thirteenth Day of January, 1930.
Witness

(Signed) J. K. Davis   (Signed) Douglas Mawson
         Master   Commanding
         S. Y. "Discovery"   Antarctic Expedition
         13.1.1930   13.1.1930

The ceremony was finalised by giving three cheers for the King and singing the National Anthem. Forty-six years later the Proclamation was retrieved by an Australian sledging party from the Mawson Base and handed over to the National Library of Australia at Canberra where it is now housed. It had suffered little deterioration.

The summit of Proclamation Island, named by Sir Douglas, was a great vantage point and magnificent views unfolded in all directions. The island was seen to be separated from low ice-cliffs of the mainland by a narrow passage of open water. Projecting on the coastline were a number of rock outcrops and many small islets offshore.

Within sight were at least 200 large bergs, mostly tabular in form with steep sides about 30 metres high. In the distance they reminded me of floating sugar cubes with the *Discovery* amongst them looking like a small toy ship. From the coastal ice-cliffs, stretching away to the east and west, the vast ice-cap rose evenly and smoothly to an indeterminate height in the distance. Many lofty mountain peaks, easily seen because of their black colouring, protruded through the ice-cap in all directions.

One large peak to the south-west was recognised as Mt Codrington, 465 metres in height, sighted and named by Captain Biscoe in 1831. It towered above a number of lesser peaks, some of which were named by Sir Douglas after members of the expedition. Biscoe had named outstanding peaks in the area after members of the Enderby family in England, but his names have been neglected on later maps and charts.

At the conclusion of the flag-raising ceremony, Sir Douglas told the party to be ready to return to the ship in two hours' time. Before leaving the ship, Captain Davis, worried at not being able to anchor his ship, had told Sir Douglas to get ashore quickly, raise the flag and come off as the ship was unable to stay. It was disappointing news as it left little time to make geological and biological observations and make collections.

Proclamation Island was found to be composed of Pre-Cambrian gneisses and schists, deposited at least two to three thousand million years ago. After a number of rock specimens had been collected, members of the party began to descend the mountain, setting off in various directions to make the most of our available time.

Falla and I began to search for nests of bird species restricted to Antarctica. About 30 metres down from the summit we came across a small colony of Antarctic petrels. These are beautiful birds with a deep brown head, back and wings and a white front. Nests were situated between rocks on fairly level, narrow ledges on the steeply sloping sides of the island. No eggs were found, but there were a few chicks in down, about a week old. A small number of adults were standing around and it seemed obvious there had been a heavy loss of eggs and very young chicks. This was no doubt due to the depredations of Antarctic skuas, present in considerable numbers and always on the prowl. The only other records of nesting Antarctic petrels were made during Mawson's 1911–14 expedition when colonies were found at Cape Hunter, Adélie Land, and Haswell Island near Queen Mary Land.

Nests of the widely distributed cape pigeons and snow petrels were also examined on ledges high on Proclamation Island. As a cape pigeon's nest was approached its occupant crouched, spreading and drooping its wings to cover the nest. At the same time it ejected a jet of clear red oily substance at the intruder. Most petrel species have this disconcerting habit of regurgitating an evil smelling liquid which they can spit unerringly for considerable distances. The record distance for sharp-shooting was held by cape pigeons with accurate throws of up to two metres and they usually made six ejections before exhausting their supply. The vile smelling liquid retains its odour for several days once it gets on clothing.

As time was getting on we carefully made our way down towards our landing place. On the way we entered the Adélie penguin rookery which was far more extensive than we originally thought. Some nests were at least 120 metres above sea level and an approximate estimate of its occupants was 10,000 birds. In the rookery, Adélie penguins have a far different appearance from the immaculate birds seen at sea. All were besmirched with mud and slush and looked most bedraggled. Their eyes are a conspicuous feature. As they look up the pupil is almost hidden, the white iris then shows up in marked contrast to the surround of blue-black feathers.

Earlier, I had shot some birds including two skua gulls which I was now carrying by the legs in one hand. Negotiating my way through the crowded rookery I was suddenly besieged by scores of enraged, loudly squawking penguins, crests erect, who began savagely pecking at the skua bodies. When lifted out of their reach they still attacked, but now my legs were their target. Carried away by the excitement, nearby nesting penguins wildly attacked close neighbours and in no time I was the central figure in an apparent madhouse.

Completely surrounded by scores of excited, struggling penguins, still attempting to reach the skua bodies, I found it difficult to move. Encumbered by a shotgun, a haversack full of rock specimens, bird bodies and two dead skuas I was at a distinct disadvantage. I forced my way through the throng, occasionally tripping and falling over birds and slipping on the smooth glaciated rock surface; my final progress was mostly on my back.

Arriving at the motor boat I found the rest of the party ready to push off and return to the ship. While we were ashore, the *Discovery* had been moved further out into more open water. Our passage to her was impeded by a considerable number of drifting floes. Sir Douglas, at the tiller, steered the boat rather recklessly through rafts of ice, ramming smaller pieces with gay abandon and bumping several larger pieces rather severely. Now and again we found ourselves face to face with crab-eater seals and on one occasion two sea leopards glared at us as we closely passed their resting place.

In open pools, Adélie penguins porpoised around our boat as we moved towards the ship. On land they appear awkward and rather comical creatures, but in the water they display a series of astonishingly graceful movements. They suddenly shoot out of the water to a height of about 30 centimetres, then they project themselves through the air in a smooth, streamlined curve and re-enter the water with barely a ripple. Seconds after, the performance is repeated, and so on.

On two occasions, apparently thinking the boat was floe-ice, penguins popped out of the water and over the gunwale into the boat. Much to our amusement, one landed on Ingram's lap, giving him quite a shock. Both birds were later skinned and added to the ever-increasing collection.

Water in the petrol again caused several engine stoppages on our way to the ship. Delays were short, for by this time I was adept in quickly draining the carburettor. It was obvious the tank would have to be removed, thoroughly drained and dried out. At last the boat ranged alongside the *Discovery* which was still drifting, but maintaining position by turning her engines over now and again. The shore party scrambled on board, tired, hungry and dishevelled.

During our absence ashore, Campbell and Eric Douglas had completed patching the tears in the seaplane wings and it was again in perfect condition for its next flight. Campbell told me that for most of the morning Captain Davis had manoeuvred the ship in all directions in search of a suitable anchorage. Soundings in close vicinity to the island were around 180 metres with occasional shallow readings. After the ship had struck a submerged rock he gave up all ideas of anchoring and moved further offshore, allowing the ship to drift.

Immediately the motor boat had been hoisted inboard and made snug, the ship steamed out from the coast and a course was set to the west. Leaving Proclamation Island, particularly in such perfect weather, was a great disappointment. Sir Douglas had planned to reach the adjacent mainland where a landing could readily have been made to raise a second flag. He had taken a flag ashore with him for this purpose, but abandoned the idea when he saw the ship had failed to find an anchorage. It was a lost opportunity to fulfil instructions to raise the flag on the Antarctic mainland as soon as possible.

Weather conditions the next morning were perfect with every prospect of another beautiful sunny day. Johnston and Marr were already at work sorting and preserving zoological material collected on Proclamation Island. Falla and I skinned and filled out birds. Earlier, Sparks reported he had been in wireless communication with the whaling factory ship *Radioliene*, out from Cape Town. This was good news to Sir Douglas. While in Cape Town he had discussed the possibility of the ship bringing coal and mail to a rendezvous off the Antarctic coast. Explicit plans, however, were not ratified at the time. We learned later that Sparks had not actually been in touch with the *Radioliene*; he had only heard them transmitting messages to various ships and the *Discovery* was not mentioned.

The ship was making steady progress in open water on a westerly course, following along a definite edge of storm-packed ice. Unbroken ice extended back to the coast for at least a mile or more.

Early in the morning a definite point was sighted where the coast turned to the south-west. It was named Cape Close by Sir Douglas. The edge of the pack also trended away in that direction and the ship's course was altered to follow it. Shortly afterwards, the ship passed a conspicuous rock formation, rising from the coastline to a height of about 450 metres. From its position, Sir Douglas concluded it corresponded with the description of Cape Ann, sighted and named by Captain Biscoe in 1831. Captain Davis did not agree with this decision. He was of the opinion that Biscoe had described Cape Ann as coastal ice-cliffs and he marked the rocky peak on his chart as Cape Biscoe. On present-day maps and charts the name Cape Ann is retained.

Land was now clearly visible and it maintained a generally uniform rising ice-slope, studded with high mountain peaks. The ship's position at midday was 66°12'S, 49°21'E, and 11 soundings during the day ranged from 204 metres at 1 A.M., to 1722 metres at 11 P.M. Leaving Cape Ann astern, we continued on a south-westerly course, following the pack-ice edge as closely as possible. Many mountain peaks were sighted and Moyes was kept busy taking bearings and marking them on his chart. Our objective was to continue on our course until the 35th degree of east longitude was reached when the ship would be turned back to the east.

About mid-afternoon, the ship was confronted by a tongue of solid compacted ice which projected from the coast and extended in a north-westerly direction. Our course was altered in that direction until the ice became sufficiently broken near its extremity to permit the ship to force her way through into open sea again. Steaming south-west, we again made contact with the coastal pack-ice and continued on a westerly course with a little southing.

The weather still remained perfect with only a light breeze, sunshine and excellent visibility. A moderate swell running in from the north-west caused little inconvenience. Late in the afternoon a line of high mountain peaks came into view. Sir Douglas named them the Tula Range after Biscoe's schooner of 150 tonnes. Still further inland and away to the south, a longer and more imposing range of rocky mountains was named the Scott Range, in honour of Captain R. F. Scott.

The high coastal ice-cliffs now turned south towards the Scott Range, finally being lost to sight in the distance. The ship could not follow them because she was blocked by solid pack-ice which extended south as far as the eye could see. Later in the evening, near the 48th degree of east longitude, ice-covered land was again sighted with a single mountain peak rising to a height of about 1200 metres. We had crossed the entrance to an extensive indentation of the coast, which Sir Douglas named Amundsen Bay.

A flight in the seaplane at this stage would have been of the utmost importance, particularly to delineate the margins of the bay and to make an aerial observation of the Tula and Scott Ranges. Unfortunately, the swell, although moderate, made take-off impossible.

At 8.30 P.M., Colbeck, the officer on watch, sighted a vessel several miles ahead, steaming towards us. Closing in, she was identified as the Norwegian research vessel, *Norvegia*. Flags had been hurriedly raised. On our approach the Norwegians dipped their flag in salute, followed by the dipping of the Blue Ensign. Sir Douglas then ordered that signal flags be run up wishing them a pleasant voyage, for which they thanked us. Engines were stopped as the *Norvegia* swung in towards us, when a voice through a megaphone said, "Commander Riiser Larsen speaking, I would like to speak to Sir Douglas Mawson if I may come aboard." Immediately, there was great activity on the part of the Norwegian crew as they began unpacking sledges, skis and other equipment from the ship's boat before it could be swung over the side.

All hands on the *Discovery* freely expressed their admiration for those on the *Norvegia*. She was a surprisingly small vessel, under 35 metres in length. Her sides were so badly scarred by contact with ice that it was obvious she had spent a good deal of time in heavy pack-ice. Two aeroplanes, lashed on deck, dwarfed the ship. A Lockheed Vega cabin plane was housed between the forecastle and bridge, its wings extending about six metres beyond the sides. A seaplane occupied the poop deck with about half the fuselage projecting over the stern. Coal was stacked high on all available deck space. We learned later that she had just coaled from the whaling factory ship, *Thorshammer*, before our meeting. The vessel was sitting so low in the water it would have taken a diver to locate her plimsoll mark. After her return to Norway in 1931, the *Norvegia* was used as a sealer, and in 1933 was crushed in ice in the Arctic.

Before the arrival of the ship's boat, Sparks handed Sir Douglas a wireless message from Australia. Before he had time to read it — it had to be decoded — the boat ranged alongside and Commander Larsen, with the ship's mate, Mr Neilsen, were welcomed on board by Sir Douglas and Captain Davis.

Commander Riiser Larsen was a tall and impressive figure, clean shaven and immaculate in leather flying clothes. While he and Sir Douglas retired for a talk, Neilsen was shown over the *Discovery*. He was very interested in seeing the cabin occupied by Captain Scott on his first expedition to the Antarctic in 1901–03, now occupied by Johnston and myself. Commander Moyes produced a bottle of sherry from some well-hidden source and toasts were drunk wishing one another good health and safe voyages.

Neilsen made no mention of their future plans, and several pointed questions were neatly turned aside. However, as the *Norvegia* was in constant wireless touch with Norwegian whaling ships, he was able to supply us with news of local happenings. We heard that Admiral Byrd had made a successful flight to the South Pole and back — an epic flight at that time. A light plane from the factory ship, *Cosmos*, had crashed in the Ross Sea, killing the pilot and the ship's doctor. Sir Hubert Wilkins was following the Weddell Sea coast in search of a suitable site for his plane to take-off for an aerial survey of that sector of Antarctica.

Questions were asked regarding survival of the *Norvegia* in heavy seas during gales and blizzards. Neilsen said they sheltered in the pack-ice, making for it at the first sign of impending bad weather. Pushing well into the pack, they escaped any movement and waited for the weather to improve. Engines were stopped and coal supply was conserved.

In the meantime, several of our crew had handed cigarettes and tobacco to the two Norwegian seamen waiting in the boat tied alongside. Attempts at conversation were not entirely successful, for they had very little command of English.

Finally, after about an hour's discussion, Commander Larsen arrived on deck with Sir Douglas and Captain Davis. As the boat left to return to the *Norvegia*, the occupants were farewelled by three cheers from all hands on the *Discovery*.

Retiring to the wardroom we eagerly awaited the arrival of Sir Douglas to hear any news he was prepared to tell us. He said Commander Larsen was not very communicative but did say that his party were unable to force the *Norvegia* through heavy pack-ice to the coast where he claimed 100 kilometres of land between Kemp and Enderby Lands. A flight was then made to a large pool of open water, adjacent to the coast, on which they landed. The plane was then taxied on to a gently sloping tongue of mainland ice. They then set off on skis to reach a mountain peak where Larsen proposed to raise the Norwegian flag. Its distance was estimated to be about five or six kilometres, but after skiing that distance the peak was just as far off as when they started. Distances are extremely deceptive in the clear Antarctic air. At this stage, with threatening bad weather, Larsen raised the flag on the ice-slope, proclaiming the land for Norway. They then retraced their steps to the plane and returned to the *Norvegia* which was drifting off the pack-ice edge.

Commander Larsen also informed Sir Douglas he had received messages from Norway advising him "not to do this and not to do that" until he was most confused. Apparently, the Norwegian and British Foreign Offices had settled differences that had arisen concerning exploratory activities in the Kemp–Enderby Land sectors, and Larsen had been advised to confine his attentions to the coast between Enderby and Coates Lands away to the west. Learning our coal supply was running low, he tentatively suggested we could perhaps obtain 50 tonnes from one of the Norwegian whaling factory ships operating in the area. His offer was not accepted by Sir Douglas.

In the meantime, Moyes had decoded the wireless message from Australia. It stated that the Antarctic Committee had learned that the position of land claimed by Larsen was on the Enderby Land coast between 52½ and 58½ degrees of east longitude. This claim was apparently later repudiated. The message again stressed the importance of raising the British flag on the Antarctic mainland.

Before leaving the *Discovery*, Larsen intimated they had completed their programme of coastal exploration and were devoting the rest of the whaling season to research and pack-ice movements. He said 150 whales had been sighted that day and that the area supported an enormous population of these creatures.

Oceanographic work carried out by the *Norvegia* included minor plankton nettings, water samples down to 500 metres and depth soundings. Their sounding machine was inferior to our echo sounder as their ship had to be stopped before a reading could be taken.

Through the night the ship continued following the pack-ice edge on a south-westerly course. Good progress was being made at full speed and on the morning of the 15th we had lost sight of land. Last seen, it was stretching away to the south or south-west. Movement in that direction was prevented by solid compacted pack-ice. Further investigations to the west appeared negative and Sir Douglas decided to turn back to Cape Ann where he said determined efforts would be made to push through to the coast, make a landing and raise the flag.

It is always so easy to contemplate in hindsight what should have been done, but it was obvious we retreated too hastily from Proclamation Island. Opportunity should have been taken of the superb weather to make a landing on the continent, which, without the slightest doubt, would have been successful.

At midday our position was 66°35'S, 45°32'E, so once again we were below the Antarctic Circle. Before heading back east, Sir Douglas decided to run a complete plankton station. There was a heavy swell, a light north-easterly breeze and the depth of the sea floor was 2310 metres. The station commenced at 2 P.M., but operations had to be suspended temporarily when the ship drifted into brash ice an hour and a half later and had to steam into open water. Trouble was then experienced with the thermometer in a water sampling bottle. The mercury thread kept breaking, which entailed taking the metal casing to pieces, heating the thermometer and then shaking the thread down until it joined. This took up a good deal of time and the station was not completed until 7 P.M.

Afterwards, the ship steamed west to longitude 44°45', where she was turned and headed on an easterly course back to Cape Ann. Miles of brash ice were encountered but caused little hindrance to the ship's progress.

Surprisingly, there was an absence of bird life, except for flocks of snow petrels and occasional Arctic terns. Knowing Falla's anxiety to obtain specimens of these terns, Sir Douglas suggested a tern watch on the forecastle head. Captain Davis had agreed to stop the ship so that birds could be recovered when we shot them. Falla and I took hourly vigils with shotguns but the terns were few in number and rarely came close to the ship. After about four hours the idea was abandoned.

Campbell and I had been most impressed by the immaculate appearance of Commander Larsen when he came on board so we decided to remove our wild and bushy beards. The transformation was astounding. I walked into Campbell's cabin and after one look he said, "I don't know you," while I countered with, "I've never met you before." We agreed that under different circumstances, recognition of one another would have been impossible. Marr and Doc Ingram stopped by and were the first to see us clean-shaven, faces washed and hair neatly brushed. Marr could only dazedly repeat over and over again, "Good God, I'm struck all of a heap." Doc said he could not believe his eyes.

It was then decided to try the effect on the others. Campbell produced leather flying garb in which we dressed ourselves. He adopted the role of Captain Holm, a Norwegian airman who could speak a little English, while I was Captain Rubbersen with no knowledge of English. Our first visit, with Ingram as guide, was to the forecastle where he introduced us to several of the crew. He said we were from the *Norvegia*, had flown alongside and had come aboard to stay the night. He was showing us over the ship and we would sleep in spare bunks in the hospital.

George, our young steward and cook's assistant, said, "I'll prepare their bunks, sir," and rushed away to reappear with an armful of blankets, wearing a hastily donned clean sweater and hair neatly brushed. Feeling the deception had gone far enough we explained who we were and hurriedly departed, not waiting to see the reaction.

Emboldened by our surprising success, we planned to visit Chief Engineer Griggs in the engine room. Simmers, who had appeared on the scene, was sent below to warn him that two Norwegian fliers were on their way down to look over the engines. Later, we descended the iron ladder into the engine room. Griggs hurried forward, wiping his hands on cotton waste, and was introduced to us by Doc Ingram. We solemnly shook hands. He then took charge of us and, in considerable detail, explained the workings of his beloved engines. Campbell and I made muffled remarks to one another which we hoped sounded like Norwegian. Finally, Campbell in extraordinary broken English, thanked him and saying goodbye, we both raised our caps. Griggs quickly raised his skullcap and bowed as we left.

Ascending the ladder we heard him say in undertones to Ingram, "How did they get on board without having the engines stopped?" Ingram explained, "Amazing piece of work, taxied alongside and were on board like a shot." "Go on," said Griggs, "smart buggers these Norwegians. I must come up and see their plane." Arriving on deck, he looked over the port and starboard sides — no plane. He approached us with a puzzled look; events were getting beyond him. Laughing, we explained ourselves. "Damn fine, damn fine," he said. He admitted he had had no idea who we were.

Both Campbell and I considered we could look just as immaculate as our Norwegian visitors, and on that note were ready to revert to our old habits — beard growth and a minimum of washing.

During the night an irregular north-easterly course was kept until, in the early hours of next morning, we headed due east. At 7.30 A.M., MacKenzie, on watch, sighted the *Norvegia* to the south and heading west. The two ships passed so far abeam that signals could not be exchanged. Apparently, Commander Larsen was returning to confine his operations to west of the Enderby Land boundary.

Our position at midday was 66°12'S, 48°12'E. Good mileage had been made since noon the previous day. We were now approaching Cape Ann and later in the afternoon the rocky peak showed up with the Scott Range away in the distance. Mountains of the range extend to the south, inland, for possibly 150 kilometres or more.

Conditions were favourable for flying and Sir Douglas instructed Campbell and Eric Douglas to prepare the plane for a flight. In the meantime, a complete plankton station was carried out and finished at 8 P.M. Assistance was now given to the airmen, but the plane was not ready to take to the air until about an hour later. Thick clouds were beginning to form and although the sea was calm, a swell from the north-east was increasing in size. The flight was postponed until early next morning. The ship was allowed to drift through the night, maintaining our position a few miles off Cape Ann.

I was awakened at 5 A.M. by Sir Douglas to assist in getting the plane over the side as the weather looked promising for a flight. As we were about to swing the plane overboard, Captain Davis came along, clearly unhappy, and advised against the flight. Heavy dark clouds were forming over the mountain range and the light wind was freshening. Sir Douglas agreed to postpone the flight.

It was then decided to do two dredgings on the sea floor; depth was 290 metres. At 9.30 A.M., our new Monegasque dredge was lowered over the stern, and with the ship steaming slowly ahead, about 750 metres of cable was paid out before the dredge rested on the bottom. The ship then drifted for an hour before the dredge was hauled in by the steam winch and hoisted on deck. It was a tremendous catch, including siliceous sponges, holothurians (sea cucumbers), bryozoans, squid and a variety of other marine organisms.

Our midday position was much the same as at midday the previous day. The wind from the north-east was increasing and a noticeable swell began to run in from the north-west. At 4 P.M. the dredge was again lowered and dragged over the sea floor for 45 minutes with the ship steaming at half speed into a fairly strong headwind. When the dredge was brought on deck it was found that the cod-end had doubled over the iron-frame opening, but there was a good catch. In addition to specimens caught in the first dredging there were crinoids (sea lilies), asteroids (starfish) and three fish.

During the day the ship had been drifting in an embayment of heavy pack-ice. It afforded good protection from a rapidly increasing north-easterly wind which later strengthened to a moderate gale. Snow began falling.

One of the crew happened to see Nigger, the ship's cat, jump from the gunwale into a sloping-out rubbish chute. Frantically clawing at the sides to save herself, she finally shot out into the sea. A cry of "cat overboard" brought all hands on deck and attempts were made to rescue Nigger who swam alongside the drifting ship. Frustrated by the ineffectual efforts at rescue, Lofty Martin jumped overboard to save his pet, but the water was so cold he barely had time to tie a rope around his waist before succumbing to the cold. Dragged to the side, he was hauled on board half frozen, but soon recovered after a change of clothes and a good nip of rum provided by Captain Davis.

In the meantime, Falla had rescued Nigger by scooping her out of the water with a long-handled landing net. Almost drowned and shivering violently she quickly recovered in the heat of the engine room and in no time was playing around the deck as if nothing had happened.

Sir Douglas and Doc Ingram spent the rest of the day sorting the dredged material. Falla and I were still skinning birds which we had collected at Proclamation Island.

Beaten Back by Mountainous Seas

I T WAS BLOWING a full gale the next morning. Captain Davis was endeavouring to keep the ship in the partly protected embayment, but was finally forced to steam out to the north into open water. Striking the full force of the gale, the ship ran before it to the south-west. The huge seas were a magnificent, but terrifying, sight. On many occasions it appeared that huge following waves would crash over the stern, but the ship always rose, usually with only a few centimetres of freeboard to spare. Erratic movements of the ship, as she surfed from the crests into the deep troughs, took the united efforts of two men at the wheel to keep the ship on course and to prevent her from broaching. Seas sweeping the deck prevented Sir Douglas and Doc from continuing their sorting and they retired below deck.

These wild conditions persisted throughout the day and night and all next day, which heralded the third month of the voyage. At midday, the ship was still running before the gale-force wind which showed no signs of lessening. We had logged 150 miles to the west and were now 40 miles past our most westerly point which we had made four days ago. At about longitude 43° 17' east, after awaiting an opportunity in the huge seas, the ship was turned and headed into the wind with engines turning over at full speed. We prepared to ride out the gale.

Late in the afternoon, winds from the north-east increased in violence to a strong gale. Not making any headway the ship was again turned — an exciting few minutes — and we ran before the wind. Although seemingly impossible, the seas had increased in height and pooping appeared inevitable. Several waves did curl over the stern and sweep the decks. The movements of the ship are beyond description. Gunwales were under water most of the time, decks were awash and the forecastle head was mostly lost to sight, as the ship, recovering from her drop into the troughs, plunged into the waves ahead.

Captain Davis was in his element under these conditions. His nickname, "Gloomy", was forgotten as he walked the bridge, half smiling and singing sea shanties under his breath. He was a figure of strength and reassurance.

All hands agreed this was the worst weather we had yet experienced and there were still no signs of any improvement; the barometer was still falling. At times, after extra heavy rolls, the ship took a long time to recover. On those occasions all conversations ceased as we anxiously waited for her to roll back onto the other beam.

Work in the laboratory was impossible under these conditions. While attempting to write my diary, an extra heavy roll caused everything to slide off the table; drawers flew out, scattering their contents in all directions, while I, thrown over the back of my chair, finished up flat on the deck. In the commotion, my pen lodged in a secret hiding place and was never found. Doc Ingram, suffering from the pangs of seasickness and temporarily resting on my bunk, could not suppress his mirth until one of the crew came along to inform him that his cabin, which housed the hospital, was flooded and most of his bacteriological research material was on the deck in fragments. Beyond a few muttered remarks, perhaps better not heard, the news had little effect; casting it from his mind he turned over, hoping for sleep to overcome his misery.

Our position at midday was 66°29′S, 43°17′E, after a very long distance run for the 24 hours. This was due to the following gale-force wind, but unfortunately our good mileage was in the wrong direction. During a brief visit to the deck I noticed a sea leopard struggling and being tumbled about in the wild seas, apparently in a state of complete exhaustion. It was making no headway and was soon swept out of sight.

Captain Davis issued an ultimatum to Sir Douglas that immediately our coal was down to 120 tonnes, he proposed to take the shortest course to Kerguelen Island. This left little margin for further exploratory work in this area as our coal supply at that moment was down to 149 tonnes.

The gale continued through the night and the next morning without moderating but the barometer was at last beginning to rise. At noon we had reached our farthest west, longitude 43°05′ east, a position only a few miles north-west of our previous day's position. Shortly afterwards, the ship was turned and headed south-east. Pitching and rolling heavily, she made little headway, making about one and a half knots with engines at full speed. Snow was falling which reduced visibility. Icebergs were numerous, but the sea was completely devoid of pack-ice, which had been swept away to the west by the strong easterly winds. There was a good chance that open water would continue to the coast.

The ship made slow progress against wind and heavy seas as she crossed the Antarctic Circle in the late morning. Several hours later the ship's course was altered to almost due east and she followed that course for the rest of the day.

In the morning the ship was still fighting her way towards Cape Ann with no moderation in the weather. The barometer was still rising. Sparks reported that wireless transmissions from the *Radioliene* were booming in, but he was unable to make contact with her. Later, a wireless message was successfully sent to London, relayed to Cape Town, and then to the *Radioliene*, asking her to communicate with us at an appointed time. Sparks could get messages through to the north, but not to the east or west. We still clung to the hope that the *Radioliene* would have coal for us.

The *Discovery* was just about making headway as she plunged into heavy seas, against strong head winds on her course to Cape Ann. The engines were turning over at full speed and consuming valuable coal. On one occasion the ship's bow, swinging to starboard, coincided with a terrific gust of wind and several consecutive huge waves. The two helmsmen were unable to bring her back and she broached. While broadside on she rolled her gunwales under, shipping tonnes of water while swinging around, and once again we ran before the wind, away from our destination. It was some time before there was an opportunity to turn back on course.

We now began to make better progress with the ship steaming at about two knots. The barometer was still rising with promise of good weather on the way. Late in the afternoon the ship's rolling had eased sufficiently to allow Sir Douglas, Ingram and myself to continue sorting the dredging catches of several days ago. Marr and Johnston were also busy in the laboratory and Falla was skinning birds.

The weather improved during the night. By morning the wind had subsided to about 28 kilometres an hour from the north-east, later veering to almost due east and easing. Seas had also moderated and the ship's speed had increased to 4½ knots.

Pack-ice now came into view, extending away to the north-east. In the distant south, ice-slopes of the continent and mountains of the Scott Range became visible. As the ship followed the pack-ice edge we passed a large glacial ice tongue, its front about 60 metres high, which extended from inland and over the coast to near the edge of the pack. It was a conspicuous feature originating from a valley in the inland mountain range.

Good progress was being maintained in open water and later we again crossed the Antarctic Circle. For the rest of the day we continued on course to Cape Ann.

By morning the ship was lying off Cape Ann, drifting with engines stopped. It had been an exceptionally good run during the night. Unfortunately, heavy pack, held in position by numerous grounded bergs, kept us some distance from the coast. Sir Douglas was keen on making a flight in the plane from an extensive pool, sheltered by large bergs. It was a perfect day for flying with a clear sky, sunshine, hardly any wind and a calm sea.

Captain Davis, however, argued strongly against a flight being made although at this stage it would have been invaluable. Reluctantly,

Sir Douglas abandoned the idea. A decision was then made to head for Proclamation Island where it was hoped conditions would be favourable for the plane to make a flight, and for a shore party to make a landing on the mainland coast.

We were again in shallow waters; 10 readings through the day ranged from 1274 metres at 4 A.M., to the lowest reading of 172 metres at midday.

Nigger had completely recovered from her swim in icy waters but apparently had not learnt her lesson and continued to walk along the gunwale, carrying on with a variety of antics. We feared she would fall overboard again. A strange cat, she completely ignored everyone except Lofty Martin, who fussed over her and combed her regularly every day. In fine weather, Nigger followed Martin around the deck but had not taken to climbing the rigging.

Late in the evening, Sparks was at last in wireless communication with the *Radioliene*. A message received from her stated that her Captain refused to communicate unless in code. One was arranged and sent off. We hoped to learn of her position and the possibility of receiving coal. Only a few tonnes of coal were needed to give us more time in the area and then continue east for further observations of the coast. Otherwise we would have to sail direct to Kerguelen Island within a day or so. There was no news from the *Radioliene* before we retired.

Proclamation Island came into view at 2 A.M. the next day but progress towards it was barred by at least five miles of heavy pack-ice and a host of grounded bergs. At 6 A.M., I was awakened by Sir Douglas and on reaching the deck I found the ship drifting off the pack-ice edge. Captain Davis had refused to force the ship south through the ice because he was worried by an impending storm. The barometer was falling, dark clouds were gathering to the north-east and a light breeze was freshening.

A dredging was decided on. At 6.30 A.M. the large Monegasque dredge was lowered over the stern and, on reaching the bottom, about 180 metres, it was dragged for five minutes before being hauled in. A remarkably good catch included an abundance of siliceous sponges, the spicules of which were a menace when sorting the material.

Wireless communication with the *Radioliene* had again been made and messages were coming and going. She was about 150 miles west of our position and had parcels and mail for us. She also had coal, but her Captain was awaiting instructions from Cape Town before suggesting a rendezvous. Hopes were high as he enquired if we were square-rigged, indicating he was planning the best method of coaling our ship.

The author and "Birdie" Falla preparing bird specimens in the deck laboratory.
(By courtesy of the Mawson Institute. Photo: F. Hurley.)

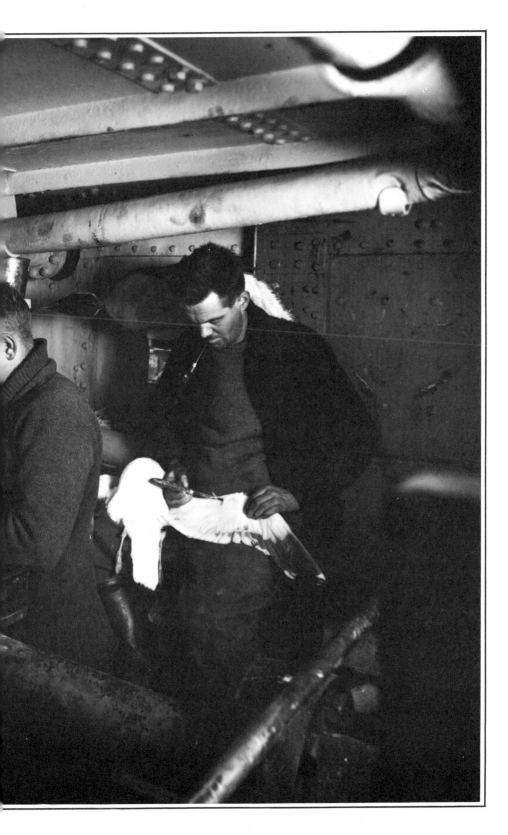

Sir Douglas informed us that if 150 tonnes of coal could be obtained from the *Radioliene*, he would keep to his earlier plan of sailing east to Queen Mary Land and raise the flag, and then instead of visiting Kerguelen Island again we would sail direct to Australia. On the other hand, if coal was unavailable, a return to Kerguelen Island must be made to restock with the coal left at Jeanne d'Arc, before heading for Australia. The latter decision ruled out any chance of receiving mail, although Captain Davis suggested his readiness to sail west, meet up with the *Radioliene* and, without coaling, proceed direct to Kerguelen. This action was unacceptable to Sir Douglas as it would prevent any further activity, even though restricted to only two days, at Proclamation Island. So much depended on further information from the *Radioliene*.

The ship had been drifting all day, tantalisingly close to the coast. At midday, a decision was made to trawl for fish, using for the first time a three-quarter size commercial otter trawl — the net having a gape of 12 metres. After being rigged, it was lowered over the stern and about 530 metres of cable paid out. Two ropes, one on each side of the net opening, were fastened to the otter boards so as to keep them pulling away from the net and thus keeping the gape open.

The net, towed at 2½ knots, caught on the bottom, causing a strong jolt of the tow cable. Immediately, the dynamometer — an instrument designed to measure pull and strain — jumped from a recording of half a tonne to two and a half tonnes. Its rope attachment then broke with a loud snap and the instrument was dragged under the water as the cable rapidly unwound from the winch. Campbell finally controlled the outgoing cable and began winding the trawl back to the ship. When hoisted inboard it was found to be badly torn and the dynamometer also suffered slight damage.

An examination of the net proved it had been dragged along the bottom instead of fishing above it. The catch included bottom-living creatures smothered in mud, while our expected good haul of fish totalled only seven specimens. At 4.30 P.M., a plankton station was begun. Near its conclusion the ship had drifted into heavy brash-ice and oblique tow nettings were not attempted.

Late in the afternoon, permission was granted to the engineers to carry out essential maintenance on engine bearings and also a check on the boilers. The amount of drift was underestimated and while the engines were out of action the ship drifted into heavy pack and nosed her way towards a large berg which had recently calved. Both large masses of ice, still lying close together, were immediately in our path. A jib topsail was hurriedly unfurled and set, giving sufficient steerage way in time to prevent the ship colliding against the berg's steep side.

With the aid of the jib the ship was manoeuvred out of the pack into open water again. Engine repairs were completed late in the evening and the ship moved about two miles from the pack-ice edge. Oblique nettings were then carried out and the complete station, No. 41, was finalised at 10 P.M. With the engines occasionally brought into use to maintain position, the ship drifted through the night. A slight swell was coming in from the north-east, otherwise the sea was a flat calm.

Weather conditions were perfect for flying the next morning. Campbell and Eric Douglas had been on deck very early and the plane was ready for an immediate flight. No time was lost in swinging it over the side and the two airmen left on a short test flight. On their return, satisfied with its performance, Eric Douglas, with Hurley as passenger, took off to take still photographs and cine-film of the area. From a height of 2500 feet he made a complete photographic record of the land features, coastline and pack-ice distribution. On their return, they reported open water adjacent to the coast, including Proclamation Island.

Sir Douglas then flew with Campbell, inland over the ice-capped mainland and to the east and west. During the flight, Sir Douglas observed at least 200 mountain peaks protruding through the ice-cap, a number of which he estimated were 2000 metres in height. Away to the south the ice-slope appeared to reach a height of 1500 metres. He also observed a narrow stretch of open water near the coast. While over land ice, Campbell dropped a flag attached to a short mast and this was later seen lying on the ice surface. A proclamation was read, but retained, claiming new lands discovered as far west as the 45th degree of east longitude.

On his return to the ship, Sir Douglas advised Captain Davis that from what he had seen there was every possibility of forcing the ship through broken pack for about a mile and reaching the stretch of open water. If this could be done a landing on the mainland was possible from the motor boat.

The ship now steamed to the pack-ice edge along which we cruised, backwards and forwards, for short distances until 6 P.M. The engines were then stopped and the ship allowed to drift. In this area the pack-ice was well broken up and appeared navigable. However, Captain Davis refused to enter, his only valid reason being the danger of the ship striking rocky outcrops obscured by ice. His decision was a terrible disappointment.

A number of crab-eater seals were noticed, basking in the sun on rafts of ice, well within the pack. Sir Douglas prevailed on Captain Davis to push the ship through the ice, so they could be shot and added to the collection. No difficulty was experienced in penetrating the pack-ice, the ship easily pushing aside broken ice until we reached a point where two seals were slumbering on a raft of ice. They were killed by Campbell with a high-powered rifle, only a single shot being necessary for each seal. Campbell and I then lowered ourselves over the side, scrambled across the ice and tied ropes around the bodies. They were then hauled on board.

As our freshwater supply was diminishing, Sir Douglas suggested that while in the pack we should "ice ship". A large piece of floe was selected as ideal for the task; its height was level with the gunwale and with the ship resting alongside, ice and snow could be thrown from the floe surface directly onto the deck. They could then easily be stacked in the condenser tanks.

Captain Davis, however, refused to manoeuvre the ship towards the selected piece of floe-ice, and began to work her back into open water. Near the edge of the pack he agreed to tie up alongside a smaller floe. A line, tied around a projecting piece of ice, could not hold the ship against a strong drift and she continued on her way leaving the rope behind. That was the end of "icing ship".

Steaming into open water, the ship was taken about a mile off the pack-ice edge and again allowed to drift. Our anxiously awaited message from the *Radioliene* had not eventuated. All hands were very disappointed. Captain Davis was adamant in his decision to leave for Kerguelen Island at midday next day. Campbell, Falla and I began the task of skinning the two seals.

The phenomenal run of superb weather continued into the next day. However, a change was threatening; dark clouds were building up to the north-west and the barometer was falling.

Several flights were made during the day. Visibility was perfect. Hurley, with Eric Douglas as pilot, made the first flight; climbing to a height of 4200 feet and flying well inland, they sighted an additional range of mountain peaks away to the south, not previously recorded. Some of the peaks were estimated to be at least 2000 metres in height. Hurley later found that the vibration of the plane had put the shutter release of his still camera out of action and a number of exposures were ruined. He was certain, however, he had secured a few hundred metres of film with his cinecamera. He described the filming of the ice plateau and projecting mountain peaks as sensational.

A calm sea with virtually no swell was ideal for the plane's landing and take-off. On the return of the first flight, Campbell again took off with Moyes as observer. He was keen to see the many features he had been charting from the air. On this occasion, while coming in to land, Campbell noticed that brash ice had drifted over the area where he was about to touch down. Opening the throttle he skimmed over the brash and landed some distance away. He taxied back to the ship and the plane was hoisted inboard. It was its last flight on this voyage. Moyes was carried away with the grandeur of what he had seen; he was also of the opinion that a landing on the mainland was possible.

While the flights were going on, the large Monegasque dredge was dragged over the sea floor, about 240 metres deep, for 15 minutes. An excellent catch resulted, similar to those of the past few days. Dredged material was piling up and its sorting would take some time. The two seals shot the previous day had been skinned, flensed and preserved. Professor Johnston had been excitedly searching through their intestines for parasites and every now and again reported interesting species.

The two leaders were exchanging notes. Captain Davis wrote to Sir Douglas stating he had to leave immediately for Kerguelen Island as the coal was down to 100 tonnes. Sir Douglas in reply regretted his decision, but, as he informed us, he had to accept the fact that the coal shortage had reached a vital stage. He was quite sure, however, that in his opinion a supply of 80 tonnes would be ample to reach Kerguelen if more use of the sails could be made. As it transpired, the ship arrived at Kerguelen Island with 60 tonnes of coal in her bunkers.

Return to Kerguelen Island

ON JANUARY 26 at 4 P.M., the ship was headed north from the Antarctic coast on a course to Kerguelen Island. It was with a feeling of disappointment, as the land gradually receded from view, that a landing on the actual continent had not been achieved. A complete plankton station was commenced at 10 P.M. and finished, after tow nettings, at midnight. The sea was smooth with a very light swell.

A message was received from the *Radioliene* early next morning informing Sir Douglas that they had no news for us. We had now come to the conclusion that no assistance was coming from that source. The ship had been drifting since the previous day, but at 6 A.M. engines were started and we continued on a northerly course, passing many icebergs.

A magnificent weathered berg later came into view, its surface sculptured into a variety of turrets and spires. The ship circled around it several times to enable Hurley to record it with his cinecamera. Ship's officers logged it as 74 metres in height but this was doubted by Moyes who estimated it to be 55 metres. These differences of opinion frequently occurred. On one occasion an immense tabular berg was entered in the ship's log as 6.4 kilometres long, while Moyes recorded its length as 1.6 kilometres.

Many birds were feeding on the water and flying around the ship. They included silver grey, snow and Antarctic petrels — species restricted to the continent. This would be our last opportunity to secure specimens. Captain Davis agreed to stop the ship so that shot birds could be recovered. Blubber, flensed from the two seals, was thrown overboard and immediately attracted the attention of many birds. The shot birds were lifted on board with long-handled landing nets.

Campbell, while securing a sooty albatross, lowered himself down a rope and handed the bird to Falla. He then found he had run out of strength and could not climb back. Willing helpers began hauling on the rope, but when he was near deck level the rope was released and Campbell plunged back waist deep in water. It was an accidental occurrence although he took a lot of convincing.

Captain Davis had been in a cheerful and more friendly mood since leaving the coast. It was rumoured he was again heard singing sea shanties; one in particular being "Rolling home, rolling home, rolling home".

The weather remained perfect and on the calm sea the ship was making good progress at about four knots on our northerly course. Many whales were sighted and late in the afternoon a school of about 30 blue whales cruised slowly past the ship. A complete plankton station was worked between 2 and 5.30 P.M. Falla and I then began skinning birds while Sir Douglas and Ingram continued sorting the remaining dredged material.

Most of the next day was devoted to running another station (No. 45) in a depth of 4350 metres. It was begun at 9.30 A.M. but not completed until 6 P.M. because of the great depth. On this occasion, water samples and temperatures were secured up to a depth of 4000 metres. Lowered to deeper water, it took the messenger 30 minutes to slide down the hauling wire to make contact with the release mechanism so that the bottle reversed as it reached 3000 metres. It then had to be hauled to the surface, emptied of its water content, temperature recorded, before lowering it to 3000 metres for its second haul to 2000 metres. At these depths the operation was very time consuming.

In the vertical plankton nets the dominant catch was krill from 1000 metres to the surface.

A wireless message from Cape Town was received by Sparks informing Sir Douglas that the decision of coaling the *Discovery* from the *Radioliene* was left to the discretion of her captain. Since there was no message from him it appeared obvious that no one wanted to take the responsibility for providing us with coal.

Good progress had been made to the north and at midday our position was 63°51'S, 54°17'E. Late in the afternoon the barometer began to fall and Simmers forecast an approaching storm. Equipment was made snug in the laboratory and Campbell and Eric Douglas started to remove the floats and wings from the seaplane, preparatory to it being lashed and bolted down.

The threatened storm eventuated during the night, and early the next morning was blowing from the north at half gale force and gradually increasing. At midday the wind had veered to the north-east and increased in violence to a fresh gale with gusts exceeding 70 kilometres an hour.

Big seas had built up and the ship was taking tonnes of water over the bow. Waves sweeping the decks made it impossible to move without the aid of lifelines. Work was impossible as the ship rolled heavily with her gunwales under water at times. With engines turning over at half speed, the ship was kept headed into the giant waves. She was making very little progress and was practically hove to. The two men at the helm were fighting against the ship's wild movements to keep her on course and prevent broaching. Heavy snow now began falling.

These unpleasant conditions continued throughout the day and night and showed no signs of abating the following day. The barometer was showing a tendency to fall even lower. Port and starboard doors leading below decks could not be used because the decks were awash. Tonnes of water was sweeping unceasingly over the bow and gunwales. To venture on deck, one had to go forward and emerge under the protection of the forecastle head. Ship's officers and helmsmen were fully exposed to the extreme cold and flying sheets of spray on the unprotected navigating bridge.

The gale, without lessening, had continued through the night. On the 31st, the ship's course was altered from due north to the north-east to Kerguelen Island where we expected to arrive in seven or eight days. Two jib sails were unfurled and set, assisting to some extent in easing the ship's movements. However, a heavy swell running in from the north-west on our port beam was causing the ship to roll heavily.

Later in the day, weather conditions began to improve and the barometer showed signs of rising. There was a noticeable decrease in the wind's strength, but seas were still heavy and confused. The ship's speed had increased and she was now making about three knots. At midday our position was 61°19'S, 53°17'E; the day's soundings ranged from 4350 to 4970 metres.

Many birds were flying close to the ship, and Falla in his hourly checking, which he rarely neglected, continued recording the various species and their approximate numbers. It was noticeable that the Antarctic nesting birds had been left behind and subantarctic species were beginning to take their place. We were also leaving the northerly limit of drifting icebergs; only a few weather-worn bergs were occasionally sighted.

In the afternoon, Sir Douglas, Campbell, Ingram and I shifted a number of cases from the scientific hold to a forward hold. It was exciting work, manhandling cases while the ship was rolling and pitching; we all suffered from bruised and cut hands.

Later, in the wardroom, we were told by Sir Douglas that he had received a wireless message from London stating that the press in Norway had published reports of recent exploratory work carried out by the Norwegians off Enderby and Kemp Lands. English papers, including *The Times*, carried the same news. Apparently it was headline news and Sir Douglas was asked to forward a synopsis of exploratory work achieved by him in that area.

By the next day the wind had eased to a light breeze blowing in from the south-west, accompanied by light to heavy snow squalls. The wind later swung almost due west causing a nasty cross sea with a heavy north-west swell. The rolling of the ship became so severe that her course was altered slightly but with no marked result. Lack of ballast was making it worse. We were now down to 90 tonnes of coal. Later in the morning, wind from the west increased and rising waves began to sweep over the gunwales on our port side.

Sails were hoisted at 9.30 A.M. because of the favourable wind. It was a busy scene on deck as the crew went aloft to unfurl the sails while scientists, hauling on the shrouds, soon had foresails, topsails, topgallants, three jibs, aft staysail and spanker set and drawing beautifully as they filled with the following westerly wind. The ship's speed immediately increased to about six knots with a marked decrease in the ship's rolling. It was a great sight to see her under full sail again.

It was rumoured that Captain Davis was keen to return to Australia via St Paul and Amsterdam Islands after leaving Kerguelen Island. The islands lie about 800 miles north-north-east of Kerguelen. On reaching them, we would run free with the prevailing westerlies to Australia. Although such a course sounded most interesting, general opinion, later proving correct, was that a direct course to Australia would be followed.

Work in the laboratory had now virtually come to an end. All the birds had been skinned and filled out and the dredged specimens preserved in jars ready for packing in cases with other material. A good run of 109 miles was logged since midday the previous day. Our position at noon was 59°30'S, 53°11'E.

Sails had been taken in, furled and the yards squared in the early hours of the next morning. The ship was still following a course east of north in a moderately calm sea and was making good progress under steam. The sky was heavily overcast; light snow was falling, later changing to a light drizzle of rain. It was also warming up and we were enjoying a deck temperature of 1°C.

A few weather-worn icebergs were still being sighted. One in the distance appeared to be half black and half white. Approaching closer, it was seen to be an overturned berg of glacier ice; the dark area was a transparent green colour, crowded with small fragments of rock picked up from a rocky surface when the berg had formed part of a glacier. It had broken off as it was forced out over the sea. The ship circled this unusual berg several times to allow Hurley, as well as all hands, to photograph it.

The sky was still overcast the next morning with thick fog, followed by rain in the afternoon. The sea was calm with a moderate swell rolling in from the north-west.

Fireman Smith was taken off duty because of a poisoned foot, leaving the two remaining firemen to work shifts of six hours. Volunteers were called for to assist in this work. Campbell and I agreed to work the first shift in the morning.

We were awakened at 4 A.M. for coal trimming and we had moved three tonnes of coal from a bunker to the plates before breakfast.

It was unpleasant work in an atmosphere laden with coal dust. The rolling of the ship caused several mishaps when a barrow load of coal would finish up overturned in places far from originally planned.

Engines were stopped at 10.30 A.M. to run a full plankton station. An echo sounding at 8 A.M. had recorded depth of the sea floor as 3950 metres. The machine then broke down and no further readings were possible until four days later. Troubles experienced during station No. 46 included occasional stoppage of the donkey engine which hauled the plankton nets, taps accidentally left open on the water sample bottles and persistent breaking of a mercury thread in one of the thermometers. As a result the station took five hours to complete.

At midday, after a distance run of 271 miles for the past 48 hours, we had reached 55°11'S, 55°55'E. The ship was still making good progress at about five knots.

During the night the wind strengthened from the south-west. The morning of February 4 was perfect with a cloudless sky. Good mileage continued under steam and sails, and at midday we had logged 122 miles for the 24 hour run. We sighted another badly eroded black and white iceberg which was possibly calved from the one seen the previous day.

Campbell, Simmers and I spent part of the day in the stokehold where we moved five tonnes of coal from a bunker to the plates at the fires. Eighty tonnes still remained and it seemed obvious we would reach Kerguelen Island with at least 50 tonnes in hand. Sir Douglas told us he was hoping to sail south again after re-coaling at Kerguelen, but was waiting confirmation from the Antarctic Committee in Australia before letting Captain Davis know of his decision.

Shortly after midnight a north-westerly wind freshened to gale force. Sails were raised, and with engines turning over, the ship was making about 7 knots. At midday, our 24-hour run was 163 miles; our good mileage was due to the favourable following wind.

Ritchie Simmers had been showing signs of fatigue and strain during the past few days. Doc Ingram, concerned about his health, advised him to rest but Simmers refused to do so. One of his many duties was to record, at regular intervals, readings of three thermometers placed in different positions on the ship including one high on the mainmast. He carried out these tasks without fail, even at the height of the strongest winds, which meant continual broken sleep.

The wind had dropped to a light breeze on the 6th. At midday we had logged another good day's run of 169 miles. Doc and I spent the morning with Sir Douglas in the scientific hold moving cases in readiness for a full check at Kerguelen Island.

In the afternoon Campbell and I retired to Doc's cabin to assist him with his X-ray equipment which he had unpacked. Several exposures were successfully taken of Doc's wrist which had caused him occasional pain since a fall on the deck of the *Nestor* on our way from Australia to Cape Town. Fireman Smith's foot was also X-rayed. Both results indicated little cause for alarm, although Doc was of the opinion that Smith's foot should have improved more than it had.

At a session of the Fiddley Club, President Moyes suggested a series of natural history talks by Falla and myself on phyla of the animal kingdom. We agreed, but it was unlikely they would take place at this late stage of the voyage. Attendance was usually no more than five members as space was very restricted. Seats were restricted to five ash buckets on a grid above the stokehold which left a mark of membership — a ring around one's stern. The club's main asset was warmth.

At 10 A.M. next day the high mountains of Kerguelen Island came into view. Soon afterwards we were welcomed by a prolific number of birds; they circled the ship and hovered overhead as we proceeded on our way. The air was literally crowded with birds of many species.

Rain had been falling most of the night, but early in the morning it ceased. A light fog then developed which soon lifted and was followed by a clearing sky and sunshine. Engines had been turning over at their maximum speed in an endeavour to reach Royal Sound before a threatened change in the weather.

Fireman Smith's foot was getting worse and causing him considerable pain. Doc Ingram thought he would have to operate and asked Campbell if he would administer the anaesthetic under his instructions. My guess was the three concerned were sincerely hoping an operation would not be necessary.

I decided to have my second shave since leaving Cape Town, revealing my features again, but on this occasion retaining a moustache. Eric Douglas also considered shaving for the first time and Frank Hurley, scenting good footage, arranged a haircutting scene. Eric Douglas was seated in a chair having a trim by Moyes who had earlier shown skill with clippers and scissors. Waiting in a queue were several others including the ship's cat, Nigger. "Good stuff," said Hurley, his cinecamera whirring away, as we waited our turn at the barber's.

A sharp lookout was being kept by the officer on watch for Salamanka Reef, usually only visible by a slight break of waves on the surface. It was sighted on our starboard quarter at 5.30 P.M., and a course was then set for the entrance to Royal Sound.

Earlier in the afternoon a light wind blowing from the north-east freshened, reaching a strength of 50 kilometres an hour and raising a nasty choppy sea. We were now only a short distance from Kerguelen. Speed was reduced so that our entrance into Royal Sound would take place early next morning.

Although conditions were not very suitable, Sir Douglas decided to carry out a dredging. The echo sounder was temporarily out of order, but a reading by the Kelvin machine recorded a depth of 150 metres. The ship's engines were stopped and the Monegasque dredge was lowered over the stern. Three hundred metres of cable was paid out until it rested on the bottom. It was then towed at a slow speed for five minutes.

While being hauled in, the dredge, bulging with its catch, jammed against the stern and became stuck. Campbell immediately stopped the winch. Sir Douglas, with a rope tied around his waist, climbed over the gunwale, stood on the sponson and made several unsuccessful attempts to free the dredge. Climbing back on board, he received an unexpected helping hand from Doc Ingram, who grabbed him by the seat of his trousers and threw him off balance. "Good God," he cried, "you almost pushed me in." He joined in our laughter as he reached the deck. Finally, several of the crew came along and, rigging a block and tackle, soon had the dredge dislodged and hoisted inboard. It was an excellent catch, but because it was late, Sir Douglas said he would call Doc and myself at 6 A.M. so that the dredged material could be sorted before reaching Port Jeanne d'Arc.

I was awakened at 7 A.M. by Sir Douglas with the explanation that although he had roused earlier, he had decided to sleep in for another hour. Sorting was started, but temporarily abandoned as the ship was off the Prince of Wales Peninsula and about to enter Royal Sound. Rain, which fell most of the night, had ceased; it was a beautiful morning with a clear sky and hardly a breath of wind.

We were escorted into the Sound by a large number of birds. It was a great, but noisy welcome. Off Murray Island we passed a ship at anchor which we learned was the *Austral*, a French sealing factory ship, due to sail to France on February 24. The *Austral* dipped her flag as we passed. In response there was an embarrassing delay as our Blue Ensign was hurriedly raised and dipped, just as we steamed out of sight into the Davis Strait.

Sorting and sieving the dredged material continued, but at the same time every opportunity was taken to once again admire the magnificent scenery of the island, assuredly one of the best of its kind in the world. Gliding over waters of millpond smoothness, the ship steamed through the narrow fjord of Davis Strait, entered the Buenos Aires Channel and arrived at Port Jeanne d'Arc shortly before midday. The motor boat was swung over the side and several of the scientists made the ship fast. Other mooring ropes and cables were then brought into use and the ship was safely berthed at 1.30 P.M.

Immediately afterwards, without warning, a gale-force wind with extraordinarily strong gusts swept down the channel and continued well into the night. Had we arrived an hour later, berthing of the ship would have been impossible. The gale was also a reminder of the treacherous nature of Kerguelen weather.

It was decided not to start coaling until next morning. Sir Douglas, Doc and I continued to sort out the dredged material, completing the task late in the afternoon. I then left to go ashore with the idea of shooting rabbits or pintail ducks for the larder.

A remarkable change had taken place on the island since our last visit. Large areas of ice and snow had disappeared and the ground was now completely covered with a matting of brilliant green plants and grasses. Ducks were conspicuous by their absence and rabbits were very shy, scuttling to their burrows at first signs of my approach. I sighted a white longhaired Samoyed dog in the distance, but it quickly loped away. I returned to the ship, soaked to the skin, with a bag of three rabbits; heavy rain had been falling continuously.

In the meantime, the buildings of the whaling station were found to be thoroughly clean, thanks to the *Kilfinora* crew. The Fiddley Club had already moved from the ship's grid above the stokehold and was now established in the deserted office building. President Moyes had quickly carried out one of his most important duties and lit a fire in the stove.

During the night the gale-force wind had eased, but the next morning it was still strong, and bitterly cold. Clouds were clearing, allowing the sun to break through now and again. A short choppy sea had developed on the channel with spray flying high as the crests were whipped by the strong wind. Suggested dredgings from the motor boat were abandoned.

Campbell and Eric Douglas were busily engaged in replacing the floats and wings on the seaplane in preparation for flights over the island. Following a request, Sir Douglas gave me permission to go on a flight if an opportunity occurred, saying if I wanted to risk my neck it was up to me.

Moyes wanted to complete his charts and Howard to compile his water analyses and temperature records, so they elected to work in the new Fiddley Club premises ashore in preference to the cold and confined space on the *Discovery*. The heating stove in the ship's wardroom had never been used; a wise decision, for we would have been loath to leave the warmth when called upon to carry out work on deck.

To make sure the ship would not be blown from her berth, Captain Davis ordered additional mooring cables, finishing up with eight wire hawsers running from the ship to bollards on the wharf and also to fastenings on shore.

Late in the afternoon, Sir Douglas organised a party to visit Swain's Haulover, a short distance away by motor boat from where the ship was berthed. Doc Ingram and I decided to walk and finished up climbing Red Dome Peak, one of the nearest high peaks overlooking

Swain's Bay and Royal Sound. Visibility was perfect and from its summit we had a splendid panoramic view of the mountain ranges and innumerable waterways. Mt Ross is 1960 metres in height and its summit, usually obscured by clouds and mist, was clearly visible, revealing two well defined peaks.

To the north and north-east the spacious harbour of Royal Sound, studded with islets of varying sizes, was laid open before us. It was a magnificent spectacle. From this elevation it was possible to determine the extent, position and relationship of the many channels to one another as they formed an intricate pattern. We traced the tortuous course of the *Discovery* through the Sound, 25 kilometres inland, to the deserted whaling station at Port Jeanne d'Arc.

Swain's Bay, with its entrance from the sea facing due south, stretches inland for about 20 kilometres and is immediately west of Red Dome Peak. Whaling and sealing vessels used to enter the bay and anchor off a narrow flat area, less than half a kilometre across, separating the bay from the Buenos Aires Channel. Ships' boats were then hauled across the narrow sandy strip to the channel and then rowed to Port Jeanne d'Arc. Hence its name, Swain's Haulover. This procedure saved vessels making a long journey from the west around the coast to Royal Sound and the run inland to the whaling station.

From the peak we could make out the tiny figures of the motor boat party, walking across the Haulover. It was too late to join them, so we decided to return to the ship. At the base of the peak a Samoyed dog was quietly watching us. We slowly moved towards it with various appropriate noises of goodwill, but they were of no avail and it quickly made off, with many puzzled backward glances.

Back at the whaling station we found the party had returned from the Haulover with two king penguins and stories of treacherous sea elephant wallows covering the low-lying sandy strip. They had also seen two dogs. Simmers's health had worsened and he had a high temperature. Doc ordered him to his bunk with instructions to remain there until he showed signs of improvement.

The next morning broke with the sky completely overcast with gathering dark clouds. Heavy rain had been falling through the night and was continuing. The wind had eased to a light breeze and it was bitterly cold. Immediately after breakfast, Sir Douglas and I brought the motor boat alongside the ship and a party set out for a morning's dredging and general collecting. Hurley accompanied us with his cameras.

We entered a small bay on the western end of Long Island and went ashore. Falla and I went to observe the bird life. We found a small rookery of rockhopper penguins with well-grown chicks in down being fed by their parents. Pintail ducks were plentiful and a number of them were shot and later handed over to the ship's cook.

I was fortunate in discovering the nest of a paddy-bird, or sheathbill. Clambering around rocks a little above water level I noticed a paddy-bird rush from a narrow crevice between rocks. Jumping on a nearby rock, it stood scolding me with excited clucking noises while watching me closely with its head on one side. Suspecting a nest, I searched and found it in a slight depression between two boulders, hidden by a mass of tangled undergrowth. Two young chicks were in the nest, not long hatched and huddled together in one corner.

Nests of these cheeky birds were not found during our earlier visit to the island. Falla removed one of the chicks and placed it alive in a cardboard box. The watching paddy-bird had by this time been joined by its mate and both were madly clucking and becoming very agitated. When we left the nest, Falla recorded the following incident in his bird notes. "They [the parents] set out to follow us at a safe distance uttering protesting clucks. After some time I stopped to examine a petrel burrow and to do so put down the cardboard box containing the young sheathbill. Unnoticed by me, the parents came up and dragged the box away. I was in time to see them bang it on some stones until it flew open, when one of them seized the chick in its bill and all made off back to the nest." I was against recapturing the young bird but Falla said it was the only young sheathbill we had seen on both visits to Kerguelen and he wanted it for the collection.

Returning to the motor boat I found Sir Douglas waiting for me to help him with shallow water dredgings. A light dredge with a galvanised iron frame opening, 75 by 30 centimetres, was used. Six short hauls were made on a shelving bottom in depths ranging from three to 20 metres. A good deal of kelp filled the net after each dredging, but also good catches of marine life including several fish. Light rain had now increased to a steady downpour and further dredging was abandoned. We picked up the rest of the party who were waiting anxiously for us in the rain. Professor Johnston had made a good collection of marine organisms from under rocks between tide marks. Heavy rain continued as we returned to the ship.

During the afternoon Doc Ingram transferred Simmers to a bed in the manager's residence on shore. He was worried about his condition as he still had a high temperature. After the transfer it was decided that Doc and I should also sleep ashore to be near him in case of an emergency.

I was awakened early next morning when Bonus Child, coming off watch from the ship, gleefully put his cold hands down my back. He then kept us awake by playing the gramophone. It was a cold morning with an overcast sky, low black clouds and occasional heavy falls of rain.

Following a decision to curtail outside activities, a fire was started under the laundry copper and this was kept going to provide an ample supply of hot water. By this time most of the scientists had arrived from the ship. It was very pleasant to be indoors, enjoying warmth from the well-stoked stove. All hands took it in turns to wash clothes and indulge in a much needed bath. For some strange reason Campbell and Colbeck decided to entertain us with an exhibition of knife fighting. It quickly came to an end when Campbell retired with a badly cut finger.

At midday, the light wind suddenly increased to gale force. This kept us indoors and we all enjoyed a relaxing day. Coal was being transferred to the ship by members of the crew, as the opportunity occurred. The latest news was that we would sail from Kerguelen on the 20th and proceed south.

The gale subsided during the night and was blowing a reasonably moderate breeze in the morning. Sir Douglas suggested further collecting and dredgings. A party set out in the motor boat and proceeded about three kilometres up channel to Grotto Bay on Long Island. A landing was made and the party separated and moved off in pursuit of their various interests. Doc Ingram and I were detailed to secure rabbits and ducks. It was an unsuccessful foray as none were seen. Several dredgings were carried out as we returned to the ship.

Campbell and Eric Douglas had almost assembled the plane. It would be ready to fly later in the afternoon, but there would have to be a marked improvement in the weather conditions before flights were possible.

In the afternoon, I continued skinning birds in the warmth of the Fiddley Club. Several members thought it was not quite the right thing to do and frowned upon my efforts. The room was a hive of activity. Moyes was still working on his charts while others were busy bringing their diaries and records up to date. I took time off to finish washing my soiled clothes — apparently not very successfully as Sir Douglas was heard to enquire, "Who's hanging their dirty clothes on the drying line?"

From the windows of the room, rabbits and occasional giant-sized Norwegian rats could be seen running about in the areas between buildings. Attempts were made to shoot them but were discontinued when Campbell, rounding a corner, had to duck for cover as shots rang out.

Several of the crew, while off duty, walked inland and blew up a number of burrows with explosives in the hope of securing rabbits, a novel but unsuccessful method. The crew had been coaling ship on and off during the past two days, but so far only ten tonnes had been taken on board.

Before retiring, Sir Douglas informed us that he had planned a two-day collecting trip to Greenland Harbour on the island's east coast. The party accompanying him would be Hurley, Johnston, Ingram, Marr, Campbell, Eric Douglas and myself. We would be leaving first thing in the morning. Our hopes for good weather were dispelled when the morning broke with a strong, icy cold wind, the sky heavily overcast, and light rain.

Ignoring the bad weather, we clambered into the motor boat with our gear and set off down the channel to the head of the Bolinda Arm, 22 kilometres away. A short choppy sea met us as we moved out into the channel. Running before a north-west wind, the boat, with only a few centimetres of freeboard, came dangerously close to shipping waves over the stern. Near the western end of Long Island we noted a small rookery of about 50 rockhopper penguins.

Crossing the entrance to Davis Strait, we entered the Bolinda Arm, receiving some protection from the wind. Closely following the northern shore, we were surprised at the large flocks of pintail ducks and numerous rabbits, disturbed by the reverberating noise of the boat's exhaust. It was decided to land here on our return journey and secure as many of them as possible to take back to the ship.

Reaching the head of Bolinda Arm, all hands disembarked with their gear on a narrow strip of low-lying land, separating the arm from Greenland Harbour. On French charts it is named Castaway's Haulover.

On shore, the party was greeted by two stately king penguins, a solitary sea elephant and numbers of the ubiquitous paddy-birds. The latter followed us everywhere with eyes alert to see what mischief they could get into. Bird life was in profusion. Overhead, large flocks of black-backed gulls were noisily screeching and flying in all directions. Skua gulls were busy feasting on the carcasses of sea elephants slaughtered by sealers the previous summer season. Very few of these mammals are now seen on the beaches and low-lying areas of Kerguelen Island.

After a quick lunch, most of the party walked across to the head of Greenland Harbour. Care had to be taken not to walk into old sea elephant wallows — a muddy ooze of considerable depth, but with an innocent looking surface. Sir Douglas and I set off to investigate a strange looking outcrop of rock with sloping smooth sides. A close inspection proved it to be a boss, a dome-like mass of igneous rock, which had intruded a coarse volcanic tuff. Sir Douglas identified it as phonolite.

Climbing to the top of the 120-metre-high dome, I found the central core had been partly eroded away and I was peering over a thin skin of the outer surface. Rapidly retreating to a safer position I stopped to admire the surrounding landscape. A cold wind was blowing and light rain was falling. Suddenly, the sun broke through the clouds and there was a dazzling display of all colours of the spectrum. It was a fantastic rainbow with colours of an intensity that I had never seen before. The end of the arch bathed the opposite mountainside with the most vivid and glorious colours.

Descending the boss, I rejoined Sir Douglas and we began to walk back to the boat. I almost stepped on a fully grown rabbit, which made no attempt to run. It allowed me to stroke it until Hurley was called from nearby and took several photographs of the strange sight. The rabbit, no doubt thinking enough was enough, then scampered off and disappeared into a burrow. Shooting it was out of the question.

We found tents erected and dinner awaiting us when we returned to the boat. After the meal we sat around a large fire built up with driftwood until it was time to retire. Commander Moyes and Doc Ingram were my tent mates. Earlier, Campbell and Marr had shown more than ordinary interest in the position of my sleeping bag. It was a comfortable and peaceful night until, near midnight, Campbell and Marr, bellowing like bull elephants, raided our tent and almost choked the life out of Moyes. Suspecting something was going on, I had changed my sleeping position. Moyes took a dim view of the escapade. I laughed for days afterwards.

The morning of the 14th was cold and miserable with a strong northerly wind blowing and heavy rain. I awakened early but made no attempt to rise as Doc and Moyes were still sleeping soundly. Hurley, who never seemed to sleep, poked his head into the tent announcing breakfast was ready and he would serve us in bed. The hot tinned sausages with bacon, toast and tea were very much appreciated.

Doc Ingram and I left on a shooting trip with good results, bagging eight ducks and two rabbits. Later, I helped Sir Douglas search for his Watkins aneroid, an instrument he valued, which he had mislaid during his walk the previous day. Retracing his steps as far as possible, we searched for two hours without success. Disappointed, we returned to the motor boat, when we were about to depart, to find it already packed with our gear.

Moving out into deep water, several dredgings were made at a depth of about 18 metres. Later, it was decided to land on shore, opposite the entrance of an extensive valley. Heading inshore, we passed over a belt of thick kelp before a landing could be made. As the tide was receding, Eric Douglas volunteered to anchor the boat in deep water and stay until the party returned.

At the head of the valley large volumes of water, cascading over rocky slopes, had turned the valley floor into a morass. We were glad we were all wearing seaboots as the party plunged over the boggy surface for about a kilometre before reaching higher and firmer ground. Doc had brought a .22 gauge rifle ashore, but despite the large numbers of skua gulls and ducks, only a few were brought down. As ducks were hit they were immediately dived on by watching skuas and carried to the ground. Sir Douglas, trying his skill as a marksman, was annoyed when he saw a duck he had shot dived on by a skua. Handing the gun back to Doc, he rushed to the spot where it had landed, waving his arms and shouting, dragged his duck from the skua's claws and with hardly a smile on his face, handed it to Doc. It was added to those already shot for the larder.

About a kilometre up the valley at a height of about 180 metres, we came across a series of small lakes. Johnston remained there for the rest of the afternoon and collected many interesting freshwater organisms. I continued climbing and at about 300 metres, found a Wilson storm petrel's nest. The bird flew from it at my approach. The nest consisted of only a slight depression on the ground in between several rocks and contained a single egg. Storm petrels are one of the most abundant birds in the Southern Ocean, but it is only on rare occasions that their nests have been found.

A heavy mist now began to fill the valley. I made a hurried return to the boat to find the rest of the party ready to leave. It was a miserable journey back to the ship. Heading into the northerly wind, the boat's bow plunged into the steep choppy waves, throwing sheets of spray over the party huddled together in the cockpit. Heavy rain was also falling.

It was a relief when we reached the *Discovery* and were able to change into dry clothing. Retiring early I was awakened through the night by a mouse running across my face. My sudden yelp awakened Simmers sleeping nearby. When I explained what had happened, he turned over and said in a sleepy voice, "Don't worry, it could have been a rat."

The wind dropped through the night and the morning was calm with prospects of a perfect day. Falla and I spent most of the day skinning birds and packing the now large collection into cases ready for stowing in one of the ship's holds. Early in the morning, Captain Davis, Colbeck, Child and Eric Douglas left in the motor boat for a day's run to the islands and fjords in the Observatory Bay area. The two engineers were busy carrying out essential maintenance on the engines.

The crew who were left to coal ship ceased work about midday. Several of them walked across to Swain's Haulover where they killed a lone sea elephant. The cook's expertise was then called upon to select sufficient steaks and other choice cuts to provide fresh meat for several days. This incident was frowned upon by Sir Douglas and those responsible later received a blast from the skipper. Apparently, they were

A shore party braves the weather in Royal Sound, Kerguelen Island.
(Photo: F. Hurley.)

supposed to have continued coaling all day.

A strong wind was blowing next morning. The sky was overcast with thick black clouds and light rain was falling. The plane was ready to take to the air but continual bad weather prevented any flights. Several were planned for Sir Douglas, Moyes and Hurley.

Scientists spent most of the day indoors completing various tasks. Sir Douglas boiled down a quantity of blubber saved from two Weddell seals shot some time before while in the pack-ice. It yielded 18 litres of oil, requested by the Hudson Bay Company for experimental purposes. Several days previously, I had lowered two seal skulls, tied to a line, over the wharf, hoping that small crustaceans would feed on the flesh, leaving the bone structure clean. Hauled to the surface, I found the experiment had been most successful. Not a vestige of flesh remained and furthermore, several small interesting crabs were found in crevices of the skulls.

Falla and I spent the next day on the Joffre Peninsula collecting birds and investigating nesting sites. A light wind, early in the morning, strengthened to gale force by midday but began to ease in the afternoon. On our return to the whaling station we learned that the crew had completed coaling and 120 tonnes were now stowed on board.

Ritchie Simmers was up and about again and had practically recovered from his illness. He was warned by Doc to ease up on his activities for at least another week. Fireman Smith's foot had also responded to treatment and was back to normal.

Early next morning a light wind was blowing from the north but with every possibility of increasing in strength later in the day. At 9.30 A.M. the plane was lowered over the ship's side and Campbell and Eric Douglas taxied it into mid channel to make a test flight. Simmers, Doc and I left in the motor boat in case our assistance was required. Conditions were not ideal for the plane's take-off. After a fairly long run with the floats smacking hard against short choppy waves and throwing up a great deal of spray, the plane lifted and took to the air.

The airmen returned soon afterwards, landed without trouble and tied up to the motor boat. In the meantime, I had taken Hurley on board with his cameras and he took the place of Eric Douglas in the plane. The wind had now freshened, waves had increased in size and Campbell was having difficulty in taking off. To start the engine he had to leave the cockpit, swing the propeller from a float, until the engine fired, then clamber back into the cockpit. By that time, the plane had swung broadside to the waves and he had to switch off the engine. While this was going on the plane was drifting rapidly down channel and into rougher water.

Throwing Campbell a line from the motor boat, we towed the plane back into smoother waters. Another attempt to take off was successful; bouncing from wave to wave the plane finally rose into the air, almost completely obscured by flying spray.

I then decided to take the motor boat further up the channel into more protected water and wait for their return. About an hour later, sighting the boat in its new position, Campbell made a good landing, taxied to the boat and tied up. Hurley was ecstatic over the flight and the photographic record, stills and film, which he had obtained. It included spectacular closeup shots of Mt Ross. On one occasion, caught in a down current of air, the plane dropped 1000 feet before Campbell regained control.

Eric Douglas took me up as passenger on a final flight. Again difficulties were experienced in attempting to take off in the choppy sea. Eric, however, would not give in and finally, after a fairly long run without gaining much speed, the plane bounced off several waves and with full throttle, became airborne. It was a great experience. Rising to a height of about 4000 feet the view unfolding below us was breathtaking. Royal Sound was a magnificent sight with its many twisting waterways, islands and islets. Numerous lakes of varying sizes, formed on the tops of most islands, were an unexpected sight. Returning from our flight, Eric flew over the whaling station where he performed some minor aerobatics before flying back to the anchored motor boat.

We had no difficulty in landing and an attempt was then made to tow the plane back to the *Discovery*. This proved impossible as the strong wind kept swinging the plane around in such a manner that towing was out of the question. Both plane and boat were going around in circles, wallowing in the waves and making no progress. Campbell then decided to fly the plane back to the ship. He took off in a shower of spray and disappeared towards the ship at a terrific speed with the strong following wind.

Rolling back to the *Discovery* in the motor boat, we arrived in time to see the pram in mid channel with Marr and Colbeck on board ready to assist Campbell. We followed in the motor boat as Campbell taxied the plane beneath the swung-out block and tackle. Colbeck attached the lifting hook and all hands on deck hauled the plane free of the water and inboard. In the meantime, Marr, unable to row the heavy pram against the wind, was disappearing down channel. We rescued him in the motor boat. And so ended a more than exciting morning.

Later, we received the expected dressing-down from Sir Douglas who had not quite recovered from several hours' anxiety about the plane's safety. He complained with the following remarks. "You've nearly buggered the expedition...wasting time flying on a day like this ... madness to go up a second time...looping the loop over the ship," and so on. A few minutes later he was happily listening to our experiences. Fortunately, at the time he did not realise I was the passenger on the second flight. He smiled without comment when he was told. Sir Douglas told us later that the scientific staff would leave in the motor boat for Observatory Bay the next morning, where we would camp until picked up by the *Discovery* on her way to Royal Sound.

The weather was superb on February 19 with a cloudless sky and the channel surface as smooth as a millpond. Permission was given to Hurley to make a flight with Campbell since conditions were so ideal for photography. Our departure for Obervatory Bay was therefore delayed although all camping and collecting gear was already stowed on board.

Returning from his flight, Hurley asked Sir Douglas if he could make further flights, but his request was refused as he was wanted on the camping trip. Campbell and Eric Douglas were to remain behind to make further flights and take aerial photographs which would assist the ship's officers in the preparation of charts.

At midday, the motor boat got under way with its gunwales almost at water level. Its occupants were divided into two groups: Marr, Simmers and Moyes sitting on the deck forward of the cabin, and Sir Douglas, Howard, Johnston, Hurley, Falla, Doc and I remaining aft in the cockpit.

Travelling up the Buenos Aires Channel, Sir Douglas produced a bag of sweets and, handing them round, said, "Don't give them any in front...I don't know how many times I have to tell them not to sit there, but they still persist...so don't give them any lollies." These were the sort of remarks made by Sir Douglas that we looked forward to hearing, and which endeared him to us. Naturally, those sitting in the bow later received their sweets. Furthermore, on this occasion they were sitting forward to keep the boat on an even keel.

Rounding the north-easterly end of Long Island, we left the Buenos Aires Channel, entered and passed through the Charcot Channel and came up to a group of small islands. The party was landed on one, while Sir Douglas and I set out to dredge and attempt tow nettings. The water was too shallow for the nettings, but two good catches resulted from dredgings in about 22 metres.

Returning to the island for the shore party, we then headed for the Enzenpergen Arm and travelled up it for about 16 kilometres. Near its head, a moraine blocked further progress except for a narrow passage which allowed us to continue for several more kilometres. We had passed from salt water into fresh water. The arm ended at the entrance to an immense valley with steep sloping sides with volumes of water cascading down it from thawing snow and ice from the mountain tops.

During the course of our excursions, we never failed to be over-awed by the typical mountain scenery and spectacular fjords. The Enzenpergen Arm was no exception. All aspects clearly showed evidence of sculpturing by great glaciers during past centuries. These had since retreated, but their effects were breathtaking.

Returning, we noticed the rock formation consisted of alternating beds of volcanic tuff and lava. The softer tuff bands had been weathered into innumerable small caverns, now utilised by Kerguelen cormorants as nesting sites. As the boat passed noisily downstream, birds waddled out onto their verandahs and gazed down at the intruders with great curiosity. Through binoculars, Falla noticed fully fledged young, and others partly in down, amongst the adult birds.

Leaving the entrance to Enzenpergen Arm, it was noticed an inspection plate on the side of the engine was leaking oil. The engine was stopped and the boat anchored while a gasket was cut and fitted. After this slight delay we set off for Observatory Bay and soon afterwards found ourselves in a maze of small islets. To check our position, Sir Douglas had to resort to a chart and finally, after several false leads were followed, we made our way into the bay. It was now late in the afternoon with light rain falling, but before it became dark, the huts used by the Gauss Expedition in 1902 came into view. A landing was made, gear carried ashore and tents erected. We all retired early.

All hands were up early in the morning to investigate our surroundings. The huts, originally built by the British Transit of Venus Expedition (Challenger Expedition), used the site to observe the transit of Venus in 1874. Concrete bases on which their instruments stood were still intact and were used again by scientists of the Gauss Expedition in 1902. Trigonometric cairns had been erected on surrounding hills, indicating how well the site had been surveyed and positioned. Two cairns near the huts gave a true north and south line.

The huts were in reasonably good condition. Du Batty carried out repairs and stayed there for a few weeks in 1910. He had walked about 20 kilometres across from the Gazelle Basin where his small vessel, the J. B. *Charcot*, was anchored.

The Gauss Expedition, when it called in at Observatory Bay on its way to the Antarctic in 1902, left two scientists with a staff of five Chinese. During their stay one of the scientists died and the Enzenpergen Arm was named in his memory. Two Chinese also died. Their graves are located on the summit of a rise overlooking Royal Sound.

One intriguing sight between two huts was an immense mound of empty wine and spirit bottles, indicative of a thirst which would be the envy of many a drinker. The ugliness of discarded rubbish, not only bottles, but all manner of refuse scattered all over the area was a nasty scar on the environment. A small islet close inshore had the remains of erected pens which had been used to house sheep.

Immediately after breakfast, Sir Douglas, Falla, Marr, Doc and I left in the motor boat to investigate the Rivett Arm. To reach it we had to re-enter Royal Sound and after a run of about five kilometres to the north we came to its entrance. Rivett Arm proved to be a magnificent fjord with steep-sided cliffs. Proceeding inland we met the full impact of a sudden gale-force wind. It roared without warning through the narrow fjord and in no time a rough sea had developed. No shelter was at hand but a slight turn in the arm offered some protection.

With the engine throttled down and just making headway, waves continually broke over the bow and water was soon over the floor boards. These were lifted to permit bailing, but it took all our efforts to cope with the intake. Water rose to fly-wheel level, resulting in a deluge of spray. The engine then began to miss, but was kept running by protecting the spark plug and magneto with a sheet of canvas. In the meantime, Sir Douglas had unshipped the oars and placed lifebelts in handy positions. We bailed continuously but the water was still above the floor boards when we reached shelter and anchored.

The sudden gales of Kerguelen Island frequently stop just as quickly as they start, so we decided to wait for conditions to improve. The engine ignition was dried and the boat bailed dry. While waiting, we were entertained by the antics of about 20 dolphins. They appeared to be playing a game of follow the leader, porpoising very closely together as they swam in a large circle.

It was not long before the wind died down and we continued on our journey to the head of the arm. When we could proceed no further, Doc and I climbed a reasonably high peak to see if we could sight the Gazelle Basin and other waterways reached from the northern coast of the island. From this point the distance would have been no more than 10 kilometres. High mountains blocked any distant views, so we retraced our steps to the boat. The party was waiting for us and an immediate start was made on our return journey to Observatory Bay.

We had been told by the captain of the *Kilfinora* that a French family, husband and wife and two daughters, lived at the Gazelle Basin. According to the terms of a lease issued to M. Boussier, continual residency by a French family was essential. In 1909, about a thousand sheep were landed at the Gazelle Basin and left in the care of the resident family at that time but mortality was high. In 1911, a flock of 20 was landed, followed in 1913 by 20 more. The idea of raising sheep was finally abandoned because of the high death rate and breeding was difficult under the extreme weather conditions.

It had been a long and tiring day and we arrived back at Observatory Bay to a huge fire and enjoyed a meal which was kept for us. Professor Johnston had spent the day collecting specimens from under rocks between tide marks and was jubilant.

The *Discovery* was expected to call for us about midday, so we stayed in the vicinity of the huts in case she made an early appearance.

Sure enough, in the middle of our midday meal she appeared in sight and slowly steamed up the bay. Reaching a position off the huts, anchors were dropped. In a mild panic, our gear was hurriedly packed in the motor boat and in record time we were alongside the ship and welcomed on board.

The ship remained anchored that night as a full day's dredging in Royal Sound was planned for the next day. Later, Campbell and Eric Douglas regaled us with stories of their flights of the previous day. On one flight they landed alongside the French sealing vessel *Austral*, lying at anchor off Murray Island. They were invited on board and entertained by the captain and ship's officers, toasting one another for some time. This to some extent, I was told, helped to overcome the overwhelming smell of seal oil and blubber which enveloped all parts of the ship. She was sailing next day to the Gazelle Basin to leave provisions for the French family and then proceed to St Paul Island where they would pick up a number of lobster fishermen and convey them home to France. I was surprised the airmen had not added some excitement to the French family by flying to the Gazelle Basin and saluting them with a few half-rolls and wing dips, but they hadn't thought of it!

Anchors were weighed at 6 o'clock next morning and the ship steamed slowly down the bay into Royal Sound. Two tow nettings were immediately carried out, fishing at about 29 metres, which resulted in catches of small medusae (jellyfish).

It was a perfect day with bright sunshine, a light westerly wind and a flat calm on the harbour surface. Manoeuvring between many small islets, the ship entered Hydrography Channel. Engines were stopped and the Monegasque dredge was lowered over the stern. It rested on the bottom at 45 metres. It was then dragged for five minutes at one and a half knots. When hauled in, the net was filled with fine mud and very little marine life. When the dredging was finished, Captain Davis ordered the motor boat to be lowered over the side, and Colbeck, with Eric Douglas in charge of the engine, set out to visit several unnamed islets. They would rejoin the ship at her Murray Island anchorage.

A second dredging was carried out on the bottom at a depth of 42 metres, but again the catch was mainly fine mud. Finally, at 1.30 P.M., the otter trawl was lowered and towed for 30 minutes at a speed of two knots. It yielded an excellent catch, including, strangely enough, only one fish. The otter trawl is designed to catch fish rather than other marine life.

The ship headed to Navalo Harbour, Murray Island, and anchored. The *Austral* had sailed the previous day. Sir Douglas, Doc and I began sieving the muddy dredged material, using sea water, and a surprising number of interesting specimens came to light. When we finished for the day, the deck and our clothing were covered with fine sticky mud and Sir Douglas decided to wash down the deck. He lowered a leather bucket over the side but its added weight, when filled with water, pulled the attached rope out of his grasp. He was most embarrassed as one of the ship's best buckets disappeared from sight.

In the meantime, Eric Douglas and Colbeck had returned from their short surveying trip. Sir Douglas was anxious to secure a representative collection of marine life from deep waters off the Kerguelen coast by dredgings, tow nettings and trawling, which meant we would stay at our anchorage until weather conditions were suitable.

Doc Ingram received a wireless message from his friend, W. M. Hughes, ex Prime Minister of Australia, asking for news of the expedition and if all members were safe. This message caused considerable speculation, particularly when Professor Johnston also received a message inquiring after his health. Sparks heard a news item on the air stating that Mr Macpherson Robertson, a generous donor to the expedition, was sailing for England. If the news was correct, he would be overseas when we returned to Australia.

During the evening, Sir Douglas informed us in the wardroom that his future plans, at the conclusion of the oceanographic programme off the coast, were to sail south to Heard Island, complete its mapping, and cross the Kerguelen–Gaussberg submarine ridge from west to east to determine its width. A visit to the nearby Murray Island was postponed the next morning because of a strengthening westerly wind which had been blowing since midnight. By midday it had eased and Eric Douglas, Simmers and myself left in the motor boat to take Hurley and his cameras to the island. We left him on shore and returned to the *Discovery*. Although it was a short distance to the island, the motor boat was deluged by spray thrown up as she buried her bow into the short steep waves. After lunch, a second party went ashore and the boat was anchored in a sheltered position.

Moyes and I walked to the western end of the island where we came across a beacon, no doubt used in the past as a guiding light for sealing vessels entering Royal Sound after dark. It was in a state of disrepair and obviously had not been in use for many years. Walking over the surface of Murray Island was most tiring. Covering the ground was a luxurious growth, mainly close mounds of *Azorella*, into which we sank almost to our knees at each step. This intense growth of vegetation was found on all the islands which did not have a rabbit population.

An interesting find was a boss of igneous rock similar to the one located at Greenland Harbour. The large rock mass, with sloping sides, was badly weathered on the western side which faced the prevailing winds. Erosion had also reduced the central core. A thin layer of outer surface rock at the top overhung the central eroded space. Weathering had reached about the same stage as the boss at Greenland Harbour and both intrusions could have occurred at the same time.

Skua gulls were numerous and we were attacked. I was interested in watching a young pintail duck evading assaults from diving skuas. Flying in rather an amateurish fashion it used instinctive defence movements, swerving, twisting and diving to escape its attackers. Surprisingly, the young duck completely eluded them and safely regained the protection of its nest.

Leaving Moyes to take sights for his charts of the Prince of Wales Peninsula and the many scattered islands, I returned to the boat and joined Sir Douglas and Doc in running lines of soundings until the light faded. It was raining heavily as we picked up the shore party and returned to the ship. Soundings varied from seven to 29 metres, the greater depth at the anchorage.

I was awakened in the morning by the shrill whistling of wind through the rigging and the ship tugging at her anchor chains. It was blowing a half gale from the west. Surface waters of Royal Sound were lashed into white-topped waves, almost completely covered with foam and flying spray. It was certainly no place for our motor boat and island visits were out of the question.

Falla and I began skinning the birds we had collected during the past few days. We had about 30, both large and small, waiting for our attention. Later in the day, I had a rest by helping Doc to complete washing and sieving the residue of the mud dredgings. There was no lessening of the wind through the day and it was steadily increasing.

Through the night, the wind increased to gale force, but had begun to ease by the morning. Taking advantage of a slight lull about midday, Sir Douglas suggested a visit to Sharbeau Island, a few kilometres up the harbour from the ship. There were eight of us in the motor boat, and after an unpleasant trip with a following sea, we moved into a sheltered landing spot. Sharbeau Island is hourglass shaped and its central formation gave us protection from wind and waves. One of our objectives was to obtain as many ducks as possible as they were proving a welcome change to our menu.

Walking inland there appeared to be a scarcity of ducks, but after firing a shot, hundreds appeared from their resting places under the thick vegetation. Taking to the air they circled overhead, offering good targets, and about 15 were brought down. Alf Howard, after firing a number of shots without success, put his gun down and began to creep up on one which was feeding. Diving at it, he just missed but caught one immediately afterwards. No mean achievement as they were running around as if being fed in a farmyard. Showing us a technique which he explained was the correct way to kill a wild duck, he bit into the duck's neck. "That's it," he said, and threw it on the ground. Unfortunately for Howard, it took to the wing and disappeared in the distance.

Hearing calls from Sir Douglas, we left the excitement of the duck shoot and returned to the boat. We were escorted by flocks of ducks calling loudly in their shrill whistling notes. No doubt, on our departure they would return to their resting places among the dense undergrowth and once again silence would prevail on the island. Falla, on his ramble, had found a colony of Kerguelen cormorants. There were many juvenile birds, some still in down, while others more advanced were in the process of trying out their wings. On a cliff face, Hurley had come across a sooty albatross nest with two chicks. As the nests are usually inaccessible he had taken still photographs and cine-film of the nest and its occupants.

Leaving the shelter of Sharbeau Island we headed for Suhm Island about three kilometres to the north-east. Moving out into exposed waters the boat wallowed in the following choppy sea. The waves were met almost broadside on because of our course and with little freeboard, we began shipping waves over the gunwales. Bailing was necessary to keep the water at a reasonable level in the boat.

We reached the island and landed on the shore of a partly protected bay on its lee side. Suhm Island, one of the largest in the area, has an outstanding spectacular feature — a high peak of columnar basalt. Simmers and I set off to climb it. Reaching its base, we found the sides much steeper than anticipated and composed of loose weathered rock fragments. As we climbed, pieces of rock broke away from underfoot, creating minor avalanches. Heavy rain had set in with an increasing wind. Under these unpleasant conditions we decided to retreat when only about nine metres from the summit. Returning to the boat we found we had to go back to the ship because of the increasingly bad weather. Falla, investigating bird burrows, had found only a few were occupied by well-grown chicks. Sir Douglas excitedly told us he had seen the world's largest sea leopard. It was about to come ashore but decided otherwise when it spotted Sir Douglas.

Setting out from our sheltered position, we soon ran into waves much higher than those experienced earlier in the afternoon; their crests were whipped into thick flying spray by the strong westerly wind. Although the engine was throttled down to permit little more than steering way, the boat was receiving a severe buffeting as it headed into the waves. Water poured inboard over the bow and bailing could not prevent it from gaining. It was too hazardous to turn back so we made for a small unnamed islet where slight shelter was found. We anchored in fairly calm water but a heavy surge kept the boat rolling and tugging at its anchor rope. After bailing the boat dry, we decided to wait for the wind to drop before making a further attempt to reach the *Discovery*, about three miles away.

Two hours later we discussed our position. There were no signs of the wind lessening and the hours of darkness were not far off. Finally, we agreed to continue on our way to the ship. Donning lifebelts, we set off and after an exciting passage drew in alongside the *Discovery*. Fore and aft lines were thrown and fastened on deck and disembarking began as the boat rose and fell on the heavy waves. This accomplished, the boat was then hoisted on board after several nerve-racking crashes against the ship's side.

Changing into dry clothes, the weary shore party were happy to sit down to a meal of roast pintail duck and tasty new potatoes. Our original potato supply had finished and we now had tinned ones twice a week. As we retired, the wind was still blowing at gale force and there seemed no possibility of the ship sailing next morning.

On February 26 I was awakened early by a choir of voices singing "Happy Birthday" and offering me good wishes and hoping I would have a pleasant and restful day. It was my 27th birthday.

There was no change in the weather, if anything it had increased in violence. The skipper of the *Kilfinora* had told us earlier that a fine day was rarely experienced at Kerguelen during the month of February. Captain Davis was of the opinion we were in the throes of early winter gales which blow almost continually. He reiterated his desire to sail directly to Australia when conditions improved. Because of our enforced delay, Sir Douglas had given up his idea of sailing south but he was still determined to carry out a programme of nettings and dredgings off the coast. The extreme turbulence of waters in Royal Sound effectively prevented any motor boat excursions. High choppy waves were breaking as they swept across the harbour in a scurry of spray and foam.

Johnston and Marr spent most of the day carefully packing jars of specimens into wooden cases and labelling them ready for transfer to the University of Adelaide on our arrival in Australia. The collections would then be distributed to specialists for research in all parts of the world. Results of their work, when completed, would be published in the expedition's scientific reports.

Crew members had been busy all day cleaning the ship. Decks were clear as it was not necessary to carry extra supplies of coal on our voyage to Australia. Washing down and painting had been going on to such an extent that Hurley remarked, "We'll arrive in Australia looking like a millionaire's yacht, rather than an exploring vessel."

Gale-force winds continued throughout the day with no signs of easing. Intermittent heavy rain also offered no encouragement for a change in conditions. The barometer was low but steady. There was a slight improvement in the weather the next morning, but it was decided that the ship would remain at her anchorage until the following day.

Huge waves thundered on the cliffs of the Prince of Wales Peninsula, the northern headland of Royal Sound. It would have been impossible to carry out our oceanographic programme in the big seas that were rolling in.

Despite the turmoil, Sir Douglas selected a party in the afternoon to land on Long Island. This islet, situated a short distance from our anchorage, is marked on du Batty's map as Ile Longue, and is distinct from the much larger island extending opposite Port Jeanne d'Arc. Setting out in the motor boat, we heard a plaintive cry from the ship; Professor Johnston had been left behind. Sir Douglas, with a mischievous smile, said, "Will we go back?" "Yes," we replied, so back we turned. Arriving at the island we had difficulty in landing as a strong surge kept lifting the boat towards the rocky shore. It was some time before the boat was safely tied up with a stern anchor out. In the excitement of getting ashore Howard dropped Hurley's full plate camera in the water. Hurley showed great restraint as he held the rescued camera aloft and sadly watched sea water drain from it.

Moving inland, Marr, Campbell, Doc Ingram and I came across a large lake literally covered with pintail ducks. It was useless shooting any as it would have meant swimming out in the icy water to retrieve them. There were no volunteers for that task. Later, Falla and I visited a colony of giant petrels situated high on a cliff face. Fully fledged young were almost ready to fly while others were making their first attempts at flying.

A rookery of about 50 rockhopper penguins was occupied by well-grown chicks still in down, their parents busily engaged in feeding them. In late November the previous year, we had visited this rookery and found the birds had prepared nesting sites but eggs had not then been laid.

Returning to the motor boat we found Sir Douglas had collected a large series of interesting rock specimens. Professor Johnston, searching around the shoreline, had filled several large jars with small marine organisms and he had also made a collection of insects and arachnids (spiders) from the vegetation. He was a zealous collector. At the conclusion of our two voyages, spiders alone numbered 444 specimens. They consisted of eight genera, one new genus and four new species.

Our enforced stay on Kerguelen Island was by no means wasted. Every opportunity was taken to collect natural history material to add to the various animal groups already in hand. Specimens from Kerguelen Island and other subantarctic islands, practically virgin fields, were of extreme scientific importance.

Our return to the ship, after some trouble in embarking because of the strong surge, was uneventful although a choppy sea was still running. Zoologists immediately began working on the collections which had been accumulating, particularly birds waiting to be skinned.

The high piercing whistling of wind, as it swept through the rigging, awakened me the next morning. It had increased to full gale force with incredibly strong gusts. The ship's departure was again postponed. Nearing midday, the wind had dropped appreciably and ship's officers Colbeck and Child, with Eric Douglas in charge, left in the motor boat to take a series of soundings. Shortly afterwards the wind suddenly increased in violence and roared across the Sound. The motor boat hurriedly turned back but an engine valve became stuck and it stopped. Quickly manning the oars, Eric Douglas and his crew ranged alongside the ship almost at their last gasp. The commotion in disembarking and hoisting the boat on board was equal to, if not greater than, the scientists' efforts earlier. In no time the surface waters were a maelstrom of white-crested waves, foam and spray. Eric Douglas later dismantled the motor boat engine and corrected the sticking valve. Falla and I were happy to have an uninterrupted day and we continued our work of skinning and filling out birds.

There was no lessening of the wind through the night and it was still blowing a full gale the next morning. Sailing was again postponed. Sir Douglas informed us that we would sail next morning for Australia irrespective of the weather. We would stop on the way to run oceanographic stations whenever conditions were suitable. Captain Davis had reiterated his opinion that winter conditions had befallen us, and we could expect continual westerly gales with very little fine weather. Sir Douglas, therefore, reluctantly abandoned any idea of sailing south to Heard Island.

Later in the morning the wind moderated slightly. The waves in Royal Sound had also subsided, not to a great extent, but sufficiently for Sir Douglas to suggest an all-day collecting trip to the Poincare Peninsula. The motor boat was swung out, lowered over the side and, with most of the scientific staff on board, we set out for the nearby shore. An attempt to land below Cat's Ears Peak, near the southern headland of the entrance to Royal Sound, was prevented by a heavy swell and a strong surge. Turning back and keeping close to the shore, the boat surfed in the following seas and caused many anxious moments as we had so little freeboard. On all our excursions the boat was usually overloaded, but it was a good sea boat and, although prone to move about a lot because of its shallow draft, carried us safely on all occasions.

After travelling about two miles back along the shore, the boat was manoeuvred into fairly calm water behind Paquito Point where a landing was made. The party divided and set out in various directions with instructions to return at about 5 P.M. Falla, Doc Ingram and I decided to walk to the Cat's Ears Peak and search for nesting birds along the cliff face of the peninsula.

We plunged across an extensive marshy area covered with the ubiquitous *Azorella*. Reaching a higher elevation, we passed over ground covered with large boulders (erratics) carried there by glacial action. To reach the Cat's Ears Peak, a large deep valley had to be crossed, its marshy floor covered with thick undergrowth. Negotiating this, we climbed on to a rocky plateau about 250 metres above sea level. It was a weird and desolate scene. Fully exposed to the strong westerly wind we had to crouch and use strength to make headway.

We arrived at the base of the peak and began our climb to its summit. Loose rocks on the steep sides slowed our progress. We were rewarded by a magnificent panoramic view on reaching the top. From a height of about 900 metres we looked down on the Indian Ocean. Huge waves rolling in crashed against the coastal cliffs and we could clearly hear the subdued roar from our elevated position. It was a wild scene and the decision for the *Discovery* to remain at her anchorage proved to be a wise one. An oceanographic station would have been impossible in the heavy seas.

About 20 kilometres to the south-east, across an extensive plateau, Mt Wyville Thomson rose majestically to a height of more than 1370 metres. It is one of the highest mountains on the island, its summit covered with ice, and glaciers, glistening even in the dull light, descending halfway down its sides. Away in the distance Mt Ross, an extinct volcano, rose above the mountain range to a height of 1865 metres above sea level.

Our descent from Cat's Ears Peak was far more hazardous than anticipated. Care was necessary not to slide when loose rocks were dislodged. These, bounding down the steep sides, created small avalanches which attained considerable speed on reaching the plateau.

We arrived at the base of the peak without mishap and set out to return to the boat. Shortly afterwards I came across an exposure of marine fossils. They were preserved in a matrix of fine-grained tuff and consisted mainly of bivalve and univalve shells, bryozoa and encrusting worm tubes. The horizontally laid fossil horizons, interbedded by bands of basalt, comprised eight to 10 layers of deposition. Several bands were almost entirely calcareous, crowded with shell remains to the exclusion of practically all of the tuff matrix. Fossils were rare in other bands. As time was getting on we hurriedly filled haversacks with selected specimens and then departed for the boat about eight kilometres away.

On the walk back we descended almost to shore level where we were faced with almost continuous marshy flats. Falla, while trailing behind, stepped into a sea elephant wallow and was up to his waist before catching hold of strong undergrowth near the edge. His repeated calls for assistance could not be heard above the noise of the wind. By the time I realised he was not following, he had laboriously dragged himself out on to solid ground. Later, when we were describing the incident, we learned that Alf Howard had stumbled into two wallows during the day.

As we neared the boat, Sir Douglas came to meet us with news that the boat was high and dry and high tide was not until 10 P.M. He was most interested when shown the fossils. I had hopes of returning to the fossil outcrop next morning, but he explained it would be impossible as the ship was definitely sailing. The collected fossil specimens, however, were sufficient to form the basis of a research paper which I completed at the conclusion of the expedition. They proved to be of late Tertiary geological age and were entombed about 15 million years ago. The paper was later published in the BANZARE Scientific Reports.

The presence of fossil marine life, originally living in a shoreline environment, but now raised to a height of 240 metres above sea level, is additional evidence that the island is in the process of emergence from an ice age. At that time the land lay buried beneath an ice covering, which, over many years, gradually receded leaving only the mountain peaks ice-capped.

Frank Hurley, returning to the motor boat and finding it aground, had managed to find sufficient driftwood to start a blazing fire. He was in high spirits having photographed, as he said, "some of the world's most spectacular scenery". After sitting around the fire for some time drinking mugs of hot tea, a suggestion was made to manhandle the boat back into the water. This was successfully accomplished at the expense of much labour and cold wet feet. We were back on the ship again at about 8 P.M. The rest of the evening was devoted to chocking movable objects in the laboratory and in our cabins. There were indications we would be experiencing rough seas in the morning.

During the night an unexpected easing of the wind prompted Captain Davis to order steam pressure raised as he proposed leaving the anchorage at 3 A.M. Inadvertently, pressure had been blown off and was not sufficiently raised again to start the engines until 9 A.M. At that time all hands manned the capstan and, accompanied by the singing of sea shanties, anchors were raised and secured.

Homeward Bound

STEAMING OUT through the entrance to Royal Sound, the ship headed south into a fairly heavy, but widely spaced swell. The wind had dropped to almost a light breeze from the north-west. At 9.30 A.M., oblique nets were towed for 15 minutes at a depth of 33 metres. A poor catch resulted, mainly krill. At midday the large otter trawl was lowered over the stern and after a sufficient length of cable had been paid out was towed for an hour at a depth of 246 metres. The catch was good, but strangely enough it included only one medium-sized fish.

In the meantime, the wind had been increasing in violence, and was now blowing at almost gale force from the north-west. Further oceanographic activities were abandoned. Marr and Johnston began sorting trawled material and Falla and I once again skinned birds.

At midday, 17 miles had been logged since leaving our anchorage. Sails were hoisted and drawing well with the strong wind and we were on our way to Australia. Our first port of call, we were told, would be Albany in Western Australia.

During the night the wind dropped to a variable light breeze. By morning it had swung to the north-east and later increased to about half gale force.

Earlier in the voyage Doc Ingram had replaced a filling which had dropped out of one of my molar teeth. All attempts to keep the filling intact failed. The tooth was causing considerable pain and Doc suggested he should extract it. Preparations were made for the operation and correct dental instruments were unpacked from his medical equipment. We decided to do without an anaesthetic. Little of the tooth remained to get a good grip with the extractor and it splintered. The cook's young assistant was then called in to help, but a few minutes later we heard a soft sigh as he collapsed on the deck in a dead faint. Time was taken off to revive him and help him to his bunk. As there was nothing of the tooth left to grip, Doc decided to dig the root from the gum. Some time later I was told the tooth was out. Exploring the cavity with my tongue I said I could still feel a tooth fragment. "No," said Doc, "it's the jawbone you're touching." It had been a painful operation and Sir Douglas, hearing of it, said I could have the next day off.

At noon, our distance run for the 24 hours was 148 miles, and we had reached 48°31'S, 73°57'E.

The favourable following wind continued through the day and, with all sails set, the ship surged ahead at about four knots.

The wind had dropped to a light breeze from the south-west the next morning and the sea was calm with a low swell. Taking advantage of the ideal conditions, Sir Douglas decided to run a full plankton station and a deep dredging. Sails were taken in at about 8.30 A.M., engines stopped and the ship was allowed to drift. Depth by the echo sounder was 2848 metres. I was excused from assisting with the plankton nets, not to enjoy my suggested holiday, but to continue skinning the backlog of birds.

The plankton station was successfully completed at 3 P.M., and two hours later the Monegasque dredge was lowered over the stern. Over 3000 metres of cable had been paid out, with the ship steaming slowly ahead, when the dredge reached the bottom. It was then towed for 25 minutes. When hauled in and hoisted on deck, the dredge was found to be clean and had obviously not been dredging. The cable had fouled one end of the frame and kept it suspended. Because of the depth of the sea floor, about 2600 metres, dredging operations had taken three hours to complete.

Before stopping for the plankton station the ship had logged 124 miles since midday the previous day. Sails were again set and, with engines running, the ship continued on her course to Albany.

The weather next day was perfect with a light breeze coming in from the north-east, bright sunshine and a calm sea with barely any swell.

At 2 P.M., the Monegasque dredge was again lowered over the stern in another attempt to dredge from the sea floor at a depth of about 3000 metres. On this occasion the ship's speed was reduced to permit the cable and heavy dredge to sink at a less acute angle. After two and a half hours about 4000 metres of cable had been paid out; time was then allowed to make sure the dredge was resting on the bottom. The ship's speed was then increased to one knot. While the dredge was being dragged over the sea floor the dynamometer recorded a strain of only one and a half tonnes, but a terrific strain was being exerted on the guiding rollers attached to the ship's gunwale, and these became unable to function satisfactorily. After a while, the strain eased and dredging continued for an hour. Campbell, driving the winch, then began hauling the dredge to the surface, a procedure taking four hours to complete. When hoisted on board, the iron frame of the dredge was twisted out of shape and the net badly torn. Specimens retained in the net included a number of manganese nodules.

Manganese nodules are an interesting feature of oceanic depths. They occur as knobbly black or dark-brown concretions ranging in size up to 15 centimetres, which form a covering layer on sea bed sediments and only at depths exceeding 900 metres. They have been found in profusion in most oceans of the world. Nodules grow by the slow accumulation of manganese and iron minerals forming a concretionary structure around a nucleus. In larger nodules this process may take several million years. Also present are other minerals such as copper, nickel, cobalt and molybdenum.

This untapped mineral wealth has recently received the attention of mining companies. Means of recovery and processing the nodules for their contained minerals have been discussed and planned at length. In 1981, it was estimated that operations on a commercial basis would cost approximately $A7,320 million.

Darkness had set in at the conclusion of the dredging, and the catch, consisting mainly of nodules, was set aside for sorting next day. Sails were set and the ship was again under way. Ninety miles were logged for our distance run. Sparks was receiving good reception from an Australian broadcasting station and one interesting item of news was that the *Discovery* had left Kerguelen Island, after the onset of winter gales, on her return voyage to Australia. We expected to reach Albany on March 21.

The light north-easterly wind of the previous day had backed to the north early next day, but the ship was making good progress under sail and help from the engines. So far, we had enjoyed phenomenal weather in the Roaring Forties and had not been subjected to the violent westerly gales for which they are renowned.

Sir Douglas was amused at a statement made by Captain Davis during a discussion on deep-sea dredging. The subject was how to determine that the dredge was actually on the bottom before dragging commenced. The skipper said, "Really, someone should invent something that would trip something and do something." No doubt spoken in jest, but we all agreed it would indeed be a useful contrivance.

Sir Douglas was awaiting word from the Antarctic Committee regarding our first port of call in Australia, which would almost certainly be Adelaide. Rumour had it that the ship would anchor off Albany on the way while the motor boat went in for fresh meat and vegetables.

All hands were in remarkably good health and practically no sickness had occurred during the voyage. After leaving Cape Town, Steward Dungey was ordered to issue a daily glass of orange juice to all hands and make sure it was consumed. There was, however, no check on the steward and he succumbed to a mild attack of scurvy on our way back to Australia. He admitted to Doc Ingram he had not been drinking his orange juice for several months.

At midday we had travelled only 70 miles for our 24-hour run. Weather was fine although thick black clouds had completely covered the sky. The barometer remained high and steady, so there was no immediate change expected in the weather.

During the afternoon, the ship suddenly ran into a blanket of thick black fog which extended north and south as far as the eye could see. The line of demarcation was so obvious that a bump would not have been unexpected as the bow cut into the fog and was lost to sight from amidship. For about 30 minutes we steamed through the fog bank. It was an eerie experience, heightened by repeated loud blasts from the ship's whistle. The ship's emergence into daylight again was just as sudden.

Work in the laboratory continued. Sir Douglas had sorted the dredged material and specimens were in the hands of Marr and Johnston for preservation. Falla and I were still skinning birds but nearing the end.

During the night the south-easterly wind had veered to the south-west and was now a following, light wind. It was a perfect day; a flat calm sea with practically no swell. Our distance run at midday was 146 miles and our position 45°53′S, 84°14′E.

At 2 P.M., sails were lowered and the engines stopped so that tow nettings could be carried out. Nets of four sizes were towed at different times for two-thirds of a mile. The most successful catch was with a mesh net with a ring opening measuring 180 centimetres in diameter. Eighteen hundred metres of cable had been paid out and it was towed for an hour. Depth of the sea floor was 3300 metres. The catch included seven different species of fish and a variety of other marine life, but unfortunately, some fragile specimens were damaged by struggling larger fish.

A complete plankton station (No. 68) was successfully accomplished the following day, finishing up with tow nettings at 3.30 P.M. Deck temperature was now 12°C; the wardroom was 4°C warmer. Lighter clothes were now becoming fashionable.

During the afternoon, Falla shot a black-browed albatross which we managed to recover with a landing net. The crew were not too happy because according to sailors' lore, killing an albatross brought on bad weather. Later, Professor Johnston, searching through the bird's intestines, excitedly announced he had found a new form of parasitic worm. Closer investigation proved it to be a length of spaghetti. Tinned spaghetti had been served for lunch and scraps thrown overboard had been snapped up by the ill-fated bird as a dainty morsel. On the other hand, sly smiles on several faces indicated that it might have been placed in the bird's intestine with evil intent.

In the evening, our usual Saturday night celebration was held when we made our usual toast to our sweethearts and wives. This occasion was enhanced by a gift of a bottle of Greek brandy from Captain Davis; rather a surprise as he never participated in the weekly gatherings. It was a welcome addition to our usual two bottles of port and it resulted in a lively and convivial evening. At its conclusion, a number of us crammed into Falla's cabin where a host of varied subjects were discussed until, heeding complaints from nearby cabins, we retired at 1 A.M.

Perhaps it was unwise of Falla to shoot the albatross. Early next morning, the wind, after being unsteady, settled down to blow hard from the south-west and by midday had increased to gale force. Under full sail with a following wind the ship was bowling along in great style at a speed of eight knots. At midday we had logged 125 miles.

The Roaring Forties were certainly kind to us. During the night the gale-force winds had dropped and only a light breeze was blowing from almost due west the next morning. A heavy sea was running. Under sail the ship steadied to a great extent and her rolling was not so marked. Good progress was being made and at midday 166 miles were logged.

At 2 P.M., although conditions were not very suitable, tow nettings were again carried out. The large net was lowered over the stern and 2700 metres of cable paid out until it was fishing at about 1800 metres. Depth of the sea floor was 2800 metres. Good catches resulted from all nettings including a variety of fishes.

Wireless programmes from stations in Australia were coming in clearly. I occasionally visited Sparks in his wireless cabin late in the evening and listened to items from stations in Paris, London and Holland. Card games had suddenly become an obsession, particularly a difficult game of patience. Hurley was the only one to attain the almost impossible — he successfully concluded the game — but he was so annoyed at the amount of time involved that he threw the cards down, muttering, "Never again."

Fine weather broke the next day with bright sunshine, a calm sea, but a heavy swell. So far, we had sailed 1162 miles from Kerguelen Island and were now 1102 miles from Cape Leeuwin, our nearest point in Australia. The ship was still making good time under sail and engines.

At 2 P.M. sails were lowered and the ship stopped for another complete plankton station (No. 70). A few minor difficulties were experienced with the vertical plankton nets and it was not until 6.30 P.M. that the station was finished.

Marr and Johnston were kept busy in the laboratory, working hard in an endeavour to cope with sorting and preserving the influx of specimens from nettings. Falla and I were now able to assist, having completed bird skinning. The collection of birds, about 150 skins, had been packed in cases ready to be taken ashore at Adelaide.

Falla had meticulously kept up his daily observations of birds. This averaged five minutes each hour between 8 A.M. and 5 P.M. From his records it was possible to define the distribution, frequency and numbers of bird species over the area of oceans traversed by the expedition.

Late in the afternoon the wind veered to the north-west and freshened. All hands assisted in hoisting sails including topgallants; the ship made good progress under full sail and with a following wind. The north-westerly wind continued throughout the night and was still blowing steadily the next morning. It was a fine day but with dark clouds developing. Later in the morning, heavy fog reduced visibility but it gradually lightened and had finally disappeared by mid-afternoon.

The ship was now sailing in the shipping lanes of vessels plying to and from Australian ports. A keen lookout was being kept for the first sighting of a ship.

A box of gramophone records loaned earlier on the voyage to crew members was returned to the wardroom. Inadvertently left in it was a poem entitled "In Authority", composed, I suspected, by Frank Marsland. It was handed back and received with relief, for they had no wish for it to be seen by the skipper or ship's officers. It read:

In Authority

The good ship *Discovery*, of Antarctic fame,
Includes in her complement the *crème de la crème*,
But of these there are seven who cannot lay claim
To the most minute shred of authority.

There is wee-guardsman Martin and lobster-pot Mac,
Fur-trapper Tommy and Swede basher Jack,
Jock, George and Young Aussie, completing the pack
Of those who are minus authority.

On Kerguelen's fair waters aspiring to float,
They approached the Chief Officer, requesting a boat,
Which was granted on terms which it grieves me to quote,
You'll return before dark to authority.

Now sadly I tell how they failed in their trust,
Returning at last 'neath the sprinkled stardust
To a much annoyed Mate who so sadly cussed
Them for daring to flaunt his authority.

Unrepentant e'en yet, though they've left that fair isle,
And they still stagger under the Chief Officer's bile,
And of favours they get none. 'Tis all done to rile
The seven who respect no authority.

They are morbid and morose and on every young face
There is now clear to see the indelible trace
Of their shocking ill doings, they are now not "quite nace",
Aren't those seven who laughed at authority.

When Jimmy the hirsute to Malvern goes back
And endeavours to master the equestrian hack,
There is one quality I know, he will certainly lack,
That's the elusive complex of authority.

When Kenneth of Rosshire joins the Dumdum once more,
We'll find that his status will not be as yore;
In fact, in the company there'll be quite a furore,
By Jings, he has lost his authority.

And fur-trapper Tommy of homicide prates
And seeks opportunities of slaying the mates,
Or the skipper or others whose lamentable fates
Have ordained they should be in authority.

And Swede basher Jack will philander no more
With the ladies of Lonsdale, but will come to the fore
As a Bolshevik Nihilist who craves for the gore
Of those bachelor's sons in authority.

And the taciturn Jock becomes even more so
Since that fateful night when he trod on the toe
Of his countryman fierce, and he now is the foe
Of all things that resemble authority.

And George remarks frequently he'll depart in haste
On arrival in Melbourne as he's now had a taste
Of his officer's ire; he'll run as if chased
By the devil himself or authority.

Now I, myself, personally am saintly and pure,
Alcoholic refreshment and females abhor,
But 'tis with joyful sensation I confess I'd endure
Just a week or so here in authority.

When our voyaging is o'er and our paydays we've got,
We'll adjourn to a pub for a fare-thee-well tot
And we'll drink to ourselves and to hell with the lot
Of all those who are now in authority.

These facetiously composed verses were read with amusement by
the scientific staff. The *Discovery* was a happy ship with scientists and

crew always on the best of terms. Only on one occasion did I see two of
the crew come to blows. It was a short-lived fight. Lofty Martin, with his
great height and strength, lifted the two combatants by their collars and
held them squirming in the air until they simmered down. Lowered to
the deck they shook hands and were good friends again.

March 14 was another fine day with a light breeze but a heavy
swell running in from the south-west. At 1 P.M. sails were lowered and
the ship gradually lost way in readiness for another complete plankton
station. Excessive rolling of the ship in the heavy swell created
difficulties in some of the operations. In the vertical net series,
slackening of the haulage wire caused severe kinking and stranding
resulting in delays. As well, as tension was released by the rolling of the
ship, the wire frequently jumped off the guiding pulleys, but quickly
stopping the donkey engine prevented undue damage. A water sample
and temperature bottle, while being lowered from the forecastle,
jammed on the donkey engine drum and snapped; the bottle with about
300 metres of wire sank to the sea floor, 4050 metres below. The station
was completed at 8 P.M., at the conclusion of several tow nettings with
small nets. Engines were started and we proceeded on our course under
steam. A school of about a hundred dolphins played around the ship for
about half an hour before departing *en masse*.

Early next morning, Sir Douglas received a message from the
Antarctic Committee informing him that our first port of call was to be
Adelaide with a stopover of three days before sailing to Melbourne.

There was very little wind and we continued on our course under
steam at a steady rate of five knots. We were then about 600 miles from
Cape Leeuwin. At midday we had reached 39°40′S, 100°19′E, and were
now north of the Roaring Forties. Ship's Officer Colbeck gave me some
interesting figures regarding our voyage. At midday we had travelled
9662 miles since leaving Cape Town and on arrival in Melbourne we
would have covered 12,000 miles. No station was held during the day
which gave the zoologists an opportunity to finalise work on previous
catches.

The weather next day was warm enough for several of us to
indulge in the luxury of sunbathing. The deck temperature was 18°C. A
light breeze was still blowing from the east, and the sea was calm and
almost flat with a lazy southerly swell. The ship continued on her way
under steam with only a slight roll at a speed of 5½ knots.

The ship's speed was reduced for another tow netting at 3.30 P.M.
Nine hundred metres of cable was paid out and the large net towed at a
depth of about 180 metres for two and a half miles at a speed of two
knots, resulting in a good catch. I spent the evening assisting Marr and
Johnston in the laboratory.

Before retiring I spent some time on deck admiring a magnificent display of flashing lights. The sea was ablaze with a brilliant phosphor-escence ahead and astern of the ship. Myriads of lights pinpointed the presence of minute flagellate protozoans of the genus *Noctiluca*. Each one was a luminous ball, producing an overall weird and memorable sight. Perfect conditions continued into the next day and a full oceano-graphic station was commenced at midday and completed at 6 P.M.

Next morning the ship headed into a gradually increasing wind from the north-east. With engines turning over at full speed we were logging four and a half knots and at midday our 24-hour run was logged at 108 miles.

Depths of the sea floor had been increasing during the day and had dropped by 1300 metres since 1 A.M. to 5540 metres at 4 P.M. At midnight the recorded depth was 4380 metres. During the day Sir Douglas had suggested running a plankton station over the Jeffrey Deep. It was planned for 8 A.M. when the ship was scheduled to pass over it.

Captain Davis was anxious to call at Albany for fresh meat and vegetables, but a decision had already been made to sail direct to Adelaide. The skipper had then compromised by agreeing to sail direct if plans to run a line of oceanographic stations across the Bight were abandoned.

Immediately after breakfast a complete plankton station was commenced. This was to be the last on the voyage. Although planned to start at 6 A.M. it was three hours later before operations began. Unfortunately, the ship had passed over the Jeffrey Deep at 4 A.M. and the station was worked in a depth almost 1800 metres less than expected. Our position at midday was due south of Cape Leeuwin.

During the night the wind swung to the south-east and at daybreak a heavy swell was holding the ship back to a speed of little more than two knots. A series of tow nettings, a trawling and a dredging were begun the next day. We were over the Australian Continental Shelf in shallow water. At 8 A.M. a depth of 155 metres was recorded and by 4 P.M. it had shallowed to 50 metres. Conditions were not ideal for oceanographic work due to a big swell and a confused sea.

A small conical dredge was lowered over the ship's stern and on reaching the bottom it was dragged at two knots for one minute. It yielded a small but interesting catch. The otter trawl was then lowered. It was estimated that if 180 metres of cable was paid out it would trawl at approximately 50 metres. After being towed at a speed of three knots for an hour the net was hoisted on board. It was a disappointing catch. Marks on the otter boards indicated the trawl had momentarily touched the bottom, no doubt spilling most of the net's contents. Two oblique nettings then completed the station, concluding our scientific programme for the voyage.

Fine weather was enjoyed for the following days before our arrival at Port Adelaide. Variable easterly winds persisted and the ship's progress was considerably reduced; engines turning over at full speed did little to combat the headwind resistance. Scientists were kept busy cleaning and packing away scientific equipment and ensuring it would be in good condition for use on the second voyage of the expedition. Natural history specimens, estimated at between 18 and 20 tonnes, had been packed ready for transfer to the University of Adelaide.

The wardroom table was covered with reports in various stages of completion by Howard and Simmers. Commander Moyes was busily engaged in completing charts of lands visited in Antarctica. At the same time he was compiling a line of soundings as we crossed the Great Australian Bight. The echo sounder had developed a hair-crack in the main casting of the air compressor cylinder, a repair beyond the facilities of the ship, but with careful handling it was still functioning with accurate results.

Early in the morning of the 25th a ship was sighted on the western horizon, changing course and making good time in our direction. Captain Davis immediately ordered all sails to be raised and the engines stopped. In remarkably fast time, all hands assisting, the ship was bowling along under full sail on a northerly tack.

As the ship came near she was identified as the *Cathay*, out from Durban and making for Melbourne under the command of Captain Dazell Niven. Flags were dipped and a message of welcome and con-gratulations received. Slowing down, she steamed past the *Discovery* at a snail's pace. Her cheering passengers crowded the rails and we faced a barrage of cameras. Our ship must have looked a grand sight — one of the last full-rigged ships still in service. An opening appeared on the side of the *Cathay* and from it a large cask was toppled into the sea. She then increased speed and with several loud farewell blasts of her siren, proceeded on her way.

Sails were hurriedly lowered, engines started and the ship made a large circle to retrieve the cask which was hoisted on deck after some difficulties. It was full of fresh vegetables, fruit and frozen chickens. A message of thanks was wirelessed to Captain Niven. Dinner that evening was magnificent, the *pièce de résistance* being a tomato issued to each person.

Sails were made fast and the ship continued on her course under steam. With all work completed, scientists relaxed on deck revelling in the warm sunshine. The crew, however, were kept busy scraping and painting, scrubbing decks and generally brightening the ship's appearance.

Late that evening a pair of tweed trousers belonging to Professor Johnston mysteriously disappeared from his cabin. They had occasioned a fair amount of comment as he had consistently worn them in preference to his issued warm clothing, which he had not worn. At daybreak his trousers were seen flying at half-mast from the mizzen. Events then moved quickly. An irate Professor Johnston demanded the return of his trousers, complaining to Sir Douglas that articles in the pockets would be lost. Peace was partially restored when Sir Douglas was assured that the articles were safe in the laboratory. His trousers, making valiant efforts to fly like a pennant in the light breeze, still remained attached to the mast.

The heavens fell when Captain Davis appeared on the bridge and sighted the offending garment. At no loss for words he castigated all and sundry as the trousers were lowered by one of the crew and restored to Professor Johnston. The skipper's main worry was that a passing ship would assume the garment to be a signal of distress. Sir Douglas refused to inquire into the incident. Professor Johnston forgave the perpetrators and it was soon forgotten.

The South Australian coast came into view on March 30. Later the next day, the ship steamed into Gulf St Vincent, anchoring for the night off the Semaphore. The light breeze we had been enjoying increased in strength during the night causing short choppy waves. The first boarding party, scheduled to leave Semaphore Jetty at 9 A.M. on April 1, changed their plans and put out from the calmer waters of Outer Harbour.

First up the gangway from the official launch was Lady Mawson, her two daughters and Mrs T. Harvey Johnston. They were followed by Senator J. J. Daly, Vice-President of the Federal Executive Council and Chairman of the Antarctic Expedition Committee; Dr W. Henderson, Director of External Affairs; Professor Sir Edgeworth David and Dr C. T. Madigan. Anchors were then weighed and the *Discovery* slowly steamed to her berth at McLaren's Wharf where she made fast at 11.15 A.M.

The welcome was overwhelming. Every vantage point from Port Adelaide to Outer Harbour was thronged to capacity. Three Moth planes from the South Australian Branch of the Australian Aero Club circled the ship as she steamed up the river. One enthusiastic spectator became so excited he overbalanced from the wharf and fell into the harbour. Swimming to the anchor chains of the *Discovery* he was helped on board by several of the crew. Although soaked to the skin he was in no hurry to leave and spent some time looking around the ship before being gently ushered down the gangplank back on to the wharf.

It was unfortunate the *Discovery* could not be opened for inspection to the public. Although it was an historic vessel, space was extremely limited and scientists and crew were still living on board. Later in the afternoon, Lord Stonehaven, the Governor-General, and the State Governor, Sir Alexander Hore-Ruthven, paid us an official visit. They were welcomed by Sir Douglas and Captain Davis and shown over the ship. They were both very interested in her compactness, and particularly in the gear used in carrying out oceanographic stations.

Frank Hurley returned to Sydney. He had exposed a great deal of footage of cinematograph film on all phases of the expedition and was anxious to have it developed as soon as possible. In addition, Hurley had taken at least a thousand still photographs which he had developed in the darkroom during the voyage.

The expedition members were welcomed at a public reception held in the Adelaide Town Hall the following day. Travelling to the reception with Lady David, I mentioned how much I was looking forward to hearing Sir Edgeworth's speech. The occasion was one in which he could give full rein to his magnificent oratory. I had heard him on many occasions and, as a student of his, had listened with delight to his lectures on geology at the University of Sydney. Lady David agreed. She told me that before his more important speeches he would usually have no idea what he was going to say. "But," she said, "I was never worried. You know, if geology had not been his first love I feel sure he would have been a famous actor."

We were surprised at the enthusiastic welcome at the Town Hall. The main hall was crowded to the doors and outside the building a large gathering had assembled. Mounted police had to control the crowds to enable us to reach the entrance.

The Lord Mayor, Mr Lavington Bonython, welcomed Sir Douglas and members of the expedition on behalf of the City Council and citizens of Adelaide, and congratulated us on our safe return.

The Governor-General, Lord Stonehaven, read a personal message from His Majesty the King on the success of the expedition. He said, "I am able to congratulate Sir Douglas not only on the success of the expedition, but also on the typical British manner in which it has been carried out. Its achievements rank with anything that so far has been accomplished."

As predicted, Sir Edgeworth David, in extending his welcome to members of the expedition, delivered a rousing speech. At its conclusion he received a prolonged ovation and it was some time before it subsided. I overheard one listener remark, "Wasn't David great. I heard him in the Sydney Town Hall when he returned from the Shackleton Expedition, but this morning he excelled himself. If we could only get sermons preached on those lines the churches would be filled."

Sir Douglas, in replying, paid a tribute to the work of the staff and the crew. He concluded his speech by saying, "The seas have been explored over forty degrees of east longitude and the coastline of the

Antarctic continent for 500 miles [800 kilometres] has been charted and indicated. We have scientific material which should be of considerable interest."

On April 3, 1930, the *Discovery* set sail from Port Adelaide for Melbourne. Professor Johnston remained in Adelaide as it was his hometown. We arrived off Port Phillip Heads five days later at 7 A.M., a journey which mail steamers did in 26 hours.

Picking up a pilot, the ship nosed into the narrow rip and with engines turning over at full speed, failed to make any immediate headway against the strong current. She then slowly forged ahead and entered Port Phillip Bay. We were escorted by three Royal Australian Air Force planes from Point Cook. They were welcoming in particular our two RAAF airmen, Campbell and Eric Douglas.

Off the Gellibrand Light a Customs launch ranged alongside and several officials came on board. They included Mr Howard who greeted his son Alf who had accompanied the expedition as hydrologist. The *Discovery* finally berthed alongside the new Station Pier, Port Melbourne, at 3.40 P.M.

At the pier, more than 2000 people had gathered to welcome our return. After several days in Melbourne the time came for the scientific staff to return to their homes and various occupations. Thus ended the first voyage of BANZARE. Our thoughts, however, as we left the ship, were on our second adventure to Antarctica later that year.

PART TWO

SECOND
VOYAGE

November 22, 1930 to March 19, 1931

New Captain Appointed

A T THE CONCLUSION of the expedition's first voyage the *Discovery* was refitted at the Williamstown Dockyards, Melbourne, in preparation for her second cruise to the Antarctic. Later, she sailed south to Hobart, berthing at Queen's Wharf where final loading, sorting of equipment and coaling took place.

On November 15, Doc Ingram, Frank Hurley and I left Sydney on the *Zealandia*, arriving at Hobart two days later where we rejoined the *Discovery* and were greeted by some of our old comrades who had arrived previously. Later, we found Sir Douglas and the remainder of the scientific staff in a nearby wharf store going through the usual pre-sailing procedure of opening cases, checking their contents and sorting equipment. When the cases were repacked they were taken on board and stowed in the various holds.

There had been a few alterations in the personnel. Captain Davis was of the opinion that a younger man should be in command of the *Discovery* and Chief Officer MacKenzie succeeded him as Captain with full authority over the ship. I was surprised to learn from Hurley that he would not have accompanied the second voyage if Captain Davis had been in command. He said that during the first voyage he had received a complete lack of cooperation in his efforts to film important sequences for inclusion in the expedition's official film production, which it was hoped would have a worldwide screening. He was expecting, however, unstinted assistance from Captain MacKenzie on this voyage. Later events proved he was over-optimistic.

Commander Moyes was unable to accompany the second voyage and his place as cartographer was filled by Lieutenant C. Oom, R.A.N. Ill health prevented J. W. S. Marr from making the second voyage and his place was taken by A. L. Kennedy, a member of Mawson's 1911–14 expedition; his main work was to be in the field of magnetics. The position of Chief Officer was filled by Max Stanton who had a wide experience in many types of ships. There were several changes among the seamen. Lofty Martin, a tower of strength on the first voyage, was promoted to the position of bosun.

All hands worked diligently for the remaining days before the ship's projected sailing date on November 22. Working gear for running oceanographic stations was overhauled and prepared for immediate use. Coaling was finished and 430 tonnes of bagged coal and briquettes filled the bunkers, several holds and every available space, including many tonnes stacked on deck.

The crew had spent days aloft checking and overhauling the rigging, and the evening before sailing day, everything was snug and shipshape. The ship was lying low in the water with the plimsoll line well submerged. It had not been all work and no play as most of us had been royally entertained by many hospitable citizens of Hobart.

A mysterious package addressed to Stuart Campbell had arrived by post. It contained a brass monkey, so well endowed as to leave no doubt regarding its masculinity. There was no mention of its sender, but an enclosed note stated: "Please take south to ice-covered Antarctica for interesting experiment."

Before our departure, Sir Douglas outlined his plans for the voyage. The *Discovery*, after leaving Hobart, would sail to King George V Land, calling at Macquarie Island where several days would be spent ashore. Further south, contact would be made with the whaling factory ship, *Sir James Clark Ross*, the captain of which had previously agreed to carry 100 tonnes of coal for us to replenish our supply. The planned rendezvous was to be off the Balleny Islands near the entrance to the Ross Sea.

After the transfer of coal, a course would be set for King George V Land where we would visit Mawson's former base, established at Commonwealth Bay in 1911. It was then planned to sail west along the Antarctic coast for further investigations of Wilkes Land, Queen Mary Land and Mac Robertson Land. On this course we would be passing many kilometres of unexplored coast. It was an exciting programme, but one that depended on less severe pack-ice conditions than we had experienced on our first voyage.

On November 22, crowds began to assemble on the Queen's Wharf to bid us farewell. Punctually at 2.30 P.M., five bells were struck, ropes were cast off and the *Discovery* began to move away from the wharf. Suddenly, there was a disturbance amongst the crowd on the wharf and a man, dressed only in his underwear, pushed his way through and leaped on board. He was a crew member who had been reported missing several hours before. When going on shore leave the day before sailing, he had approached Captain MacKenzie and requested his back pay. It was reluctantly given to him with a warning that if he got into the wrong hands it could be stolen from him. This had happened and he arrived on board without his money and clothing.

As the *Discovery* backed away from the wharf we were farewelled by hundreds of fluttering handkerchiefs and loud and prolonged cheering. It was a heartening farewell, further enhanced by a large escort of small craft which followed the ship down the Derwent River.

Darkness had set in as we rounded Tasman Head and headed towards Macquarie Island, 850 miles to the south.

A strong wind was blowing from the south-west with fairly rough seas into which the heavily laden ship plunged and rolled. Some of the scientists began to feel the ship's movements and hurriedly retired to their bunks.

At midday next day we had logged only 65 miles, averaging three knots. Our slow progress was due to the thick marine growth covering the hull. It was hoped that most of this would fall off as we entered cold water or be scraped off by contact with pack-ice. In the meantime our progress was painfully slow.

At 2.30 P.M. Sir Douglas decided to work an oceanographic station. Depth of the sea floor was 1550 metres, proving we were still over the Tasmanian Continental Shelf. We left it behind early the next morning; the depth increasing to 2790 metres.

Conditions were by no means ideal for working a station. The stationary ship wallowed badly in the seas, creating difficulties in hauling and lowering plankton nets and reversible water sampling bottles. The operator on the outboard platform had an unenviable task as he removed catches from the plankton nets, reset the closing mechanism and released the messenger to close the net at determined depths. With each roll of the ship, waves lifted the platform on its hinges threatening to jam it against the bulwarks, at the same time soaking the operator to his waist. It was impossible to prevent the hauling wire and net from striking the ship's bottom. Several catches were found to contain barnacles and weed scraped from the hull. Oblique nettings, dredging and trawling could not be carried out because the winch house and aft deck were stacked with coal.

Falla began his daily observations of bird species. Cape hens and prions had been following the ship since leaving the Tasmanian coast. A solitary grey-headed mollymawk and a sooty albatross were sighted during the day and it was thought the same two birds followed the ship until near Macquarie Island.

The ship's floundering movement, as she headed into an increasingly heavy swell from the south-west, was not helping those who had not yet gained their sea legs. I was sharing a cabin (the hospital) with Doc Ingram. It was situated well forward near the crew's quarters and galley from which we received various odours as meals were prepared. These were not greatly appreciated by Doc who had finally succumbed to his usual bout of seasickness. We had the greatest admiration for the cook's vocabulary; rich in curses even in general conversation, he excelled himself when an extra roll of the ship scattered his pots and pans in all directions.

The ship was still laboriously steaming south the next morning at a maximum speed of three knots. A south-easterly wind freshened later, and in the afternoon it had reached a velocity of 40 to 50 kilometres an hour. The sky was overcast with occasional showers of rain.

Plankton catches from the previous day's station were concentrated and preserved by Professor Johnston. For the moment there was little to do except read or listen to the gramophone. Following a suggestion by Eric Douglas, some members, including myself, had their hair shorn to the scalp. We were told this would induce a much better and more luxurious growth. The immediate result was an unpleasant array of shiny pates and three days' growth of beards.

Later in the evening, Sir Douglas issued staff members with their Antarctic clothing. Measurements of new members had been forwarded to the manufacturer, but in some cases errors had crept in. "Grandpa" Oom later walked into the wardroom wearing his woollen pyjamas with sleeves hanging to his knees and trouser legs trailing well behind. After the merriment had subsided we learned that all his clothing was too big. Oom's height was about 162 centimetres and it seemed that the manufacturer had assumed the measurements were incorrect and had made all his clothing to fit a man over 180 centimetres in height. Although extensive alterations were attempted, Grandpa would never have won the title of the best dressed man of the year.

The following morning a strong wind persisted from the south-east with a disturbed sea. The ship's course was altered slightly to the west and for the first time since leaving Hobart, fore and aft sails were broken out and set. Her speed increased to six knots.

Doc Ingram was the only member still suffering from seasickness. For the past few days he had been sleeping and recuperating in the chart room away from the smells of cooking and below-decks fug.

At 8 A.M., readings from the echo sounder showed a sudden rise in the depth of the sea floor from 1974 to 1630 metres. Soundings then remained virtually the same until at midnight the depth again dropped to 2520 metres. We were sailing over the Mill Rise, a plateau of the sea floor comparable in extent to that of Tasmania. It was originally located by soundings from the *Aurora* during Mawson's 1911–14 expedition.

Early in the morning, a slight detour off course was made to pass close to the supposed position of the Royal Company Islets. These were reported and charted by the captain of a sealing vessel early in the last century. Many efforts have been made to locate them and it is now generally thought they do not exist. We saw no signs of the islets, but several large masses of floating kelp were sighted.

A start was made in the afternoon to remove coal from the aft deck and winch house. Sir Douglas, Simmers, Campbell and I carried bagged coal to the bunkers until they were filled. It was essential to clear this area as soon as possible to permit use of the winch and carry out oblique nettings and dredgings. Coal consumption with loose coal was 6.5 tonnes a day whereas with briquettes it was only five tonnes.

At midday, our distance run was 93 miles and our position was 46°33'S, 146°50'E. The southerly breeze had caused a drop in temperature to 7°C on deck and 3°C at the masthead. The barometer was rising.

The wind had eased to a slight breeze the next morning. The sea was calm with a slight swell running in from the south-west. We had hardly seen the sun since leaving Hobart and the sky was still heavily overcast. Sails were taken in at 2 P.M. and the engines stopped for the working of another plankton station. It was successfully completed in three hours. While the ship was drifting, an attempt was made by crew members to scrape some of the marine growth from the ship's side. Although a good deal was removed with long-handled scrapers it made no difference to the ship's progress.

While the station was in progress, the light breeze swung to the north-east and began to strengthen. It was from an unusual quarter as prevailing westerly winds are usually expected in the Roaring Forties. All sails were hoisted with the assistance of the scientific staff and with a following wind, which later increased to gale force, the ship surged ahead at six knots.

Captain MacKenzie entered the wardroom late in the evening and announced it was his birthday. Several bottles of Yalumba port mysteriously appeared and toasts were drunk to his good health and a good voyage for his first command.

Gale-force winds continued throughout the night and all next day. There was no rest from the ship's convulsive movements as she rolled, plunged and wallowed in the terrific seas which had now developed. Waves swept over the bow and gunwales, flooding the decks. Under difficulties with the rolling of the ship, I assisted Professor Johnston in concentrating and preserving the plankton catches of the previous day's station. The afternoon was occupied in continuing to shift coal from the deck and winch house to the bunkers. The bagged coal had been used up and we were now transferring the more easily handled briquettes.

During the night a change in the wind worked up a turbulent sea and the ship's buckjumping efforts were so severe that sleep was impossible. Several scientists complained of bruised parts of their anatomy from being hurled out of their bunks. The next day was depressing with heavy black clouds overhead, continual drizzling rain and fog. Seas moderated during the day, but water kept coming on board and the decks were continually awash. Briquettes were carried to the bunkers, while Hurley, Eric Douglas and I stacked five tonnes in the stoke hold between the boilers.

The ship was making good progress and, with no halt for working a station, we had logged 135 miles in our 24-hour distance run. Macquarie Island was about two days away.

During the night the strong north-easterly wind dropped completely and sails were taken in and furled. At about 3 A.M. a thick mist developed, restricting visibility. It cleared at midday and seas began to moderate, but they were still rough and confused.

All hands assisted in moving the last of the coal from the aft deck and winch house the next morning. A chain of scientists was formed and ten tonnes of briquettes were thrown from one to the other, finally filling the bunkers; the remainder were stacked in the stoke hold. The winch house, containing the large trawling winch, was naturally in a filthy state. After being swept out, Hurley got to work with the fire hose to wash down the walls and floor. Professor Johnston happened to be bending down cleaning out one of the scuppers and Hurley, unable to resist the temptation, turned the hose with great effect on his backside. With a loud yelp of distress Professor Johnston turned and, with a complete loss of words to express his displeasure, went below to change. The incident was thoroughly enjoyed by all, especially as he was wearing the same discoloured tweed trousers he had worn on the first voyage.

At 2 P.M. Sir Douglas suggested working an oceanographic station. A heavy sea was still running and Professor Johnston and Falla queried whether the conditions were suitable. Several of us accompanied Sir Douglas on deck where he was to make a decision. No sooner had we gained the deck than a wave curled over the gunwale, thoroughly soaking him. Unfortunately, Falla laughed and the decision was no longer in doubt, the station was on. The depth of the sea floor was recorded as 3850 metres.

A cold, cutting wind was blowing with continual drizzling rain. Doc Ingram had recovered from his sea sickness and assisted Johnston and myself in working the vertical plankton nets. Because of the rough sea the outboard platform could not be used and all operations were carried out, with more difficulty, from the deck. Catches obtained from 1000 metres to the surface were rich in plankton.

Sir Douglas and Kennedy experienced trouble lowering reversible water bottles from the forecastle. The first bottle was lowered to 3800 metres from where water samples and temperature were secured. On a later haul the wire kinked preventing the messenger from reaching and reversing the bottle. About 2000 metres of wire had to be wound in, the wire straightened and the bottle lowered again. The large winch was still

The expedition prepares to leave Queen's Wharf, Hobart, on its second voyage.
(Photo: S. Campbell.)

not in use, so oblique nets and the trawl could not be towed. The station was not completed until about 6 P.M.

At 8 P.M., readings from the echo sounder showed a remarkable rise of the sea floor from 3850 to 1720 metres in a distance of about 30 miles. Its position was 52°14'S, 152°48'E. Both Campbell and Oom were at the machine when the shallow reading was recorded. Ninety minutes later, over a distance of about eight miles, the depth had returned to 3910 metres. Time did not permit further investigations of this interesting area. By returning over our course, continual soundings would have proved or disproved the single low reading. Had it been correct we would have discovered an extraordinary submarine plateau rising to heights of up to 2000 metres.

On Saturday night we gathered in the wardroom to drink our usual toast to our sweethearts and wives. On this occasion Sir Douglas produced, besides Yalumba port, several bottles of Cascade beer. During the toasting, Sparks came below with a wireless message he had just received from my fiancée in Sydney. A special toast was drunk to her with cheers.

I was awakened early next morning by the sound of waves crashing on the deck and the ship's erratic evolutions which it saved for bad weather. During the night the wind had chopped to the south-west and gradually increased in violence through the day. All sails were set and we were sailing on course at a speed of seven knots.

The days were now getting longer with daylight from 3.30 A.M. to 9.30 P.M. Towards evening the first icebergs were sighted on the port bow. A group of six included a large weather-worn berg about 24 metres high, over which the big seas were dashing in clouds of spray. The remainder of the bergs were almost completely awash and just visible.

At midday our distance run was 148 miles. We had logged 964 miles since leaving Hobart and expected to sight Macquarie Island about noon next day. Owing to the continual bad weather and incessant mists there had been an absence of birds following the ship. All hands by this time had gained their sea legs and even Doc Ingram, who usually felt off colour when black clouds appeared in the distance, was his old self again, completely ignoring the ship's crazy antics.

Westerly gale-force winds persisted throughout the night making sleep impossible. On the morning of December 1, big seas were running and foggy conditions, to some extent, had lessened visibility. Navigation during the hours of darkness was hazardous because of the icebergs.

Macquarie Island was sighted through a slight mist shortly after midday. The ship pitched and wallowed as we slowly approached from the west with a strong following wind. We skirted the dangerous Lord Nelson Reef and, heading around the northern end of the island, arrived off Hasselborough Bay. At this point, partly protected from the westerly winds, a large dredge with a rectangular heavy iron frame was lowered over the stern until it rested on the sea floor at about 100 metres. It was then dragged at a slow speed for 30 minutes. The catch contained a quantity of fine-grained grey sand, a profusion of bivalve shells, mainly the one species, together with other organisms including several large crabs and two fish. A second dredging in slightly shallower water consisted largely of small rocks of island origin, almost to the exclusion of any marine life.

At the conclusion of the dredgings the ship, now escorted by an abundance of birds, made her way into the nearby Buckle Bay and, moving close inshore, dropped anchors in 22 metres at 5.30 P.M. Scientists spent the evening preparing equipment and camping gear ready to go ashore first thing in the morning.

Island of Penguins

MACQUARIE ISLAND is an isolated, inhospitable subantarctic island lying about midway between Tasmania and the Antarctic continent. In shape it is long and narrow tending in a north–south direction. Its length is 33 kilometres with a varying width of up to five kilometres. Its surface is an elevated undulating plateau with steep cliffs descending to the sea or to occasional low-lying coastal flats or beaches. Usually shrouded in mist, the island bears the brunt of almost continual westerly winds frequently blowing at gale force. The sun is rarely seen and it is not unknown for rain to fall every day in the year. A number of mountain peaks of black volcanic rock rise to heights of 425 metres from the plateau. Dangerous reefs run out from both ends of the island, terminating at the Judge and Clerk Rocks, eight miles to the north, and the Bishop and Clerk Rocks, 19 miles to the south.

Macquarie Island was discovered in 1810 by Captain Frederick Hassellborough. About that time, captains of many sealing vessels had moved eastward towards New Zealand and southward towards the Antarctic continent, sailing over uncharted waters in the hope of finding new islands. Great competition existed among the sealers and new discoveries were kept secret until the seal populations were exploited.

On discovering Macquarie Island, Captain Hassellborough landed a party of six men with provisions and a ship's boat and instructions to start sealing operations. He then sailed to Sydney to notify the owners of his discovery. He restocked with provisions and took on board an additional quantity of salt to cure the fur seal pelts. To explain his unscheduled return to port with six of his crew and a missing ship's boat, he circulated a story of a storm during which the men and boat were lost.

Returning to Macquarie Island, the slaughter of fur seals continued without interruption until the end of the season, reaping a rich harvest. At that time fur seals were sought after and killed for their pelts which had a high commercial value. The number of pelts reaching the market annually from all sealers was estimated to be 112,000. This rate continued for many years until the fur seals became virtually extinct. As the fur seal population on Macquarie Island declined, the sealers' attention was turned to the slaughter of sea elephants and later, king and royal penguins, for their oils.

More than a century ago rabbits were introduced on the island and they flourished to such an extent that, following a survey in 1972, their numbers were estimated to be 50,000. A few years later the census was 150,000. They ravaged the island's vegetation and at the same time provided a source of food for domestic cats which were perhaps accidentally liberated on shore and became feral.

About that time Macquarie Island came under the jurisdiction of the National Parks and Wildlife Service of Tasmania. It was proclaimed a sanctuary and immediate steps were initiated to protect the native flora and fauna from the introduced predators. Cats had already wiped out the only two species of land birds — the Macquarie Island rail and a species of parakeet.

The introduction of the rabbit flea had an immediate effect. The disease they carry, myxomatosis, reduced the rabbit population by 95 per cent. Feral cats were hunted, with a marked decrease in their numbers, but both animals will never be completely eradicated. However, unlike the fur seals, the sea elephant and penguin populations have now practically regained their original numbers.

Back on the *Discovery* in Buckle Bay, scientists had gathered on deck at 8 A.M. with their equipment and camping gear, anxious and ready for their two days' stay on shore. It was a dismal morning. A strong westerly offshore wind was causing the ship to roll, putting a strain on her anchor chains. A heavy mist with rain and snow squalls added to the gloom.

The motor boat and dinghy were lowered over the ship's side and after clambering on board and stowing the gear we headed for the beach with Sir Douglas at the tiller. The boat was anchored close inshore and sheltered from the wind. It took three dinghy journeys through a quiet surf to land the party on the beach. We threaded our way carefully through closely packed sea elephants and royal and rockhopper penguins. The broken-down sealers' huts offered no protection from the elements, so we erected our tents near the ruins of old boiling-down buildings. From inscriptions on the few remaining walls, we gathered that sealing operations ceased in 1918, two years *after* the island had been declared a sanctuary.

The party now separated and set out in various directions, more or less according to a plan previously arranged by Sir Douglas. Ingram and I climbed a steeply sloping cliff to reach the plateau where we met the full force of the cold westerly wind. Rain was still falling with occasional snow squalls. The plateau surface was mostly a morass. Time and time again we sank almost to our knees in the soft boggy ground and progress was slow and fatiguing.

We climbed Mt Elder, 370 metres high, and were rewarded with a view, somewhat restricted by rain and fog, of the southern part of the island. Close by was a series of freshwater lakes of varying sizes. After descending the mountain we visited one of the lakes and collected samples of organisms.

We then decided to make for the royal penguin rookery at Nuggets Beach and to keep a look out for nesting birds on the way. Strangely enough there were no petrels to be seen; their burrows appeared to be unoccupied. Many were badly damaged by the Stewart Island woodhens, also known as rails or wekas. This species is not native to the island but was introduced by sealers from Stewart Island, south of New Zealand, in 1879. They now occur in great numbers on all parts of the island and have definitely been a factor in reducing the numbers of burrowing petrels. Several of these introduced birds were observed excavating burrows in the soft soil on the hillside while others were seen entering large burrows. Nesting of the woodhens was well advanced and there was an abundance of chicks. Seven adult birds were caught for the collection.

Descending from the plateau, Doc Ingram and I arrived early in the afternoon at the Nuggets royal penguin rookery where we joined up with Hurley, Falla, Campbell and Eric Douglas. Hurley had already exposed a few hundred metres of cine-film and was still busily engaged in taking short sequences of the penguins' behaviour in their nesting groups.

The Nuggets rookery was a spectacular sight, covering about five hectares and containing about a quarter of a million birds. The beach was closely packed with hundreds of birds continually shooting in on high breakers and, on gaining their feet, waddling ashore fighting against the backwash. Just as many walked down the beach, dived into the waves and quickly swam out to sea. In the midst of the penguins, part of the bow of a small sealing vessel, the *Gratitude*, wrecked in 1898, was still projecting upright from the sand.

Extensive nesting areas, about a kilometre inland, covered slightly sloping ground in an amphitheatre among the hills. Access to the nests was largely by a well-worn track alongside a shallow creek bed, but many birds took devious routes on their uphill journey. Falla and I spent some time watching the closely packed procession of penguins as they unceasingly marched along the track; some going to the beach, others returning. Although there seemed to be a tendency to keep to the left, there was a marked amount of jostling to maintain position and direction. Returning birds were immaculate, their white front feathers beautifully clean while those off to the beach were generally bespattered with mud.

Joining the procession we moved uphill to a smaller rookery which was closely packed with sitting birds. We estimated seven nests in a square metre; each nest consisting of a ring of small stones. In the near distance five large nesting groups, almost merging, were seen on sloping ground about 120 metres above sea level. We estimated the total number of royal penguins in the entire rookery to be about 400,000. A fairly accurate calculation made more recently was that rookeries of the royals covered six and a half hectares on various parts of Macquarie Island and that the number of birds exceeded a million.

The rookery we were visiting was about 60 metres above sea level. It contained nests, on which both parents took it in turns to sit on a single egg, or protect the newly hatched chick. The parent not on duty leaves for the beach and swims offshore to find food for the chick. When the parent returns, at least 10 or 12 hours later, it is faced with a traumatic ordeal in reaching its nest. Sitting birds not only spend most of their time continually quarrelling with their neighbours, but any passing bird pushing its way through the throng infuriates them and they savagely peck at the passerby in a mad frenzy. The noise of their squawking was deafening.

We watched a penguin returning from the beach and its endeavours to reach its nest were very well described by Falla, whose official report said, in part, ". . . he began to make his way warily through the crowd, with frequent stops to allay any suspicion that he might be going anywhere, for a bird with an obvious mission seems to arouse furious resentment among the sitting birds. He did not get far undetected, and was soon being pecked on all sides and, abandoning his former caution, 'made a bolt for it'. The din aroused other sleepy birds ahead, and soon his arrival was anticipated all along the line. In the last 20 yards [18 metres] the buffetings were so severe that the victim was not only staggering, but at times almost spinning along. At last he reached his waiting mate, stopped breathless in front of her, and with flippers held back and neck forward, announced his arrival with an expressive gasp. The female showed no outward concern as he recovered his breath, and on his shuffling closer, till the two birds' toes were touching, transferred the newly hatched chick to his feet and moved away. She was still standing by when we left 10 minutes later. In the meantime, the chick had been induced to raise its head and take regurgitated food from the throat of the male."

Time had passed more quickly than we thought, absorbed in our bird observations. We noticed the others had already left, so Falla and I set out to return to the camp, being the last to arrive there at 7.30 P.M. We ate in the partial shelter of the broken-down digester house. Rain was falling, having rarely ceased during the day.

All hands retired early and I was having a warm, comfortable night until awakened at 4 A.M. by Sir Douglas with his cries of "rise and shine". Scrambling out of my sleeping bag I discovered I had been resting against a sea elephant that had moved alongside me through the night and had settled down. Only the tent fabric separated us.

As we gathered together in a rather disconsolate group, Sir Douglas informed us that a sudden strong gust of wind had overturned the tent that he shared with Kennedy. It was not worthwhile re-erecting it, so they decided to have company and an early breakfast; hence his early call.

It was another miserable day. A cutting cold wind was blowing with light drizzling rain. After a hot breakfast we were in a more cheerful mood and ready to start our day's activities. A party of six, including myself, left with Sir Douglas to visit the area around Hassellborough Bay. On the way we looked at the site of a base established by Mawson's 1911–14 expedition. A party of five scientists had been left there in December 1911, with the intention that they would stay there for a year. However, due to unforeseen events they were not relieved until December 1913.

Continuing on, we skirted the southern shore of Hassellborough Bay and came to a low-lying expanse known as the Feather Bed Terrace. There was a luxurious vegetation, including Maori Cabbage, from which Professor Johnston collected a rich variety of insects. The grey ducks that inhabit the island had been sighted only on rare occasions and never more than a pair. A flock of 12 birds rose from the Feather Bed Terrace on our approach and I was fortunate enough to shoot one as they flew overhead. No nests were found. Their numbers were being kept down by the introduced feral cats.

At Aerial Cove, Hurley, Falla and I came across a nesting colony of the Macquarie Island cormorant occupying a low level rocky area. It contained about 200 nests, each with three eggs on the point of hatching. Sitting birds were generally females with attendant males perched on the nest rims. The cormorants showed little concern as we moved among the nests and Hurley filmed the sitting birds. During our visit of about an hour, the birds remained quiet with no birds arriving or leaving the colony. The common European starling was a late addition to the bird fauna of Macquarie Island. It was not plentiful, and only on a few occasions was the species observed, usually flying in pairs.

On our way back to Buckle Bay for lunch we located a spacious cave in which it is recorded that 19 men and one woman, survivors from a ship wrecked on the coast, lived for two years. They existed on seal and penguin flesh and Maori cabbage. On the day of their rescue the woman died from malnutrition and exposure. She was buried in an unmarked grave shortly before the rescuing ship's boat reached the beach.

After lunch some of the party visited North Head with instructions to return in time to be transported to the *Discovery* at 4 P.M. Punctually, members, their gear and collections were conveyed through the surf in the dinghy to the motor boat anchored outside the line of breakers. Nearing the ship we met the full force of the strong westerly wind which had not ceased blowing since our arrival at the island. Ranging alongside, trouble was experienced in climbing on board, but by 6 P.M. we were all safely on deck, soaked to the skin.

All hands were called early the next morning to assist in weighing the anchors. The ship steamed out of the bay and a course was set along the coast to reach Lusitania Bay at the southern end of the island. A thick mist enveloped the island and only occasional glimpses of land could be seen although it was less than half a mile away.

At 9.30 A.M., the ship dropped anchors in Lusitania Bay. The westerly wind had strengthened and a big sea was running in the bay. It was obvious that an attempted landing would be dangerous, but all hands volunteered to go ashore. The motor boat and dinghy were lowered over the ship's side and, clambering on board with our gear, we set off in a heavy rain squall and fog for the beach.

On our way the boat had to negotiate thick masses of writhing kelp extending parallel to the beach a short distance offshore. Big seas rolling in threatened to throw the boat on to submerged rocks or into the breaking surf. Realising a landing was impracticable, we headed back through the kelp and went around the beach until we came to partly protected, quieter waters. We moved in again over the kelp and anchored the boat. The party landed through a fairly quiet surf in the dinghy. Eric Douglas and Kennedy volunteered to stay on the motor boat and look after it in case the anchor dragged. An unenviable vigil which would last all day.

Our landing place was about a kilometre from a king penguin rookery. On the way, Falla, Doc Ingram and I visited a royal penguin rookery of several thousand birds which occupied a large flat area. Most of it was fairly well drained although many nests occupied marshy areas with a good deal of permanent water. Conditions were much the same as at the Nuggets rookery. The majority of birds were sitting on eggs, although many newly hatched chicks were in evidence. Royal penguins are native to the island and occur in great numbers.

Moving on, we arrived at the king penguin rookery. King penguins are about 90 centimetres in height. They have a patch of golden yellow on either side of the head and a noticeably long beak. The rookery covers a large area which is completely devoid of vegetation, the soil having been washed away over the years, leaving the ground covered with stones of varying sizes. The king penguins have difficulty in walking over these and generally stumble along as if inebriated. Unlike other penguin species on the island, they invariably walk in single file and long lines of birds were seen coming and going to and from the rookery. Groups of adult birds were closely packed together sitting on their nests hatching eggs. Crowding among them were many young, some newly hatched, others covered in down and in varying stages of moulting.

Returning early to where we had landed, Doc and I shot and skinned two immature sea elephants. These creatures were in considerable numbers and the roaring of bulls never ceased. Great care had to be exercised to avoid their wallows when walking above the beach line. Strangely enough, heavy sea elephants, after wallowing for hours, have no trouble in reaching solid ground.

Rabbits were particularly numerous at Lusitania Bay. Mostly they scampered away on our approach, but some remained motionless, crouching with ears back. It was possible to stroke their backs while they remained perfectly still, as if paralysed.

It was late in the afternoon when members of the party returned to the landing spot. Eric Douglas and Kennedy were pleased to see us, having spent a trying day on the motor boat which had showed no signs of dragging its anchor after all. Professor Johnston arrived with an interesting and comprehensive collection of marine life from the rocky shore and beach. Sir Douglas had two haversacks filled with rock specimens. Frank Hurley had a disappointing day as rain and mist had restricted his photographic activities to a minimum. During our three days on the island Falla recorded 28 species of birds including two non-marine forms — a grey duck and the common starling. After an exciting run to the *Discovery* we were all safely on board at 7 P.M.

Before retiring, Sir Douglas informed the staff that the ship would be leaving Lusitania Bay at 3 A.M. the next day. All hands would be needed to assist in weighing the anchors and to carry out a dredging immediately the ship left the bay.

The *Discovery* steamed out of Lusitania Bay at 3 A.M., and after dredgings were made off the Macquarie Island coast, a course was set for the Antarctic coast. Five hours later the ship was slowed down and a dredge was lowered over the stern, reaching the bottom in 70 metres. After a 15 minute tow it was winched in and yielded a fine haul of bivalve species, an interesting lamp shell and several small but rather battered fish.

A course was set to pass to the east of the Bishop and Clerk Rocks which lie at the southern end of a shallow submarine ridge extending 19 miles from Macquarie Island. The strong westerly wind had eased slightly, but a thick fog made navigation of the ship hazardous in these waters. Fragments of ice were passed and two large weathered bergs, looming out of the fog, caused the ship to alter course.

Eric Douglas with sea elephants on Macquarie Island.
(By courtesy of the Mawson Institute. Photo: S. Campbell.)

ANTARCTIC DAYS WITH MAWSON

At midday we were about a mile and a half off the Bishop and Clerk Rocks. As we moved closer, the lifting fog revealed the rocks, which consist of three islets: two are about six metres above sea level and the other rises to about 30 metres. A gentoo and a royal penguin rookery were seen on its lower slopes.

The echo sounder was recording depths from 33 to 73 metres and big seas rolling into the shallow waters raised tremendous waves. The weather showed no signs of improvement and the barometer was falling. South-west of the Bishop and Clerk Rocks a large grounded iceberg was sighted. Its estimated height was 30 metres and its length about five kilometres.

The islets were soon lost to sight in the fog as the ship headed south. She rolled alarmingly in big seas running in from the north-west. Waves continually crashed over the starboard rails, sweeping the decks with surging water. We were now in waters with recorded depths of more than 3600 metres. A fore and aft sail was raised on the mizzen in an attempt to steady the ship but it made no difference.

During the night the wind veered to the south-west and gradually increased in violence. The next morning showed no change and it promised to be a wild day with drizzling rain and an icy wind. The barometer was still dropping and a full gale was expected. While the *Discovery* was in Melbourne, dodgers had been fitted over the navigation bridge rails. This innovation, refused by Captain Davis on the first voyage, offered some protection from the elements to the helmsman and officer on watch.

Soundings recorded a rise in the sea floor from 3765 to 1484 metres. Shallow depths then continued for four hours (about 20 miles) when the sea floor gradually dropped again to around 3600 metres. This shallow area in latitude 56° was named the Hjort Rise by Sir Douglas in memory of a noted Norwegian oceanographer.

An island is shown approximately in the position of the Hjort Rise on several old charts. Since it was supposedly discovered and named Emerald Island early in the last century, all endeavours to locate it have been unsuccessful. It is now generally accepted that the island does not exist.

However, our discovery of comparatively shallow waters in the vicinity was supporting evidence that the island could be present and its charted position incorrect. Sir Douglas was disappointed that time and the extreme weather conditions prevented a search being made which may have located it. At midday we had logged 165 miles for our distance run and had reached 56°48′S, 159°37′E. We were now in the degrees of latitude aptly known as the Shrieking Fifties.

It was Saturday night again and while toasting our sweethearts and wives, Sir Douglas produced several extra bottles to celebrate a double birthday — Doc Ingram and Eric Douglas.

Throughout the night the weather continued to deteriorate and early next morning the wind had increased to gale force. Sails had been taken in and furled the previous day and the ship was now labouring her way south through colossal seas at half speed. We had reached the latitudes where daylight continued for 24 hours each day.

Many icebergs of varying sizes and shapes were sighted. Smaller ones in the turbulent waters were difficult to see against the background of white-crested waves, lashed by the wind into a seething mass of foam. Waves swept over the ship's bow and forecastle head, throwing spray onto the bridge while on her weather side seas crashed over the gunwale, waist high on the decks. Work in the laboratory was impossible and scientists spent the day below decks trying to read or write between convulsive movements of the ship. The gale raged through the day with no signs of breaking, although in the late afternoon the sun managed to periodically break through the slightly clearing black clouds. It was the first sunshine we had seen for several weeks.

Frank Hurley took advantage of the occasional bursts of sunshine and, braving the elements, climbed the foremast. He took cinemato-graph shots of the mountainous seas as they rolled by and the ship's struggling efforts to combat them as she rose and fell on her southerly course. Hurley was overjoyed with the spectacular scenes he had recorded. They were featured in the official film of the expedition.

Everyone below decks was by this time heartily fed up with the inaction caused by the gale and heavy seas. There was no respite from wind shrieking through the rigging, groaning of the ship's timbers and the thud of waves crashing on the deck.

We had been instructed that under no circumstances were we to use the door on the weather side of the ship when entering or leaving below. Our irrepressible Chief Officer, Max Stanton, with a game of Russian roulette in mind, decided to come below through the forbidden door. Waiting his chance he dashed for the door in between waves, fumbled with the catch and opened it in time to receive the full force of a wall of water as it crashed over the gunwale. It hurled him headlong down the companionway and at the same time flooded the wardroom. Soaked to the skin he slowly regained his feet to face a group of glaring and jeering scientists. Chuckling to himself he walked away to change his clothes, saying, "I'll do better next time."

At midday, our distance for the 24-hour run was 87 miles. Our course was altered later in the afternoon, to ease the tossing and rolling of the ship, and we ran before the gale until midnight when the ship was brought back on to our southerly course.

On December 8, conditions had moderated, although big seas

were still running and there was no lessening in the ship's erratic movements. It was possible for work to continue on the collections from Macquarie Island. Campbell and I flensed and preserved the two young sea elephant skins with occasional interruptions by seas rolling on board. Falla and I spent the rest of the day skinning birds, including a king penguin.

Our distance run was 101 miles and our position was 59°16'S, 160°57'E. We would soon be leaving the Shrieking Fifties and entering the Silent Sixties, which, on many occasions, belied its name. We were now heading south down the 160th meridian to locate the *Sir James Clark Ross* which carried our coal supply, but so far wireless communication with her had been unsuccessful.

Late in the evening there was a noticeable moderation in the weather conditions. A rising barometer indicated the worst of the gale had passed.

The wind had dropped the next morning to a light breeze from the south-west; the sky was clear and we were enjoying the benefit of continual sunshine. Seas, although reasonably calm, were still confused. The ship was making good progress with 108 miles logged at midday. Her movements were now reduced to a slight, steady roll which was much appreciated by all hands. We passed many icebergs of fantastic shapes and form. The deck temperature — below freezing point — was bracing and exhilarating. At 2 P.M. the ship was stopped and a full plankton station was run in 2800 metres, taking three hours.

During the early hours of the 10th, the ship entered an area of broken pack-ice and I was awakened by the noise of ice grinding along the vessel's side. The sea was a flat calm except for a gentle swell which caused picturesque undulations of the ice. The southerly extent of the ice field could not be determined because a thick fog developed after breakfast, reducing visibility. Several hours later, the ship emerged into open deep-blue water with an oily flat surface.

Later in the afternoon, the wind swung from the south-west to the south-east and, slightly freshening, began to lift the fog. Birds were again gathering around the ship after a total absence during the prolonged gale. A few subantarctic species were still with us, but the majority were those restricted to the Antarctic with Antarctic and snow petrels dominating. Whales were also increasing in numbers.

Wireless contact was made with the *Sir James Clark Ross* towards evening. Her position was given as well east of the Balleny Islands, practically north of the Ross Sea. We still had an estimated 483 miles, or five days' steaming, to reach her position. The south-easterly wind coming in from the Antarctic continent brought with it a drastic lowering of temperatures. It was minus 4°C on deck and minus 2°C in the wardroom. Everyone began seeking warmer clothing.

Clear weather continued the next day. We were navigating along the edge of compact pack-ice trending north-west and passing through areas of loose ice. Contact with the ice had removed a good deal of the marine growth from the ship's hull, resulting in a slight increase in her speed. Our daily distance run logged at midday was 116 miles.

At 4.30 P.M. the echo sounder recorded a sharp rise of the sea floor from 2582 to 1411 metres. Two hours later it had dropped again, this time to 2760 metres. Falla and I spent the day skinning and filling out birds, leaving only a few to be dealt with.

Within the limits of the pack-ice, many bird species were observed feeding in open lanes or pools opened up by ice movements. These included Antarctic, snow, silver-grey petrels and cape pigeons. Obtaining food was no problem as the water abounds in krill, their staple diet. They had plenty of leisure time which they spent sitting and resting in groups on floes and bergs. At the onslaught of a blizzard they would immediately make for their nesting areas, flying low and gaining distance against the wind by long tacks.

We continued on a direct course towards the *Sir James Clark Ross* for the next two days while maintaining constant wireless communication. Good progress was made through belts of loose floe-ice and occasional open water, logging 239 miles for the 48 hours. Icebergs were in considerable numbers and many whales were observed. The weather was perfect; the sea was a flat calm as ice to the north effectively blocked any swell. Our course was altered on the 13th to the north-east to reach more open water, but after several hours steaming the ship was again headed south on a direct course to the *Sir James Clark Ross*.

Perfect weather continued throughout the next day. The sea was as flat as a millpond. About 40 or more icebergs, ranging in size to a kilometre in length and over 30 metres in height, were in view at the one time. They provided a magnificent sight; immense floating masses of crystalline ice glistening in the sunshine and showing up in strong contrast to the deep blue of the surrounding waters.

We steamed past many bergs of unsurpassed beauty. Weathering had sculptured many of them into fantastic shapes and form. One end of a remarkable berg opened into a magnificent arch about 35 metres high; three deep caverns, their interiors bathed in blue and purple colours, ranged alongside it.

All hands lined the rails, or had climbed into the rigging, to photograph the many picturesque bergs. Conditions were ideal for photography. Hurley was in a state of rapture over what he termed "sensational shots" which he had taken with his various cameras.

Later in the day a horrible smell pervaded the ship. It appeared to be coming with a light breeze from the south. Shortly afterwards, a black object was sighted a good distance ahead, surrounded by birds.

Closer investigation proved it to be a dead blue whale, about 24 metres in length and floating belly upwards in the water. It had obviously been dead for some time and its body was blown up like a balloon. Scavenger birds had penetrated into the stomach and were making a loathsome meal, fighting and squabbling for good positions. The whale had been shot by a whale chaser, but why it had not been towed to the factory ship brought forward many theories. The stench was overpowering. For hours afterwards it clung around the ship, even below decks and on our clothes.

The *Sir James Clark Ross* was sighted on the 15th, and after buffeting our way through fairly thick pack-ice, we arrived off the vessel at 8 A.M. Owing to the scarcity of whales around the Balleny Islands the ship had been moved east to near the 180th meridian. This was well east of the proposed, although tentative, rendezvous, costing the expedition a loss of 10 days and a gain of only 40 tonnes of coal.

Captain MacKenzie was hailed through a megaphone from the factory ship's bridge to first of all cockbill our yards (swinging them to lie up and down the masts) and then move in alongside their port bow. Mooring ropes smothered with blubber and blood were thrown on board and the *Discovery* made fast. To prevent the two ships bumping, a large blue whale, about 24 metres in length, was placed between the vessels, together with long strips of blubber, suspended on chains from over the ship's rail, which also effectively served as fenders.

A rope ladder was lowered from the factory ship and Sir Douglas, with Captain MacKenzie, climbed on board to pay their respects to Captain Neilsen, commander of the vessel and her fleet of chasers. In the meantime, Sir Douglas had given permission for Hurley to accompany a 27-metre chaser, the *Star X*, which was about to leave in search of whales. He planned to make a cinematograph record of the methods used in hunting whales.

The frightful stench of whale emanating from the factory ship was indescribable; nothing in the world can be compared with it. The smell mingled with other shipboard odours seemed to lie on the air like an inescapable, invisible fog.

Without any waste of time, bags of coal in a large wire net were slung from a forehold of the factory ship on to our deck. Scientists and crew, working together, carried them to openings on the deck where they were shot down into the bunkers. Below decks, a gang stowed and trimmed the overflow of coal from the bunkers. In no time, all hands were working in an atmosphere laden with coal dust. When space ran out below the remaining bags were stowed on deck.

Transferring the 100 tonnes of coal continued without a break and was completed in five hours. Fresh water was also pumped into the ship's tanks. After a hurried clean-up a number of scientists, accepting an invitation from Captain Neilsen, climbed on board the factory ship to look it over and watch flensing operations.

My first view of the flensing deck, the ship's centre of activity, left me bewildered by its scene of carnage. It was running boot deep in blood and grease, the scuppers spouting continual streams of blood and filth into the sea. Men working like demons were removing blubber in long strips from a large blue whale, which shortly before my appearance had been winched up the slipway or ramp at the ship's stern to its present position. Two other carcasses being similarly treated were already in the late stages of disintegration.

Cranes on an overhead gantry assisted flensers by lifting strips of 15-centimetre-thick blubber, slowly rolling them back, while flensers, with their razor-sharp, long-handled knives, cut the blubber from the flesh. The resulting long strips were then cut into chunks as the crane lowered them to the deck. Stripped of its blubber, men waded knee deep among the one and a half tonnes of bulging intestines and removed the meat. Finally, buzzing steam saws cut the bones of the remaining skeleton into small sections.

Blubber, meat and bones were continually being dragged by other workers over the blood-covered deck and thrown down their respective chutes to the factory below decks. Blubber went to the steam boilers where the oil was extracted; meat went to a refrigerating plant for cutting, dehydrating and canning, and crushing machines converted bones into fertiliser. The intestines, having no value, were thrown overboard, providing an endless supply of food for birds and killer whales. Work continued in 24-hour shifts each day when whales were plentiful.

The products obtained from a blue whale about 27 metres long were: 26 tonnes of blubber, which would yield about 13 tonnes of oil; 57 tonnes of meat and 22 tonnes of fertiliser. It took just over an hour to process a whale.

Proceeding below decks I inspected the factory working at full pressure and creating an incredible confusion of deafening noises. An interesting interlude was a visit to the ship's piggery where 20 well-fed pigs looked the picture of contentment and good health. I stayed there for some time as the pigsty smell was heavenly in comparison with the pervading stench of whale.

Returning to the flensing deck I carefully made my way across its gory surface to rejoin the *Discovery*. Plenty of whales were being caught at the time of our arrival, but few had been caught before reaching their present position. Fifteen whales were floating belly upward in the sea astern of the factory ship, waiting their turn to be winched on board and converted into dollars for the whaling company. According to international law, every whale must be on the flensing deck within 33 hours of its being killed.

The crew were still making valiant efforts to clean the *Discovery*'s decks and surrounds of a thick coating of coal dust. As Sir Douglas was about to leave the factory ship he was presented with a quantity of whale meat and liver which, I assume, was accepted with reluctance.

At 7.30 P.M., mooring wires were cast off and the *Discovery* moved out to a position a little over a mile from the factory ship to await the return of the chaser *Star* X with Hurley on board.

A chain of unfortunate incidents now occurred. It was discovered that Eric Douglas had been accidentally left behind on the *Sir James Clark Ross*. Third officer Bonus Child was instructed to row across in the dinghy and bring him back. In the meantime, the *Star* X had returned to the factory ship with two whales. Hurley, on finding his cabin mate marooned on board, decided they would both go on another trip on the chaser as he required more film of whale-catching.

Child returned with this information after rowing more than two miles in a heavy dinghy and a rising sea. Taking advantage of the dinghy being overboard, Falla and I spent an hour or more shooting birds, which were in great numbers, as they circled overhead and fed on offal thrown from the factory ship.

There was a threatened change in the weather the next morning. A freshening easterly wind brought with it intermittent snow squalls, but had at the same time cleared away a fog which had developed in the early hours. The *Discovery* was still lying off the factory ship awaiting the return of the chaser with Hurley and Eric Douglas on board. Sir Douglas was getting more impatient every minute. At 10 P.M., the chaser ranged alongside and Hurley and Eric Douglas climbed on board. They expected a severe reprimand, which they duly received in no uncertain manner. The ship had been delayed for 24 hours waiting for their return from an unauthorised trip. Hurley said later it was well worth the towelling as he had got some superb pictures. The ship now got under way, following a north-westerly course on our journey to Adélie Land which we expected to reach in about 14 days.

Hurley recorded his experiences on the *Star* X. The following extract is from a copy of the notes he gave me:

The chaser, Star X, is 90 feet [27 metres] long, steel with curved, well-flared bow, falling steeply away from the bow to amidships where it is only three feet [one metre] above sea level . . . the gun platform is about 12 feet [3.5 metres] above water level — muzzle loader gun balanced in a frame so that it may be readily raised and lowered or swung around at any angle. Harpoon weighs 116 lb [52 kilograms] and is 42 inches [106 centimetres] in length — a nose piece, or shell, is screwed into the harpoon and this explodes when the whale is struck, delayed action about 1–2 seconds. Immediately below the gun is about 120 feet [36 metres] of 1¾ inch [44 millimetres] manilla rope coiled in a special receptacle so that it uncoils as the harpoon speeds towards the whale. This rope passes over fair-leads to a powerful block on the mast and then around a braking device before entering the hold where it is spliced on to another rope 4800 feet [1460 metres] in length. The block on the mast is suspended by a steel rope which passes down into the hold where it is secured to an ingenious system of powerful spring buffers. These take up any sudden bursts of energy and especially the first dash for liberty when the whale is first harpooned ... Each chaser has a wireless direction finder so that the factory ship can be reached in any kind of weather. Engines develop 750 h.p.

... at last a thrilling intimation comes from the crow's nest that a whale is in sight and we go in pursuit ... Drawing near, the telegraph is turned to slow, the engineer standing by, hand on valve all the time and the response is instantaneous. The whale has sounded, but we are not free of loose floe-ice and our chances in open water are better. Captain Jacobson rushes down the emergency bridge to the gun ... a hiss of mist with a sound like a steam engine shoots up almost under our bow. The gun challenges with a deafening roar — the line leaps like a springing cobra. There is a vortex of blood-dyed foam — a sullen thud as the bomb explodes in the body of the whale and out swirls the line ... the line continues running out and spinning the brake drums. The gun is hurriedly reloaded, this time with a killing harpoon — a weapon without barbs but headed with a more powerful bomb. The whale's desperate dash for freedom is waning and the engineer is applying the brakes. Line already out is 2400 feet [730 metres] and there is still enough strain to draw us along. The Star X was then put at full speed ahead and steamed away parallel to the course of the captive so as to form a large loop with the rope offering tremendous resistance to the whale. The whale was soon tired out and the chaser then steamed in towards it until 30 yards [27 metres] away the second harpoon was fired — again that horrible significant sound — the delayed action bomb and that was the end. The winch clanked in the loose line and the carcass began to sink until the line became taut. The winch clanked away with the tremendous weight until the back of the whale appeared alongside. A tube was then pushed through the blubber into the body cavity and air pumped in until well inflated ... Wind and mist had now arisen and the chaser was 30 miles from the factory ship. Arriving there we found at least 16 whales floating at the stern awaiting treatment.

The 17th was foggy with limited visibility. There were heavy falls of snow and although the barometer was high and steady, the outlook was threatening. During the day, a light wind from the south-east veered to the south-west and then to the north-west, but without any appreciable increase in strength.

We had logged 84 miles at midday and our position was 64°41'S, 178°29'E. Since leaving the *Sir James Clark Ross* we had been heading west with a little northing as we skirted the northern edge of heavy pack-ice. Occasionally we passed through tongues of loose pack, but otherwise the sea had been remarkably free of ice, except for many icebergs. Amongst the typical tabular shaped ones were a number of large weathered and wave-worn bergs of fantastic shapes and weird designs.

Hurley asked that the ship alter course slightly to pass close to the more spectacular bergs so they could be photographed and filmed. His requests were refused by Captain MacKenzie who lately seemed to be continually worried and had retreated within himself. He now rarely spoke to the staff and was quite a different person to the one we knew on the first voyage, even allowing for necessary restraints because of his increased status.

The awful smell of whale was beginning to disappear from below decks. Whale steaks cut from the meat received from the factory ship were served at our evening meal. After a mouthful or two it was firmly rejected and the remainder, including the liver, was thrown overboard.

The next six days were spent sailing, under steam and sail, along the northern edge of heavy pack-ice. This extended away to the south in an almost unbroken field as far as the eye could see. Sir Douglas had hoped that our western course might have been set to pass close by the Balleny Islands, but the pack was keeping the ship well to the north of them.

Good progress was being made in a calm sea mostly free of ice, except for occasional areas of loose pack and innumerable icebergs. Work in the laboratory had finished, including bird skinning. Deep sea dredgings could not be carried out as the aft decks were still covered with bags of coal. As coal was consumed each day, bags were thrown into the emptying bunkers and the deck was finally cleared.

On the morning of the 21st, the ship was stopped and a full plankton station was completed in four hours. Whales were frequently sighted and attempts made to identify them by their spoutings. A sperm whale is readily recognised by its jet of vapour being exhaled at a diagonal angle due to the position of its nasal cavity or vent. Blue whales exhale a jet of thick feathery vapour which rises straight upwards. Fin whales spout a very thin vertical column of vapour.

We never tired of admiring the drifting icebergs, the white sparkling islands of floating ice which studded the sea in all directions for most days. On one occasion we had the good fortune to see one which

became top-heavy and slowly rolled over. Majestic in its slow movement, it raised circles of waves which spread out into the distance before
the berg came to rest. Its previously submerged portion was riddled
with numerous caverns and projecting pinnacles, clearly revealing the
great extent of melting by sea water.

Campbell and Eric Douglas began assembling the Moth seaplane.
Its parts were contained since the first voyage in large cases stacked on
the winch house. Sir Douglas was looking forward to making several
flights from the base he had established during his 1911–14 expedition at
Commonwealth Bay, near the western border of King George V Land.

Shortly after completing a plankton station there was a change in
the weather. The wind swung to the north-east and as it freshened a
thick wet fog developed. For two days we nosed our way on course to
the south-west with only occasional liftings of the fog. The barometer
was falling rapidly and the sails were taken in and furled as wind and
seas increased. Work on assembling the seaplane was temporarily
abandoned.

The ship had now entered an area of fairly thick pack-ice which
was being tossed about under the influence of a heavy swell rolling in
from the north. Swinging masses of ice repeatedly crashed against the
ship's side with nerve-racking sound effects as she forced her way
through the pack.

On the 23rd, the wind veered to the south-west and the expected
bad weather suddenly developed. The wind increased to moderate gale
force and several hours later was blowing a full gale. The ship had
passed through the tongue of thick pack and was again in open water.
The foggy conditions we had been experiencing for the past two days
disappeared with the change of wind. Keeping north of the pack-ice
edge, the ship headed into the gale and although only a moderate sea
was running we were making no more than one knot on our west-south-
west course.

Gale-force winds continued through the night and most of the
following day. All hands were busy in the wardroom making sledging
harnesses under the direction of Frank Hurley. We expected to do some
sledging after landing at Commonwealth Bay. Later in the day,
Christmas Day preparations were in full swing. Decorations began to
appear in the wardroom and a Christmas dinner menu was prepared.
Sir Douglas, Doc Ingram and I brought up cases of Christmas gifts from
one of the holds and began unpacking presents.

Weather conditions improved slightly during the night, but

Whales moored alongside the factory ship, Sir James Clark Ross, *with a chaser in
the distance.*
(By courtesy of the Mawson Institute. Photo: F. Hurley.)

Christmas Day broke with an overcast sky; a strong wind was still blowing from the south-west, bringing with it heavy falls of snow. I was awakened by Christmas carols played on the gramophone and selections continued until a service was held at 11 A.M. All hands except those on watch were present.

Gifts were then distributed to every person on board. Children of the Woodlands Church of England Grammar School at Glenelg, South Australia, sent numerous Christmas cards of their own design and drawing. Presents were also received from the wives of members of the South Australian Geographical Society, from Lady Mawson and from students of the Church Grammar School at Mowbray Heights, Launceston, Tasmania. The cook excelled himself in producing a Christmas dinner which was thoroughly enjoyed. Toasts were drunk and conversation, with hardly a break, increased in volume as members endeavoured to make themselves heard.

The wind had dropped to a light breeze the next morning. The sky had cleared and we enjoyed bright sunshine. Simmers pointed out that this was the third period of sunshine since leaving Hobart more than a month ago. However, it was not of long duration; about midday the clouds gathered again and snow began to fall.

Coal received from the *Sir James Clark Ross* had been practically consumed and in the morning 13 tonnes of coal briquettes were transferred from a forehold to the bunkers. Heavy consumption of our coal was a constant worry. In a calm sea we covered about 110 miles in 24 hours, burning six tonnes of coal. However, in bad weather the consumption of coal was alarming with as much as eight tonnes being consumed to cover a distance run of only 20 to 30 miles. Coal was also used when the ship was held up in heavy pack-ice, running before blizzards and gales, then having to retrace many miles to reach our original position. The sails helped, but these could only be used in open water and when conditions were favourable.

The ship was stopped in the afternoon and a full station was carried out. Depth of the sea floor was 3070 metres. At midday, after a distance run of 99 miles, our position was 65°16'S, 147°32' E.

Large flocks of birds were now beginning to gather around the ship, some wheeling overhead, others feeding on surface organisms by hovering above the waves, head to wind, and frequently plunging with outspread wings. Occasionally, birds would disappear entirely under water for several seconds to catch food. Falla recorded most Antarctic species, but Antarctic petrels were in the greatest number. Adélie penguins were now being frequently sighted, resting on floating ice. Now and again a solitary emperor penguin was noticed standing erect and unperturbed on low rafts of pack-ice.

We encountered heavy pack-ice later in the day as we continued on our south-westerly course. An almost compact ice field stretched away to the south, but ahead of the ship, the ice was broken with occasional open leads along which we weaved our way.

The ship continued through heavy pack during the night and was still fighting her way to the south-west by next morning. Ice conditions became so bad that it was decided to turn the ship north and reach open water. Most of the day was spent in battering our way through heavy ice until we emerged from the pack into open ice-free water. The ship then steamed along the pack-ice edge which trended in a south-westerly direction. We were approximately 180 miles north of Cape Gray on the King George V Land coast. A vast compact ice field stretched east and west for hundreds of miles. As the summer months advanced, and under the influence of blizzards sweeping from the continent, most of the pack-ice would eventually break up and drift to the north.

The ship made good progress on the 28th as she skirted the northern edge of the pack-ice which was now running almost due west. A sharp lookout was being kept for a promising change in ice conditions which would allow the ship to make southing as we were now approximately north of Commonwealth Bay. Whales had been sighted on previous days, but we were now in an area where they were in considerable numbers; spoutings could be seen in all directions.

The *Kosmos*, a Norwegian whaling factory ship of 22,000 tonnes, the largest whaling vessel afloat at that time, was operating off the Adélie Land coast. Sparks had been trying to make wireless contact with her, but so far without success. Sir Douglas was hoping that her captain would be able to supply us with much needed coal.

Early in the afternoon, the pack-ice fringe swung away to the south and good progress was made in that direction for about six hours. Heavy ice then forced an alteration in our course to almost due west. At midnight, the sky had partly cleared of clouds and for the first time on the voyage we witnessed the setting and immediate rising of the "midnight sun".

A light breeze was blowing the next morning with an oily smooth sea, but a heavy swell was running in from the north-east. The *Kosmos* had been sighted in the distance. Heading towards her we passed three chasers and several floating flagged whales. At 9.30 A.M. we had come up to within hailing distance of the *Kosmos*.

Sir Douglas set off in the motor boat to meet Captain Andraesen, who, in an earlier wireless message, had agreed to let us have 50 tonnes of slack coal. This was a most generous offer and indicated the Norwegians' goodwill towards our exploratory programme. Both ships were rolling to such an extent that coaling the *Discovery* seemed impossible.

Although our ship was drifting some distance from the *Kosmos*, we were again becoming immersed in the indescribable stench of dead whales. Chasers were returning with their catch, towing a whale on each side of their vessel. The whales were moored with others at the stern of the *Kosmos*, waiting their turn to be hauled up the ramp to the flensing deck. Most of the whales being caught in this area were fin whales and we learned later that nine chasers had captured 45 of these whales the previous day. Fin whales are a much smaller species than the blue whale and yield about 60 barrels of oil per whale, so that 3000 of them would have had to be caught to fill the tanks of the *Kosmos*, which held 180,000 barrels. Six barrels equal about one tonne.

Finally, after a long wait, Sir Douglas returned to the *Discovery* with arrangements for coaling — and a gift of whale meat! Our yards were cockbilled and at 4.30 P.M. we moved in alongside the factory ship and made fast. Two whale carcasses in between the two vessels served as fenders. Both ships then slowly steamed ahead into the swell to alleviate rolling. Slack coal was then poured down a chute which was projected over the side of the *Kosmos* on to our foredeck where all hands endeavoured,with little success, to keep pace with the flowing torrent of coal. Some of it was bagged, carried and emptied into the bunkers, while a quantity was removed and stacked on the aft deck. It was a scene of feverish activity.

Coaling was completed by 6.30 P.M. and the captain of the *Kosmos* sent 20 men to assist in bagging the residue of the coal on deck. Lines were cast off at 8 P.M. and the *Discovery* slowly steamed away. The transfer of coal was a successful operation under adverse conditions. Slight damage occurred to the port side bulwarks of the *Discovery* during the process of ranging alongside the *Kosmos*, but this was soon repaired. Captain MacKenzie, who was unhappy during the coaling, was heard to say "he wouldn't go alongside a 22,000 tonner again in such a swell for 50 tonnes of gold let alone coal."

As the *Discovery* laid off to hoist the motor boat on deck the scene was reminiscent of a busy port rather than a position about 100 miles north of the Antarctic coast. Chasers were coming and going and an oil tanker, the C. V. *Brovig*, had hove in sight and was now standing by to take off the 60,000 barrels of oil from the *Kosmos* which she had collected up to that time. Afterwards, the C. V. *Brovig* would sail direct to New York. To make room for the whale oil, 100 tonnes of fuel oil was pumped overboard from one of her tanks.

Battered by Hurricane Winds

AFTER A FAREWELL TOOT on the ship's siren at about 10 P.M., we proceeded through loose pack-ice on a southerly course towards Adélie Land. By morning the ship was making good progress through fairly open water with only occasional areas of loose pack-ice. At about 10 A.M., the light breeze from the east veered to the south-east and by midday it had increased in strength to gale force. It brought with it heavy driving snow which reduced visibility to a drastic extent.

In an attempt to seek shelter, the ship was headed into heavy drifting pack-ice and hove to after making some distance. The depth of the sea floor was recorded as 220 metres, which put us on the Continental Shelf. Many grounded bergs of varying sizes were in sight and anxious moments were experienced as the ship was manoeuvred to prevent collision with them on our drift. The main wireless aerials were carried away just before midnight.

Gale-force winds continued throughout the night and had increased in strength to an average of 100 kilometres an hour the next morning with gusts attaining at least 160 kilometres an hour. It was blowing a hurricane. In the meantime, the ship had emerged from the pack-ice and was fighting her way through a wild storm-tossed sea in which occasional bergs and growlers were a continual navigational hazard. Flying spindrift and snow shut out almost all vision. Attempts to keep the ship on course were unsuccessful as she refused to answer the helm against the terrific force of the wind. A large berg suddenly loomed in sight and the ship was unable to avoid colliding with it. Great lumps of decaying ice crashed on the decks from the impact.

In between falls of snow it was noticed the ship was being blown towards a line of heavy consolidated pack consisting of large masses of ice including weather-worn bergs. Waves pounding against the ice front were throwing spray about 20 metres in the air and it was then swept by the hurricane in horizontal sheets across the pack. Wind and heavy seas had set the pack-ice in motion, heaving, wildly swinging and grinding, one against the other. It was a frightening spectacle.

Only one course was left open to us; we had to penetrate far enough into the pack to seek shelter. After some difficulty the ship was manoeuvred to hit the pack head on, and with two jibs set and engines turning over we began to force our way through to less turbulent conditions. For a time it appeared the ice was too consolidated for the ship to make headway. She was receiving a terrific battering as swinging masses of ice crashed against her sides with occasional sounds of splintering timber. Little could be seen as the ship was being deluged with flying spray and heavy snow.

Gradually, the ship made headway and we eventually escaped through a belt of pack-ice into an ice-encircled pool of fairly calm open water. For about five hours we maintained position by steaming into the wind, but later in the afternoon the open water began to close in with drifting pack. Fortunately, we were able to make the shelter of a mammoth sized tabular berg which had grounded in about 180 metres. Pack-ice drifted past on either side at about one knot, but in its lee was a fairly wide stretch of ice-free water.

We were in an insecure haven as later powerful eddies of wind swinging around the iceberg blew the ship back into the pack despite all our efforts. This time it was more menacing than previously experienced; ice towered above the bulwarks and swung heavily. It was difficult to keep balance with some of the violent bumps and the continual grinding of ice against the ship's side. It was a most unpleasant sound. Large dagger-shaped pinnacles of ice, formed by the effects of underwater erosion, crashed against the ship's planking as the ice rolled, with the sound of straining and snapping timber.

The ship was securely locked in the grip of drifting pack-ice and there appeared to be no prospect of any immediate escape. The scientific staff spent the day on deck ready to assist when necessary, but there was little we could do. Below decks the noise of ice hammering against the ship's hull was alarming and in the confined space it sounded much worse than it really was. No one appeared unduly worried as we had great confidence in the ship's construction to withstand ice damage. The ship's carpenter had been below sounding the wells and there was no sign of any leakage of water.

We were therefore very surprised when Sir Douglas came along to inform us that the situation was critical and it was touch and go whether the ship would survive the battering it was receiving. It seemed out of character with him to be so pessimistic. His announcement had little effect and perhaps increased some of our unspoken, innermost doubts. We did not want to believe him and so the only reaction was increased jocular remarks amongst ourselves. It was an unusual way to spend New Year's Eve, waiting for the New Year to be blown in on the wings of a hurricane.

Working sails and steam, we escaped from the heavy jostling pack and emerged into a large pool formed by an immense grounded berg cleaving the drifting pack into two streams. The ship nosed up close to the berg, which towered high above our masts, where we received protection from the undiminished screaming hurricane-force winds. It was now midnight but no thought was given to celebrations.

Fortunately, the pool remained open during the night and on New Year's Day the ship was still maintaining her position with some difficulty. Weather conditions were unchanged with the wind still averaging about 110 kilometres an hour and gusts exceeding 145 kilometres an hour. Light snow was falling and the deck temperature was minus 20°C. Heavy pack drifting to the north-west and grounded bergs covered the sea in all directions. Our plan was to remain in the shelter of the big berg until the weather improved or as long as the water remained open.

Two chasers from the factory ship *Kosmos* were observed the next morning, sheltering in the pack about a kilometre away. In bad weather they made a break for the pack, or sought protection in the lee of icebergs. Their knowledge of ice movements and their remarkable seamanship, power and speed enabled the small vessels to manoeuvre within the pack but the slightest error of judgement could have spelt disaster.

At midday our position was 66°00′S, 139°25′E. We were not far north of the Antarctic Circle and within reasonable steaming distance of Adélie Land. Another chaser drifted within hailing distance late in the evening. The skipper told us his vessel had a damaged stern post and when the weather improved he would be leaving for Cape Town for repairs. It was a 3000-mile journey in the world's worst seas and he hoped to be back before the end of the whaling season.

Shortly before midnight, heavy black clouds began to roll away and patches of clear sky appeared. The southern horizon became bathed in a golden glow as the midnight sun, a magnificent red disc, set, only to rise again a few moments later. It was a cheering sight after a day of endless anxiety. However, gale-force winds still continued unabated.

The wind, still coming in from the south-east, showed no signs of easing the next morning. The sky had again clouded over. At about 3 A.M., pack-ice had closed in on the pool in which we were sheltering, forcing the ship back into heavy pack. This was negotiated and an hour later we emerged into open water with the pack trending to the south-east. Suddenly, an increasing wind blew the ship back into the pack edge and again we became entrapped in wildly swaying ice. While attempting to regain open water, the propeller hit a solid mass of ice and, with a horrible thud, brought the engines to a standstill. Damage to the rudder or propeller was always uppermost in our minds as any impairment of them would be disastrous.

Fortunately, the engines started up again and their smooth running was a good indication that no harm had resulted. Reaching open water again, the rest of the day was spent steaming head on into the wind and heavy seas. The ship was on a course towards Adélie Land, but progress was a little less than two knots although the engines were turning over at full speed.

The weather began to improve during the afternoon with occasional bursts of sunshine. Land was sighted late in the evening. A faint line of coastal ice-cliffs could be seen extending along the southern horizon about 40 miles away. Depths of the sea floor recorded during the day ranged from 508 to 144 metres. Continuing on our course, we passed many large grounded tabular icebergs.

An expected moderation in the weather did not eventuate and early on January 3 a strong wind, still from the south-east, had a strength of about 65 kilometres an hour. The sky was again thickly clouded over. The ship's speed had decreased to about one knot as she plunged head-on into a rough sea with waves continually covering the forecastle head and sweeping knee-high along the decks.

Our position at noon was 66°25'S, 141°22'E after a 24-hour run of 74 miles. It was almost the same position as the one we had reached four days ago before the onslaught of the hurricane. Our estimated distance from Commonwealth Bay was still about 40 miles. The wind backed more to the east in the afternoon, but still continued to blow at almost gale force. Light snow was falling.

For most of the day ice-slopes, rising inland to about 600 metres, had been visible in the distance. Even with the aid of binoculars, no distinguishing features could be made out. Cape Alden came into view as the ship moved in towards Commonwealth Bay. As it was Saturday night, the scientific staff drank their usual toast to their sweethearts and wives, but on this occasion there was an added air of excitement. We had reached our destination and all hands looked forward to going ashore next day.

The wind had increased during the night and continued all next day. The sky had cleared of clouds early in the morning and the sun shone brilliantly, making conditions more pleasant. Fighting her way through a turbulent sea with breaking waves, the ship steamed slowly past Cape Alden and the Mackellar Islets into Commonwealth Bay on the western border of King George V Land. It is a huge U-shaped bay 30 kilometres wide with the rocky headland of Cape Gray to the east and Cape Alden to the west. Cape Denison, the site of Mawson's 1911–14 expedition's main base, is situated at the centre of the bay with an area of about two square kilometres of rocky outcrops.

At an Imperial Conference held in 1926, Britain and Australia asked the French Government to move back the eastern border of Adélie Land so that Cape Denison would be in King George V Land. On the cape, facing the sea, is a large cross erected by members of the Mawson expedition as a memorial to Dr Mertz and Lieutenant Ninnis.

France agreed to the request, realising the cape's indissoluble association with Australian history.

Great difficulty was now experienced in finding a suitable and safe anchorage. Terrific gusts of wind sweeping down from the ice-slopes and across the bay made navigation of the ship an arduous and exhausting task. It took the united efforts of two men on the helm to maintain the ship on a straight course. After steaming up and down the bay several times with continual soundings, the anchor was dropped at 2 P.M. in 33 metres, but even with the engines turning over it began to drag and had to be raised. The ship then steamed into waters in the lee of a glacier front 55 metres high. In this position the wind, sweeping off the ice-slopes, passed over the ship, striking the sea some distance offshore. The anchor was lowered in 35 metres and held. We then waited for the wind to subside before attempting a landing.

Sir Douglas, Hurley and Kennedy were revisiting Cape Denison after an absence of 17 years. They had been observing their old quarters through binoculars with keen interest and were anxious to get ashore as soon as possible.

Campbell and Eric Douglas began to assemble the seaplane. Securely lashed down during the hurricane, it had suffered no damage and they expected it would be ready to fly the following day if conditions were favourable. Members of the scientific staff were busily engaged in getting together their shore equipment, including camping gear.

All hands were up early on the 5th to be greeted by perfect weather. The sky had cleared and it was sunny and warm. Wind had dropped completely and the sea within the bay had subsided to a flat calm. No time was lost in lowering the motor boat over the ship's side. Equipment was stowed and with all the scientific staff on board we set out for Cape Denison about a mile to the east. No difficulty was experienced in finding a landing spot in Boat Harbour and scientists moved off in various directions to carry out their particular duties.

Some of us hurried over to inspect Mawson's old quarters to see how the huts had stood up over the past 17 years against the worst winds in the world. The walls of the main hut consist of two layers of strong pine wood, anchored to piles sunk into holes blasted in the rock and wedged in with ice. The outside timber had been snow blasted to such an extent that it was about 12 millimetres below the nail heads. The interior of the hut was filled with ice and embedded in it were articles of equipment and furniture. The roof had suffered from the ravages of time and was almost at the point of collapse.

Campbell and I were given the task of picking out the ice which had filled the hut, so that Kennedy could determine the magnetic dip from exactly the same base as it had been ascertained regularly during

1911–14. We uncovered a wooden shelf on which were three cakes of chocolate. They were frozen solid and in perfect condition and made good eating later. With the ice completely removed, Kennedy placed his instrument in position and later informed us that his readings indicated the Magnetic Pole had moved its position considerably closer towards Cape Denison over the past 18 years.

Several years ago the Australian Government agreed to restore the hut to its original condition to be preserved as a national monument to honour Sir Douglas Mawson who had played a major role in making known the Australian Antarctic Territory. Restoration of the hut would be carried out by the Antarctic Division of the Department of Science. Work began during the summer season of 1981–82. Many tonnes of compacted ice within the interior were removed and preliminary reconstruction work commenced.

At midday, all hands gathered together for the claiming of land ceremony. Captain MacKenzie raised the flag while Sir Douglas read the proclamation which claimed the Territory of King George V Land and its extension under the name of Oates Land situated between longitudes 142° and 162° east of Greenwich and between latitudes 66° south and the South Pole, including the Curzon Archipelago, Hodgeman Islands, Way Archipelago, Dixson Island and Mackellar Islets.

The proclamation, signed by Sir Douglas and witnessed by Captain MacKenzie, was then placed in a sealed container and deposited in the cairn at the base of the flagpole. A board was also attached to the cairn on which had been carved, "The British Flag was raised and British Sovereignty asserted on the Fifth day of January, 1931".

Falla, Doc Ingram and I spent the rest of the day collecting birds and observing the habits of Adélie penguins in their rookeries, which occupied practically all the ice-free rocky areas. The number of birds in the Cape Denison rookeries was estimated to be over 10,000, but much larger rookeries established on the Mackellar Islets, about two miles offshore, contained greater numbers. During the 1911–14 expedition the total population was estimated to be 200,000 birds. A hurried visit to the islets the following day revealed what Falla thought to be twice that number.

Emperor penguins were not to be seen and it was not until much later, when we were off the Queen Mary Land coast, that groups of up to 10 birds were observed resting on ice-floes. Weddell seals were numerous and many had laboriously made their way well inland where they slumbered on the ice-slope.

Late in the afternoon the shore party, with the exception of Sir Douglas and five others, returned to the ship. Tents were pitched and a meal was prepared. We retired early and spent a comfortable night in our warm reindeer skin sleeping bags.

The sky had clouded over during the night but the next morning was fine and sunny. Doc Ingram, Campbell and I left for the ice-slope to try our hands at skiing. Our efforts met with little success on the smooth ice surface, free of any snow. We could only stop by throwing ourselves sideways and skidding to a halt. We then hauled a sledge well up the ice-slope and with the three of us lying flat, Campbell with his legs over the end to steer, started off down the ice-slope. Gaining speed we eventually found the sledge heading for a Weddell seal fast asleep on the ice. Frantic efforts by Campbell to steer past it were to no avail and we slammed into it amidship. We were hurled forward onto the seal's back where there was a wild floundering of bodies. The seal voiced its displeasure with loud roars and groans and resumed its sleep.

We spent the rest of the day visiting the Mackellar Islets and dredging in the bay. At 3.30 P.M. the shore party returned to the ship with cases of tinned foodstuff that had been left in the open for 17 years. An 18-litre tin of petrol, without the slightest sign of rust, was later used to run the motor boat.

During our two days on shore, the sun reflecting off the ice had caused minor sunstroke to several members of the party, even though the temperature was minus 18°C. In the Antarctic the full strength of the sun is felt because the air is completely free of dust, in comparison with that on the southern Australian coast where the air was laden with dust.

Stuart Campbell, disappointed that no use of the plane had been made, was informed by Sir Douglas that a flight would be made next day to determine the extent and disposition of consolidated pack which blocked further progress to the west.

At 5.30 P.M. the motor boat was hoisted on deck, anchors were weighed and the ship got under way. Shortly after leaving Commonwealth Bay the ship was stopped while oblique and vertical nettings were carried out. These were completed at 12.30 A.M. on the morning of the 7th. The weather was perfect with bright sunshine, a light breeze from the south-east and the sea a flat calm.

After steaming a short distance the ship was again stopped close to a large tongue of pack-ice held together by grounded bergs. The large dredge was lowered over the stern in 585 metres and settled on the sea floor after about 1370 metres of cable had been paid out. It was then dragged for 15 minutes. While being hauled in it struck the bottom again in much shallower water so that the catch possibly included specimens from that depth. Results were very good with a variety of forms.

We steamed north along the edge of a vast field of consolidated pack-ice extending out from the Adélie Land coast. According to reports Cape Robert projects well to the north, against which the pack

builds up. The ship reached open water at 8 P.M. and Sir Douglas decided that Campbell and Eric Douglas should make a flight to examine the ice conditions. The airmen made a half-hour flight to the south and west and reported there was no sign of the cape; the coast seemed to trend away to the south. The pack-ice was about 65 kilometres wide and stretched away to the west as far as they could see. The plane was hoisted on board and lashed down and the ship proceeded along the pack-ice edge to the north-east.

On the 8th the ship was still following the pack-ice fringe. Our noon position was 66°17'S, 140°15'E. Soundings through the day varied from 1045 to 395 metres. It was a magnificent sight as the ship glided through fairly open sea, passing bergs which sparkled in the sunshine. The deep blue of the sea showed up in strong contrast to the vivid whiteness of ice.

Sir Douglas and Doc Ingram spent most of the day sorting the dredged material from the previous day. Professor Johnston preserved the specimens as they came to hand. Falla and I began to skin birds collected at Cape Denison and the Mackellar Islets which included Adélie penguins, Antarctic skuas and Wilson storm petrels.

Early in the afternoon it was decided to alter course slightly west of north and push our way through the heavy pack-ice to reach its northern edge. We were steaming over shallow waters. At 4.30 A.M. there was a sudden rise of the sea floor from 800 to 137 metres. Four hours later it descended to 314 metres followed by another rise to 126 metres. For the rest of the day we were still in shallow waters ranging from 208 to 342 metres. Extending back to the coast, the shallows accounted for the vast sheet of consolidated pack around which we were now steaming. Scattered grounded bergs over the area had held up pack-ice over the years and had consolidated to form a permanent barrier against westward progress along the coast.

The ship emerged from heavy close pack early next morning and, skirting its northern edge, we proceeded on a westerly course. Good progress was made and the ship rolled for the first time for days as she felt the effects of a moderate swell from the north-west. A cold westerly wind caused a fall in the temperature to minus 20°C. Falla and I had difficulty skinning birds in the laboratory and every now and again we had to plunge our hands into a bucket of sea water to restore feeling in our fingers.

The barometer began to fall about midday and heavy clouds appeared on the eastern horizon. During the afternoon the westerly breeze dropped, its place taken by a light breeze from the east. The

Expedition members inspect the Mawson buildings at Cape Denison.
(Photo: S. Campbell.)

BATTERED BY HURRICANE WINDS

expected change in the weather did not take place until noon the next day when the wind, veering slightly to the south, began to increase in strength. It freshened later to a half gale which came from the right quarter. All sails were set and we were making an incredible speed of nine knots. Snow began to fall accompanied by wind-driven sleet.

The wind continued to blow at about 65 to 100 kilometres an hour throughout the day. Sails were later taken in and the ship rolled and wallowed in big following seas. These conditions persisted during the night with no sign of the weather moderating; the barometer was still falling. We reached 65°51′S, 129°39′E, after a record run of 138 miles, at noon the next day. We had now skirted the long compact tongue of pack-ice which had forced the ship to the north. Our position was about 130 miles north of the western border of the Wilkes Coast lying between longitudes 136° to 130° east. Sir Douglas planned to go south and reach the uncharted coastline in this area. Captain MacKenzie favoured taking advantage of the strong wind to proceed under sail to Queen Mary Land which was one of our main objectives about 1100 miles to the west. In the meantime, the ship was practically hove to waiting for the weather to improve.

A move was made towards the south about midday, but soon afterwards further progress was blocked by a line of heavy pack. The ship was headed back clear of the ice. We were now steaming broadside on to huge waves raging in from the south-east, causing the ship to roll so heavily that her weather gunwales were repeatedly submerged. Tonnes of water sweeping on board covered the deck waist high. Later in the afternoon the wind increased to gale force; visibility was too bad to continue and the ship was hove to with engines turning over just sufficiently to maintain position as she headed into the wind.

January 12 brought no moderation in the weather. The ship was still heading south-east into tremendous waves, making only enough progress to maintain steerage way. Two men were at the helm each watch and it took all their efforts to prevent the ship from broaching. Later, the wind moderated and with the barometer rising it appeared the gale would soon blow itself out. The barometer suddenly began to drop again; the wind increased in violence and was accompanied by thick driving snow.

The ship's movements were almost beyond description. She pitched and tossed and developed a fantastic corkscrew motion as she dived from wave crests into the deep troughs. To add an air of cheerfulness in the wardroom, Eric Douglas played a record. His unfortunate first choice was entitled "I'm dancing with tears in my eyes because the

The Discovery *passes through loose pack off Wilkes Land.*
(By courtesy of the Mawson Institute. Photo: F. Hurley.)

271

girl in my arms isn't you". It was received with loud sounds of distress and anger from occupants of the cabins with cries of "take if off . . . take it off." Eric quickly complied and gave up his attempts to lighten our lives.

New Lands Discovered

THE GALE BEGAN to moderate during the night and by the next day, January 13, the wind had dropped to a light breeze. The sky cleared of clouds and the sun shone for the first time in several days. The sea had subsided and visibility was perfect. The ship moved into open pack and drifted. Progress was made to the east-south-east in an attempt to reach the Wilkes Coast although a strong ice-blink to the south indicated the absence of open water.

Today was the anniversary of our first landing on the Antarctic Continent at Proclamation Island, Enderby Land. To commemorate the occasion, Hurley, Eric Douglas, Falla, Campbell and Simmers staged a burlesque show in the evening. All the items were well received including one entitled "Dodgers of the Pack-ice".

Early next morning progress towards the Wilkes Coast was blocked by a barrier of heavy compact pack and further attempts to reach it were abandoned. The ship was then turned and headed west. It was a perfect day. Our position at midday, after a distance run of 87 miles, was 64°56′S, 128°46′E. Good progress was made under sail for the rest of the day as we made our way along the unbroken northern edge of the pack. Birds, markedly absent during the gale, were again beginning to follow and circle the ship in increasing numbers.

The ship was still skirting the pack-ice margin on her westerly course the next morning. The heavy consolidated ice stretched away to the south as far as the eye could see. Where the edge confronted the open sea it formed a remarkably straight and sharp line of demarcation. A keen watch was kept for any possible access to the south but none was observed.

The sea was smooth with only a slight swell from the north-east. Conditions were ideal for a reconnaissance flight. At 10 A.M., Campbell and Grandpa Oom took off and ascended to 8000 feet. In their absence the ship moved in close to the pack and a series of oblique and vertical nettings were carried out.

On the return of the plane, Oom reported that land had definitely been sighted at a distance of about 100 miles. A cape was observed from which the coast ran east on one side and south-south-west on the other. This feature was later named Cape Goodenough by Sir Douglas and placed on the chart. Campbell reported that the pack-ice presented an unbroken vast field of ice extending from the ship to the coast, through which it would be impossible for her to force a passage. Temperatures recorded on the flight were minus 1°C at sea level, 1.6°C at 1000 feet and minus 6°C at 8000 feet.

While hoisting the plane inboard, the rolling of the ship caused it to crash against the ship's side on several occasions, but fortunately only minor damage resulted. We then continued on our course to the west; sails were raised and with a following wind we were making about five knots. Birds were plentiful including Arctic terns which had been increasing each day until flocks of more than a hundred were not uncommon. Seals were numerous and a crab-eater, asleep on an ice-floe, was shot and hauled on board for fresh meat. It provided quite palatable steaks.

I was awakened early on the 16th by the noise of ice crunching against the ship's side. Our westerly course had been interrupted by a tongue of loose brash ice through which the ship was passing. Perfect weather still continued with bright sunshine, a calm sea and practically no swell. Icebergs were becoming more numerous again. Two massive bergs, their icicles glistening in the sunshine, presented a spectacular sight. On the top of one, weathering had produced a series of jagged spires towering to heights of 75 metres above sea level. The fanciful shapes of towers, battlements and other structures were all reminiscent of a mediaeval castle. On a fine sunny day the most beautiful and awe-inspiring sight imaginable was the dazzling white of gigantic bergs rising vertically from a millpond surface of a deep-blue sea.

At midday, our position was 65°03′S, 121°27′E. Depth of the sea floor was 3070 metres. The ship was stopped at 4.30 P.M. and the plane lowered over the side. Eric Douglas and Oom took off, in a flurry of spray, to determine the conditions of the pack. They were soon lost to sight flying to the west. Eight finner whales swam close alongside the ship. They were about 12 metres in length. After staying long enough to be photographed, they continued on their way. Simmers sent up a meteorological balloon and its movements, indicating upper air currents, were recorded until it was lost to sight at 50,000 feet.

The airmen returned after 90 minutes and reported that the pack-ice extended southward in a thick mass for about 40 miles to clear water. This continued for approximately 30 miles towards ice-covered land which they considered to be about 100 miles distant. While the plane was being hoisted inboard on to its staging, Sir Douglas and Captain MacKenzie discussed the situation. MacKenzie, strangely enough, was eager to push south in an attempt to reach the open water, but on the understanding that if difficulties arose we would retreat. From what we could see of the pack it was a hopeless exercise. However, the ship was headed south, pounding into the floes and receiving a severe buffeting. We were completely surrounded by ice almost to the exclusion of any visible water. Progress became painfully slow as we faced an impossible task. Finally the ship was turned with difficulty and we made our way back into open water. We continued on our course to the west, skirting the edge of the pack-ice.

Following the flights made in the last two days, Sir Douglas claimed land, observed from the plane, lying between 120° and 130° east longitude. He named it Banzare Land after the expedition. It is now marked on the latest maps of Antarctica as the Banzare Coast. The course of the *Discovery* in this area was further south than any previous expedition.

The *Discovery* continued on a westerly course the next morning along the shore-like edge of heavy compact ice. The weather was still fine with a calm sea, but the sky was rapidly becoming overcast with thick black clouds. The barometer, however, was rising. The ship was stopped in the afternoon and a full plankton station was completed in four hours. Low clouds prevented a flight being made so we continued west. Whales were plentiful, their spoutings identifying them as mainly finners and blues.

Shortly before midnight engines were stopped and the ship was allowed to drift in the hope that the sky would clear of low-lying clouds and allow another flight over the pack-ice. We were in an interesting area. In 1839, Captain John Balleny, when in 64°58'S, 121°E, recorded in his log, "Saw land to the southward, the vessel surrounded by drift-ice." The next day he made a further entry, "every appearance of land". It was apparent that this supposed landfall did not exist in the position he charted.

On the 18th the ship was still drifting and waiting for the sky to clear. As this seemed unlikely to happen for some time, the plane was swung overboard in readiness for a flight. At 7.40 A.M., Sir Douglas, with Campbell as pilot, took off in a choppy sea, but could only attain a height of 3000 feet because of low clouds. Visibility was so poor towards the south that Sir Douglas could not be sure whether he saw low ice-covered land or compacted pack-ice in the distance. The pack appeared more broken to the west and there was a possibility that the ship could force her way through to the south in that direction.

The ship, in the meantime, had stopped to run a dredging and a tow netting. A large mesh net with a ring opening 180 centimetres in diameter, was lowered over the stern and 1370 metres of cable paid out. It was towed for an hour at a depth of 460 metres at about two knots. The catch consisted of an interesting mixed collection of plankton. The large Monegasque dredge was then lowered and 2895 metres of cable paid out until it rested on the sea floor at a depth of 2265 metres. With the ship steaming at less than one knot the dredge was dragged over the bottom for 50 minutes. It yielded an excellent catch of bottom-living organisms. Included were relatively large sea-spiders, anemones (Coelenterates), various echinoderms and several species of coral. The corals belong to a group known as the Madreporaria which includes species living at depths of up to 5500 metres in all oceans of the world. They are distinct from the reef corals which inhabit depths usually not exceeding about 45 metres and with a water temperature of 20°C or higher.

During dredging operations, which had taken nine hours to complete, the sky had become more overcast with low, moving clouds, restricting visibility. Sir Douglas decided to wait for a clearance in the weather so that he could make another flight to observe the coast.

The ship headed into thick pack-ice for a short distance the next morning. Engines were stopped and the fires banked to conserve coal. Heavy snow was falling and large pieces of pack under the influence of a north-easterly swell were swaying and repeatedly hitting the ship's sides with resounding thumps and grinding noises.

Large numbers of Adélie penguins were observed travelling over the pack from the south towards open water. The majority of these deviated from their course to inspect the ship and at times we were ringed by birds gazing wide-eyed at the strange object. Their curiosity satisfied, they moved off and their places were taken by others. Five penguins in different stages of plumage were added to our collection. Seals, mainly crab-eaters, were also plentiful. From the crow's nest, Hurley counted 190 of them resting and sleeping on the ice.

Our noon position was 64°16'S, 115°36'E. During the past week no progress had been made south with only a short distance made to the west. In the afternoon a team of scientists transferred ten tonnes of coal briquettes from the forepeak and anchor chain lockers to the main bunker. The crew were given the more enviable task of "icing ship"; our stock of fresh water was diminishing and needed replenishing. Bouts of snow-balling took place and there seemed to be signs of disappointment when the task was completed.

The next morning the Discovery was still stationary in heavy pack-ice which stretched away to the south as far as the eye could see. A few lanes of open water were observed well to the west. A light breeze was blowing from the south-east, but otherwise it was a depressing day. The sky was still covered with low clouds and there were occasional falls of heavy snow. The pack-ice in which the ship was lying had a westerly drift of about 12 miles a day. Latest information was that we were to stay drifting with the pack until the weather cleared. It seemed unlikely that a further flight would be possible in this vicinity since there was no sign of any improvement.

A solitary emperor penguin was sighted some distance away on the ice. Falla and I climbed overboard and wandered over the pack in an attempt to reach it, but the surface became broken with gaps in between floes and so the penguin was left in peace. Returning to the ship I joined Sir Douglas, Doc Ingram and Campbell in moving four tonnes of coal briquettes from the forepeak to one of the bunkers.

Sir Douglas, during his flight with Campbell two days ago, had sighted what he thought was either land or a line of jammed icebergs in about 66°S, 117°E. If it was land, he proposed to call it Sabrina Land after one of Captain Balleny's two ships which was lost in a gale with all hands. The name Sabrina Coast is now applied to the coast of Wilkes Land lying between Cape Waldron and Cape Southard.

The next day saw no change in the weather. The ship was still beset by ice and was drifting with it to the west. A sea leopard and a crab-eater seal, resting on ice close to the ship, were shot by Campbell. We had difficulties dragging them to the ship's side where they were hoisted on board by block and tackle. The sea leopard measured 320 centimetres in length. I put off the task of skinning them until later in the day.

Engines were started at midday and the ship was forced through thick pack to a large open pool which had been seen from the crow's nest and estimated to be about six miles to the south-east. It took four hours of continual battering against the ice to breach passages along which the ship could make progress before we emerged into the pool.

A smaller type of Monegasque dredge with a rectangular heavy iron frame, 120 by 30 centimetres, was lowered over the stern. Almost 3000 metres of cable was paid out before the dredge rested on the sea floor at a depth of 1720 metres. The dredge was dragged for ten minutes along the ocean floor. It was a poor catch, consisting mainly of grey ooze and a few rock specimens.

Assisted by Doc Ingram and Campbell, I began skinning the sea leopard. It was an enormous creature, weighing about a tonne, with a beautifully shaped head and a mouth full of sharp, cruel-looking teeth. Professor Johnston was standing by, excitedly waiting to examine the intestines for parasites. The pool in which the *Discovery* was drifting could be likened to a vast aquarium, occupied by fin and pike whales, seals, sea leopards and porpoising Adélie penguins. It was an interesting and unusual sight.

During the early hours of the 22nd, pack-ice began to close in on the pool. It was decided to reach open water again, north of the pack. A passage was forced to the north-west and at 11 A.M. the ship emerged into the open sea. Five days had now been spent waiting for the weather to clear sufficiently so that another flight could be made over the pack-ice. Sir Douglas was still hoping for an improvement in the weather but it seemed as far off as ever. The barometer was falling rapidly, the light breeze had backed to the north-east and had increased to a strength of

50 kilometres an hour. It was bitterly cold with continual snow falling and poor visibility.

The ship, drifting close to the fringe of the pack, was rolling steadily under the influence of an increasing swell running in from the north. Sparks Williams reported he had been in wireless communication with the whaling factory ship, *Neilsen Alonzo*, which was operating off the Queen Mary Land coast.

Skins of the sea leopard and crab-eater seal were removed and I spent the rest of the day removing the thick layers of blubber. Every vestige of fat has to be removed before the pelts can be preserved successfully. The blubber is stripped with a sharp knife, usually in short bursts as every now and again feeling has to be restored in the hands which become half frozen with the intense cold.

The next day was spent in riding out rough seas which developed from the gale-force winds. The weather had deteriorated instead of improving; the wind, veering to the south-east, had increased in strength to about 80 kilometres an hour. The ship, rolling heavily, was taking on board tonnes of water over the gunwales and forecastle head; the decks were awash. As a precaution against worse conditions, we steamed slowly north for about eight hours. The ship was then turned and headed back towards the edge of the pack.

There was a decided improvement in the weather throughout the night and by morning the wind had dropped. The sun was making valiant efforts to shine through clearing low clouds. A heavy swell prevented any thought of the plane taking to the air, but with that possibility still in mind, the ship was headed into loose pack and the engines stopped. Sir Douglas was anxious to make a survey flight to the south as we were close to where Wilkes had reported sighting land in 1840 which he charted and named Budd's Land. We found from our observations that land did not exist in his charted position but lay well to the south.

Doc Ingram, Simmers and I bagged and stowed about two tonnes of ashes. For some time, ashes from the fires, instead of being thrown over the ship's side, were bagged and stowed in empty coal holds and acted as ballast. One tonne of ash was usually the residue from the consumption of five tonnes of coal.

During the afternoon a vertical station was worked in loose drifting pack. Depth of the sea floor was recorded as 1940 metres. Trouble occurred when a plankton net, at 460 metres, drifted and fouled the wire of a deep-water bottle being lowered from the forecastle head. It became jammed and the untangling resulted in a loss of 275 metres of wire from the drum of the plankton net winch. The water bottle and net were not damaged. Because of the mishap the station took almost seven hours to complete.

The weather had not improved on the 25th. Low-lying clouds persisted, light snow was falling and a light breeze continued from the south-east. The ship was still drifting in the pack, rolling steadily under the influence of a moderate northerly swell. Most species of Antarctic breeding birds had continually gathered around the ship in large numbers. Falla was interested in the increasing numbers of Arctic terns and during the previous days had recorded flocks of more than a thousand birds. Four immature females and one male were shot while resting on a nearby ice-floe. They were skinned and added to the collection.

Our position at noon was 64°55'S, 111°40'E, practically the same as the previous day except for a few miles of westerly drift. A sounding at 11.30 A.M. recorded depth of the sea floor as 2270 metres. The ship later moved out of the pack and proceeded on a westerly course following the pack-ice edge which was becoming more broken with occasional leads which, however, did not extend any great distances to the south.

Sir Douglas pointed out a marked change of sky conditions on the southern horizon, mainly to the south and south-east, which, in his opinion, indicated the presence of land. We agreed, for land was certainly lying in that direction, but as later events proved it was in latitude 67°, a great distance from the *Discovery* at that time. We had spent a lot of time in this area and Sir Douglas was determined to make a further flight before moving west to Queen Mary Land. He was anxious to make an air survey of the coast of Knox Land, sighted and charted by Wilkes in 1840. At 9.30 P.M., the ship was again headed into pack-ice and the engines stopped to await suitable flying conditions.

The ship remained stationary in the pack through the night. She pushed her way clear into open sea the next morning and we proceeded west along the edge of the pack. A variable wind was blowing from the south-east; snow was falling continuously and there was a confused swell. The ship's speed was reduced to slightly less than two knots at 10 A.M. while a large and a small net were towed over the stern. Catches in both nets were excellent. At 2.30 P.M. there was a spectacular rise in the sea floor from 2520 to 820 metres. Shallow readings continued through the day, varying from 490 to 477 metres.

Longitude 109°22' east was reached at midday. The sky remained heavily overcast with no signs of the low-lying clouds clearing. Snow had been falling continuously and visibility was extremely limited. Early in the afternoon the ship was again stopped while our small Monegasque-type dredge was lowered over the stern. Depth of the sea

Mawson revisits huts built during his 1911–14 expedition at Cape Denison, Commonwealth Bay.
(Photo: S. Campbell.)

floor was recorded as 490 metres. The dredge rested on the bottom after 900 metres of cable had been paid out. It was dragged for five minutes and then hauled in. The net was full but its contents were covered with a fine grey mud. There was no dearth of volunteers to clean and sort the dredged material. Time was beginning to hang heavily and any activity was welcomed as a respite from continual games of huff patience. Introduced by Doc Ingram, this game had proved popular with most scientists and helped to pass the time. Sieving off the mud revealed many interesting specimens including a large sponge, a great number of crinoids (sea lilies) and a variety of rocks.

Since leaving King George V Land we had been separated from the land by a belt of impenetrable pack-ice 60 to 90 miles wide. The general feeling was that we should sail west, make southing and continue with our exploratory programme. However, late in the evening the sky began to clear and the ship once again entered the pack and the engines were stopped, in the hope that a flight would be possible the next day.

The south-easterly wind had freshened in the early hours of the next morning. The ship cleared from the pack and with sails set headed to the west. Although visibility was improving, a fairly heavy swell running in from the north-west against the south-easterly wind was causing a confused, rough sea. We were still in shallow waters and soundings averaged about 550 metres throughout the day. At 8 P.M., the ocean floor had descended to 1440 metres, but two hours later rose again to 490 metres. A dredging was carried out in the morning in about 510 metres with excellent results. The catch included a variety of life dominated by many echinoderms (sea lilies, starfish, brittle-stars and a single heart-urchin).

Sir Douglas decided that a flight should be made shortly after midday. Eric Douglas agreed to make an attempt although conditions were unfavourable. Sails were taken in and the *Discovery* came to a stop in the shelter of a large iceberg. The seaplane was lowered overboard and Sir Douglas, with Eric Douglas as pilot, set off. As they taxied out the plane had to be stopped on several occasions when the floats became temporarily buried under water. Eric Douglas said in his report of the flight, " . . . early in the take-off run it became evident I would need all my skill to get the plane off safely, for as we picked up speed and planed over the tops of the swells it was thrown repeatedly into the air without proper flying speed. It was touch and go, but we made it with about 100 yards to spare before we cleared the dangerous pack-ice . . . "

Climbing through clouds to 6000 feet, they could see a thick layer of unbroken cloud below them which extended to the horizon in all directions, except to the south where a line of clear sky showed up in strong contrast. They flew south for about 20 miles and sighted what appeared to be undulating ice-covered land in the distance. After about 45 minutes Eric glided the plane down through clouds, located the ship and made a successful landing close by. The ship was rolling badly and it was obvious we would have difficulty in hoisting the plane on board.

With the ship steaming slowly ahead into the swell, Eric Douglas, on his third attempt, taxied under the lifting tackle and Sir Douglas hooked on the plane's lifting sling. At the same time a big wave lifted the plane before it could be hauled up. It then dropped as the wave passed, stopping with a violent jerk as the slack tightened. Part of the lifting sling on the plane broke away, leaving it hanging vertically with one wing and the tail under water.

Sir Douglas fell into the sea but managed to grasp a strut while Eric scrambled on to the nose. A few minutes later the lifting sling broke away completely and the plane fell into the water and began to drift astern. The motor boat was hurriedly lowered, picked up Sir Douglas and Eric and towed the plane back to the ship. It was finally hoisted on board looking a complete wreck. The damage was found to be not nearly as severe as it appeared and the airmen and Hurley set about repairing it. The whole exciting incident was filmed by Hurley.

It was an unfortunate ending to a disappointing flight. Nothing was achieved except the reporting of a white line sighted to the south, probably land in the vicinity of Knox Land. However, Sir Douglas did observe that the western pack-ice edge trended slightly in a northerly direction and the pack was studded with numerous large grounded bergs, some of them having the appearance of low ice-capped islands. Later in the evening a course was set to the west and we were definitely on our way to Queen Mary Land.

At about 1 A.M. we were passing through a vast accumulation of the grounded icebergs, observed from the air by Sir Douglas. Many were badly weathered into irregular shapes; all of mammoth size and averaging at least 60 metres in height. The majority were embedded in the pack and the others in open water. One ice mass, estimated to be about 25 kilometres long, was almost certainly an ice-capped island, but heavy pack prevented a close examination. All hands were on deck photographing the magnificent and picturesque scenery. Shortly before midday, a large dome-shaped ice mass, 320 metres high, was observed in the pack at a distance of about 20 miles. It was definitely an ice-capped island and was named Bowman Island. Its position is 65°12'S, 103°15'E.

Changes in the depth of the sea floor were interesting. A sounding taken each hour during the day showed a rise in the morning from 1370 to 665 metres, falling to 1435 metres towards midday. It was followed by a substantial rise to only 325 metres at midnight. It was an area where one would expect to find islands.

Later in the afternoon we had cleared the accumulation of grounded bergs. All sails were set, including topsails, and with a following wind, good progress was made on our westerly course. Sparks had been in wireless communication with the whaling factory ship *Neilsen Alonzo*, operating off the Termination Ice Tongue some distance west of our present position. The captain had offered to provide us with 25 tonnes of coal.

Nearing midnight the south-easterly wind backed to the east and increased to gale force; big seas developed and heavy snow fell. The weather worsened during the night and next morning the wind was maintaining a steady 100 kilometres an hour with gusts of at least 110 kilometres an hour. The ship was forced to run before it and headed north-west, making seven knots with bare poles. Huge, precipitous waves continually crashed on board; the ship rolled alarmingly, registering a maximum roll of 43 degrees. Later, she was turned into the wind and plunging waves, barely maintaining steering speed with the engines turning over at full speed.

The viciousness of the seas was appalling. Captain MacKenzie suggested the use of oil to calm the seas. Grandpa Oom and I volunteered to attempt the exercise. We were given an 18-litre tin of oil, punctured to allow its contents to drip through. Our instructions were to lash it to the bow railing. After a hazardous climb, in between rolling and pitching of the ship, we reached the forecastle head and lashed the tin in position.

We very soon realised that MacKenzie's suggestion sadly lacked forethought. The dripping oil was swept back horizontally by the strong wind, covering the forecastle head, deck and bridge. It smothered MacKenzie, Colbeck and the two men on the helm with a thin coating of oil, transforming them into negroes. It was a mad, unreal scene. Grandpa and I, every time the ship rolled, had to grab the railings or deck fixtures and hang on. Grandpa on one occasion misjudged and slid across the oily surface, almost disappearing overboard as he grabbed and held on to the railing.

In the meantime, one of the more experienced seamen attached a thick wad of cloth to the end of a line. This was handed to us with instructions to immerse it in oil and lower it over the bow, then occasionally haul the wad in and replenish the oil. This was carried out with an immediate result. Seas surrounding the ship attained a smooth, oily surface, but otherwise there was no spectacular or effective change. The operation "oil on troubled waters" was finally abandoned. Several days later the crew were still cleaning oil from the decks and ship's forward fixtures.

At midday we were again running before the gale to the north-west. Good progress had been made aided by the strong following wind.

Our position was 64°02'S, 99°20'E. Throughout the day readings from the echo sounder recorded a gradual drop in the sea bed from 523 to 2120 metres.

Sparks was still in communication with the *Neilsen Alonzo* and learnt that her position was 64°S, 98°E. We passed due south of her, at no great distance, at about 4 P.M. Under the stormy conditions, no thought was given to approaching her. Late in the evening the wind eased slightly and the ship was manoeuvred to lie in a sheltered position behind a large tabular berg. However, strong, gusty eddying winds made our position untenable and we moved out once again to run before the gale. Seas were mountainous and threatened to break over the ship's stern as she surfed into the troughs. The scientific staff, keeping watches, assisted the helmsman and also kept a lookout for icebergs. Continually falling snow limited visibility.

It was estimated early next morning that we were about 15 miles north of the charted position of Termination Ice Tongue which projects from the coast for more than 160 kilometres. Weather conditions had slightly moderated although the barometer was still falling slowly. At 6 A.M., the ship was headed to the south-west, still running before the strong wind, with engines just turning over.

Our course was altered at 11 A.M. to the south-east to gain the shelter of the ice tongue. On reaching its charted position there was no sign of the tongue, only open water with scattered bergs as far as the eye could see. The ship was then headed south from latitude 63°40' south and after passing innumerable grounded bergs, reached 64°13'S, 97°E. Depth of the sea floor had gradually increased to 3270 metres from 4 A.M. to midday. The sea floor then commenced to rise to 1680 metres at 10.30 P.M., shoaling to 390 metres at 11.45 P.M., a sudden rise of 1290 metres.

Campbell, Eric Douglas and Hurley were spending long hours each day repairing the seaplane and it was beginning to regain its old appearance. The fuel tank, crumpled almost beyond recognition, was repaired by Hurley, a miraculous job which gained the admiration of all hands.

The ship had stopped, during the early hours of the 31st, amongst a group of large grounded bergs. There was a marked and welcome change in the weather. A light wind was blowing from the south-west; the sky was clearing with the sun occasionally breaking through and the sea was calm. The ship was literally surrounded in all directions by bergs of various shapes and sizes. These may have been remnants of the Termination Ice Tongue which had obviously disappeared since it was last seen 17 years earlier by Mawson's 1911–14 expedition. It either broke up or separated from the continental ice-cap and drifted north as a gigantic berg. Hurley subscribed to the latter theory because he remembered reading that a few years previously a whaler had reported seeing an iceberg about 200 kilometres in length in an area north of our position.

The ice tongue had been most effective in holding back the pack from encroaching on the Queen Mary Land coast and the adjacent Haswell Island. Its disappearance meant a passage had to be forced through the pack to reach land. Sir Douglas had received instructions to land there and raise the flag.

The ship continued on a westerly course, skirting the pack-ice edge until 5.30 P.M. when an effort was made to force our way south. At this point we were approximately 60 miles from the coast. After penetrating heavy close pack for about six hours it was seen from the crow's nest that further progress was impossible. With some difficulty the ship was turned, we steamed back to open water and continued our passage west.

At noon the following day the ship was directly north of Queen Mary Land and a position where a western party of Mawson's 1911–14 expedition had established a base hut. However, all thoughts of reaching it through the intervening compact pack-ice had to be abandoned. This was a great disappointment to Sir Douglas and the scientists, for we had been looking forward to visiting the hut, if it was still standing, and also two emperor penguin colonies discovered by members of the party in 1913. One of these is on an island they discovered, named Haswell Island, and was occupied by at least 7500 emperor penguins. Further to the west they discovered Masson Island on which a colony of emperors numbered about 20,000. Of these, 7000 were chicks from the previous winter's nesting.

Emperor penguins, unlike all other penguin species, breed during the winter months when temperatures may reach minus 50°C or more, and blizzards regularly sweep down the ice-slopes with terrific velocities. They are regal looking birds with attractive golden coloured ear patches. They stand 120 centimetres in height and average about 32 kilograms in weight. A record weight is 43 kilograms.

Emperors lay a single egg during the months of May or June. Only the males incubate, standing erect on an ice surface with the egg resting on their feet and covered by a flap of loose skin. The birds remain huddled together, living on their reserve supply of fat for at least two months. The females then return from feeding at sea, crossing many miles of frozen sea to the rookery where they rejoin their partners.

If the egg is not hatched it is transferred to the feet of the female. If presented with a newly hatched chick, kept alive by food stored in the male's crop, she takes over the feeding and care of it. The male, who has by this time lost considerable weight, then sets out to reach open water at least 50 miles or more to the north. After a month or two swimming and feeding in the open sea, he regains his normal weight. It is then time to return to the rookery and his partner. Walking and tobogganing, he crosses the sea-ice and arrives at the beginning of the summer months. The ice begins to break up and journeys to open water to secure food are much shorter. Finally, the parents take their growing offspring, now clothed with thick down, to the threshold of the open sea.

No other bird species in the world has to breed under such extraordinary conditions. Chick mortality is exceptionally high. Eggs are broken as birds are blown over and over again by fierce blizzards. Many newly hatched chicks die from the severe cold and starvation when a parent fails to return. In many cases chicks are killed when females, who have lost their young, make savage attempts to snatch newly hatched chicks from other parents.

The ship continued on a course to the west, making good progress with a following wind blowing at about 40 kilometres an hour. Snow had been falling since early morning. The wind moderated in the mid-afternoon and the ship was turned into the pack and engines stopped. A vertical station was commenced at 7.30 P.M. and completed two hours later. Shallow waters had been left behind, depths of the sea floor ranging from 2780 to 2400 metres during the day. Afterwards the ship was made fast to a large floe and all hands assisted in icing ship. It was hard work but we all enjoyed ourselves as it invariably led to snowballs being hurled indiscriminately at all and sundry. The ship remained drifting with the pack during the night.

It was estimated our position was about 40 miles north of Drygalski Island, but with no chance of reaching it through the thick pack. Sir Douglas, worried by the loss of valuable time and diminishing coal stock, finally decided to leave the area and make haste to more unexplored coasts to the west. He was possibly frustrated, to some extent, by Captain MacKenzie's reluctance to venture the ship any great distance into heavy pack-ice.

Early on the morning of February 2, engines were started and the ship proceeded west through loose pack and lanes of open water. Snow was falling from low-lying grey clouds and a light breeze was coming in from the south-east; the sea was calm.

Simmers and Kennedy released a meteorological balloon to observe upper air currents, but it was soon lost to sight behind low clouds. Most hands were engaged in moving 28 tonnes of coal briquettes from No. 3 starboard hold to empty main bunkers. A long chain was formed and briquettes were quickly thrown from hand to hand for several hours, leaving us dog-tired, but pleased with the speed of the task. Accumulated ashes were then bagged and taken below as additional ballast.

Our position at midday was 64°57'S, 90°21'E, and we were about

100 miles from the coast. Depth of the sea floor was 3040 metres. Later in the afternoon the pack gradually became more broken up with open leads. The ship was headed south at 6 P.M. and, forcing her way, made fair progress for six hours. She was then faced with consolidated ice and came to a halt. Seals and Adélie penguins were prevalent. Emperor penguins, only occasionally observed previously, were more numerous during the day. Groups of three to nine birds were frequently seen on the larger ice-floes. At this point the greater number of birds were well-developed young, indicating the continued existence of the rookeries at Haswell and Masson Islands.

During the night the ship had moved into more navigable ice and was punching her way to the south-west in the morning. Thick falling snow restricted visibility to such an extent that we stopped for four hours until the weather cleared. At 7 A.M. the ship again got under way and headed south in between large grounded bergs and broken pack. An estimate of our position was 55 miles from the coast.

Coaling was resumed and 30 tonnes of briquettes from No. 4 hold on the port side were transferred to empty bunkers.

Our noon position was 65°39'S, 89°31'E, our farthest south since January 9. A sudden rise of the sea floor was recorded at 3 P.M. from 2288 to 1390 metres. Shoaling rapidly continued until the depth was only 395 metres at 5.30 P.M.

The ship later steamed into a wide open pool; engines were stopped and a dredging was carried out in 400 metres. Our large dredge reached the bottom after 600 metres of cable had been paid out and was dragged for 10 minutes at a speed of one knot. When hauled in it was found that the cod end of the net had been caught over the mouth of the dredge and prevented the entrance of any catch. Vertical nets were then run (Station 100) and completed at 11 P.M.

I was awakened early the next morning by the engines starting up and the ship's movements as she got under way. To my surprise the ship had turned and we were retracing our track of the previous day. Coming on deck Sir Douglas had noticed ice closing in on the pool and suggested to MacKenzie that the ship should force her way back north to the open sea. It was a move readily supported by the captain, even though a good water sky was visible to the south.

At 7.30 A.M. the ship had steamed into loose pack with a few scattered bergs and was making good progress. The weather was fine except for an overcast sky and light falling snow. At this stage Sir Douglas admitted that perhaps he had made a hasty decision to turn north. Some of the scientific staff transferred about seven tonnes of briquettes from the sail locker to a bunker. Others bagged ashes, which had accumulated, and stowed them in No. 3 starboard hold, now emptied of coal.

Adélie penguins were in great numbers while many emperor penguins were either resting on ice-floes or diving in the sea, feeding on squid or krill. Observations have proved that emperors can dive to depths of 200 metres and can remain under water for up to 10 minutes. Most of the flying species known to breed on the continent were identified and listed by Falla as they followed the ship and circled overhead.

Our course had brought us well north to latitude 63°25′ at midday. Late in the evening, the ship moved in alongside a large floe, was made fast and the engines stopped. For some time now we had lost the midnight sun and were gradually returning to night and day. It was now quite dark at 10 P.M. and light again by about 2 A.M.

At daylight the ship started off and began following the pack-ice edge which was trending to the north-west. Officers on watch were asked to keep a look-out for lanes of open water leading south as a water sky indicated open water apparently at no great distance. Max Stanton, our cheery Chief Officer, admitted that while on watch he had passed a good lead at 7 A.M., but for some strange reason had not drawn attention to it.

The distance run for the 24 hours was 180 miles and our position at noon was 64°44′S, 86°39′E. Depth of the sea floor was 3306 metres. There was a great improvement in the weather; clouds had partly dispersed and a welcome warm sun was shining. Snow had ceased falling and visibility was perfect.

A Norwegian whale chaser, *Ornen III*, steaming east, passed quite close to the *Discovery*, but little interest was shown, and no signals were exchanged. It could have been an everyday event on Sydney Harbour. A few hours later another chaser was sighted in the distance, towing a whale, and it was also steaming to the east. There was no sign of a factory ship and Sparks had had no wireless communication with her. At 9 P.M. the ship was stopped and a vertical station was run in very open pack. Lights were rigged and work finished at midnight.

Early on the 6th we continued north-west, skirting pack-ice which later formed a wide tongue extending well to the north. To make westing, the ship was headed into the tongue, finally emerging into a great bay at least six miles across to its western boundary. Our course was then altered to the south.

Good progress was made through loose floes into open water when shortly afterwards a vessel was sighted to the south from the crow's nest. Steaming closer two vessels were observed: a collier, the *Listris*, and a factory ship, the *Falk*. When within hailing distance Sir Douglas was invited on board the *Falk*. The motor boat was lowered over the side and Sir Douglas set out. His main objective was to obtain a supply of coal. Twenty tonnes were offered.

While the yards were being cockbilled, a boat from the *Falk* came across with instructions to move in alongside and to hurry as both vessels were ready to leave; the *Listris* was to leave for Durban for another cargo of coal and the *Falk* to the east to continue whaling. All hands were on deck awaiting events when Simmers said, "I can hardly believe my eyes." Two women were looking over the rail of the *Falk*; one with bare arms and the other in a thin dress.

A number of embarrassing incidents now eventuated. MacKenzie had misunderstood the instructions and brought the *Discovery* alongside the *Listris*, the wrong ship. There was no comment and the *Listris* prepared to transfer 20 tonnes of her coal. When made fast, two whale carcasses acting as buffers kept the *Discovery* too far away from the cranes to lower the coal on our decks. The captain of the *Listris* suggested taking one of the whales away so that our ship could move in closer. Even though the sea was a flat calm MacKenzie refused to coal if it was taken away; he was rapidly losing his temper. A voice from the *Falk*, through a hailer, told MacKenzie that if he didn't follow instructions we would get no coal. Finally, doing as he was told, 20 tonnes of coal were soon transferred. All hands on the *Discovery* were working like demons, bagging coal and disposing of it in various parts of the ship.

While coaling was proceeding, the captain of the *Falk*, Lars Andersen, who was also manager and part owner of the whaling company, came on board with his secretary. He told Sir Douglas that 40 factory ships and 240 chasers were operating off the Antarctic coast.

At 6 P.M. the *Discovery* cast off from the *Listris* and we proceeded south. Several hours later the ship was stopped to allow Campbell and Eric Douglas to take off in the seaplane; the first flight since it was repaired. The plane flew with a slight list to the right, but was considered by the airmen to be airworthy. They ascended to 1000 feet and on their return had little to report. Heavy pack continued as far as they could see for about 40 miles to the south with no sign of open water. After the plane had been hoisted on board the ship proceeded to the north-west, following an extension of pack-ice in that direction. Towards 10 P.M. the moon came up — the first sight of it for many months.

Next morning the ship was continuing a course to the north-west in open water. The pack-ice edge, instead of forming a definite line of demarcation, now consisted of many small embayments and tongues of ice extending for varying distances. At 11 A.M. the ship was headed into an ice tongue of heavy floes, finally emerging into open water stretching away to the south. Our course was then altered and the ship steamed

Emperor penguin rookery near Mawson, Mac Robertson Land.
(By courtesy of the Antarctic Division. Photo: R. Wills.)

south towards a water sky to the delight of all hands.

At midday, after an alteration in our course, we had made good mileage to the west, reaching longitude 81° east. Only a few miles had been gained in a southerly direction. A sounding was recorded at 3600 metres. The weather remained fine although an easterly wind had freshened to an average strength of about 50 kilometres an hour. A fairly heavy swell running in from the north-west caused the ship to roll and wallow in the troughs. Although the sea was free of pack-ice, many bergs of varying sizes and shapes, mainly tabular, were scattered in all directions.

A line of heavy compacted pack-ice forced an alteration in our course to the west late in the afternoon. Skirting its edge for some distance, we came to an area where it had broken up and the ship, pushing her way through, again entered open water and continued south. Bonus Child, who was on watch at midnight, reported an unexpected sight this far south — a ship's navigation lights. He estimated the vessel, undoubtedly a chaser, to be about six miles north of our position and steaming east.

The ship continued south in open water the next morning. The only change in the weather was an increase in the easterly wind which averaged about 65 kilometres an hour. Our distance run was 138 miles and our position at midday was 66°04′S, 78°34′E. Good southing had been made and was continuing.

Earlier in the morning we had seen several chasers and a large factory ship, the *Tafelburgh*; five hours later we passed one of Lever Brothers' fleet, the *Southern Empress*. From what we could see there was little activity on the flensing decks and there were no whales tied astern. Sir Douglas had been in wireless communication with both vessels with his usual request for coal. He received an offer from the captain of the *Tafelburgh* of 50 tonnes which could only be made available on March 1, about three weeks away. This, of course, was unacceptable.

Steady progress to the south continued until we reached latitude 66°12′ east, when a line of solid pack forced the ship west. At 6.30 P.M., another factory ship hove in sight which proved to be the *Thorshammer*. Flags were dipped as we passed close by. Captain Lars Andersen had told Sir Douglas that she was operating in the area and from all reports there were more ships than whales.

During the day we crossed the southerly course of the *Discovery* from Heard Island on our first voyage on December 13, 1930. On that occasion we had reached latitude 67°30′ south when Sir Douglas sighted

Open pack-ice off Queen Mary Land, photographed from the mainmast of the Discovery.
(Photo: S. Campbell.)

what appeared to be land: rising ice-slopes far to the south. The ship then had to turn north-west to escape heavy pack. Good progress was being made to the west with occasional southing until darkness intervened. The ship was then stopped and we drifted until daybreak. For the first time on the voyage we were south of the Antarctic Circle.

It was a clear morning with a light breeze from the south-east, a clear sky and bright sunshine. Visibility was perfect and conditions were ideal for flying. The *Discovery* had got under way at first light and pushed through slack pack into open water. A fairly big swell coming in from the open sea prevented the seaplane from taking off but after moving into the lee of an immense iceberg it took off with Sir Douglas and Campbell in 66°30′S, 76°E.

At 6000 feet, Sir Douglas observed solid pack-ice stretching south as far as the eye could see. He saw what appeared to be a line of ice-capped land stretching to the south-east. To the west, a belt of broken pack extended north about 20 miles from the ship, but beyond that there was every appearance of open water leading south. Smoke from the factory ship, *New Savilla*, which we knew was operating in that area, was also seen by Sir Douglas.

Following the return of the plane at 4 P.M., the ship continued through loose pack until reaching an open pool five hours later. A vertical station was worked until midnight and we again proceeded slowly on our course.

At daybreak the ship emerged from loose pack-ice into open water. A course was set for the position of the *New Savilla*. Soundings from the previous day had shown a gradual rise of the sea floor from 3502 metres, which continued through the night. At 4 A.M., there was a marked decrease from 2020 to 1188 metres, followed two hours later to 433 metres. These shallow readings continued with only minor changes through the day.

The ship was stopped at 7.30 A.M. and a small dredge, attached to 350 metres of cable, was paid out before the dredge reached the bottom. It was dragged for eight minutes and then hauled to the surface, the complete dredging taking 80 minutes. The net contained mainly various rock types of continental origin but also included specimens representative of several invertebrate groups.

At about 10 A.M. we finally arrived off the *New Savilla*, which was flying the British flag. Sir Douglas went on board to meet the captain. He returned about an hour later and informed us that his request for coal had been refused; they had none to spare, but Norwegian vessels working off the Kemp Land coast would almost certainly make some available. He was also told that 50 miles to the west land could be reached by passing through a sea covered with icebergs but free of pack.

The ship was then headed south and steaming at full speed

continued until confronted by scattered pack which appeared navigable. Sir Douglas decided to send the plane up to reconnoitre before making a decision on our next move. Eric Douglas and Grandpa Oom went aloft, but low-lying clouds prevented an ascent of more than 2000 feet. After a 30-minute flight they returned and reported that broken pack stretched south as far as they could see. They also said there was a complete absence of icebergs. A decision was made by Sir Douglas to steam south-west. Bird life was prolific and in the pack many sea leopards, far more than we had seen at any one time previously, were resting on the floe-ice. Three crab-eater seals were noticed asleep on one floe alongside a sea leopard, in the sea a ferocious and deadly enemy.

The ship steamed through the night in clear weather at her maximum speed of about five knots. At 7 A.M. we came to a barrier of large grounded tabular bergs, rising to heights of at least 60 metres. Passing through them, we entered an open ice-free sea stretching away to the south. We continued on and sighted land to the west at 9 A.M. Snow covered, with ice-slopes rising from the coast to about 600 metres, it extended in a north and south direction. This was the eastern extremity of Mac Robertson Land, seen from the crow's nest the previous year.

Moving in towards the coast, the ship steamed south at about five knots until, at midday, we were faced with a belt of pack-ice and bergs. Forcing her way through, the ship emerged again into clear water extending south as far as could be seen from the deck. We were now heading into a moderate swell from the south-east and a light south-westerly breeze. It was a beautiful day, sunny with perfect visibility. Deck temperature was minus 29°C. The sea was too rough for the plane to take off and we continued south until the ship was stopped in the lee of a big iceberg at 5 P.M. Our position was 68°14'S, 70°10'E.

It was decided that a flight should be attempted. The plane was swung overboard and Campbell, with Oom as observer, taxied out to a position where he could take off in the restricted area of sheltered water. Campbell gained flying speed just before reaching a patch of brash ice. He cleared it and gradually ascended, making off in a north-westerly direction.

During their absence a plankton station was worked in 268 metres. Oblique tow nettings were not carried out. A feature of this station was the extraordinarily low temperature of the sea water, which, no doubt, accounted for the great number of dead fish floating on the surface. Some of them were added to the collection. They were mainly 12 to 15 centimetres in length and too small for eating.

In the meantime Hurley, with a crew member, had set off in the dinghy to investigate a large opening on a nearby iceberg. It proved to be an ice-cave, eroded by weathering. Its entrance was 12 metres high and 15 metres wide. They rowed in for about 50 metres from where Hurley took some spectacular pictures, including one of the *Discovery* in the distance.

The airmen returned after a flight of 90 minutes with interesting information. They had ascended to 6000 feet and flew north-west for about 20 miles to the coast which forms the eastern boundary of Mac Robertson Land. Its northern extremity, named Cape Darnley by Sir Douglas, was in open sea extending away to the west and south. They then flew south over the ice-covered land which has a plateau surface about 1200 metres in height. Campbell had dropped a flag at 68° 11′S, 69° 15′E, a position directly west of the *Discovery*.

Flying further south, they then flew due east. On this stretch they saw no high land to the south. It is now known they were looking across a vast ice shelf covering the sea for at least 160 kilometres to the south. After flying east for 50 miles they observed ice-covered land about 900 metres in height which extended north for about 100 kilometres to Cape Amery, also named by Sir Douglas.

From that point, high ice-covered land stretched away to the east. It was named Princess Elizabeth Land. Its boundaries were charted as 86° and 73° of east longitude. Near its western border a group of rocky peaks was named the Munro Kerr Mountains. This land was previously seen by Sir Douglas and Campbell during a flight on February 9, when in longitude 75° 57′ east the appearance of high land was recorded about 90 nautical miles to the south-east. The present flight proved that the *Discovery* was lying in a huge embayment of open sea which extended south, including the ice shelf, for about 160 miles. Sir Douglas named it the MacKenzie Sea.

Late in the evening the ship got under way and steamed north-west. At midnight, several bottles of champagne were produced and the scientific staff celebrated the approach to new land.

At 4 A.M. on the 12th, the ship passed through a great congestion of large tabular icebergs. When these were cleared four hours later, we rounded Cape Darnley, the western headland of the MacKenzie Sea, and a course was set west along the Mac Robertson Land coast.

The weather was unchanged; bright sunshine and a calm sea, except for a freshening of the south-east breeze. In clear water the ship steamed close inshore along the glacier cliffs of the land. It was a spectacular sight; a sheer wall of sparkling ice, 45 metres in height, stretched east and west as far as the eye could see. Sloping gradually inland the ice-cap rose to 6000 metres. A landing was impossible. About 20 miles to the west, several mountain peaks could be seen projecting through the ice-cap.

At midday our position was 67° 08′S, 68° 40′E. We had been well south of the Antarctic Circle since early the previous day. We had been passing over a shallow undulating sea floor with three distinct shoalings; the shallowest reading was 45 metres at 9.30 P.M.

In the afternoon the wind had increased from the south-east and the barometer showed signs of falling. The ship was stopped during the dark hours and remained drifting close to land until daybreak. At 6.30 A.M. on the 13th, the ship had reached a part of the coast where four steep rocky mountains rose to heights of 400 to 600 metres. One of these, named the Murray Monolith, rose steeply from the water's edge to 400 metres.

It was decided to attempt a landing. The motor boat was lowered overboard and a party, led by Sir Douglas, set out to reach the coast, about half a mile distant. A stiff wind was blowing at 70 kilometres an hour and a fairly big swell was running in from the north. We were soon covered with freezing spray; the temperature was minus 10°C. On reaching the shore, we found waves breaking on sloping rock and a heavy surge which threatened at any moment to crash the boat against projecting rocks, making a landing impossible. As we rose on a wave, Sir Douglas threw a proclamation, sealed in a canister, on to the sloping rock but it rolled back into the sea. It was retrieved and thrown high and dry on the second attempt.

The motor boat then returned to the ship and was hoisted on board. A dredging was later carried out in 145 metres. The catch proved to be a remarkably rich one, including sponges, ascidians (sea-squirts), sea-spiders, starfish, marine worms and several erratics. The dredging was completed at 8.30 A.M.

After cruising along the coast for a short distance we hove to nearby a second mountain which rose straight from the sea to a height of more than 300 metres. A landing seemed possible and the boat was again lowered and a party set off. We found a likely spot to land in a small cove surrounded by steeply rising cliffs except for a platform sloping at an angle of about 45 degrees from the water level. A landing was made on this by leaping from the boat as it surged close in. Campbell was the first to land, followed on successive surges by Sir Douglas, Falla, Hurley and myself. The others missed their opportunities and had to move the boat out to await our return.

The shore party clambered up the rocky cliff face to a level area of jumbled rocks where the flag was raised. A second copy of the proclamation was read by Sir Douglas, sealed in a canister and deposited at the base of the flag pole. It claimed land extending continuously from Adélie Land westward to Mac Robertson Land and off-lying islands, including the islands of Drygalski, Hordern, David, Masson, Henderson and Haswell, situated between meridia 138° and 60° east of Greenwich and south of latitude 64° as far as the South Pole.

We were permitted to observe the bird life while Sir Douglas collected rock specimens. The rock on which we landed, named the Scullin Monolith, supported a surprising population of birds, particularly Adélie penguins. All accessible slopes of the rocky foreshore were crowded with them while steep winding tracks led to many colonies hundreds of metres above sea level. Similar crowding had been observed on the Murray Monolith and Falla estimated the penguin population in both areas to be at least 300,000. Other nesting sites were those of Antarctic, silver-grey, and snow petrels. The breeding season was almost over and most chicks were in similar stages of development.

We returned to the landing spot where the boat was brought in and after many hesitations we jumped on board and set off for the ship which had moved further out to sea. At midday, the motor boat had been hoisted on to its staging and once again we were on our way west, following a spectacular coast of sheer ice-cliffs with occasional rocky outcrops. We had travelled 70 miles since noon the previous day and our position was 67°45'S, 66°58'E. We were passing many small islets and grounded bergs. From time to time the echo sounder indicated the presence of shoals and submerged reefs. At 3 P.M. an exposed reef, over which waves were crashing, was sighted 15 miles offshore and named Martin's Reef after the ship's bosun. Shortly afterwards we passed a large needle-like rock, rising about six metres above sea level. The ship was stopped nearby and a dredging was carried out in 220 metres. We then continued to the west.

Charting the coastline and inland mountain peaks kept Oom exceptionally busy while Sir Douglas named prominent features. Cape Fletcher was named after me in 67°41'S, 65°38'E. I hope it remains in position and does not drift away to the north as some coastal projections have been known to do. Inland we could see the ice-cap gradually rising to a plateau surface of about 1200 metres and a number of rocky peaks at least 2000 metres above sea level.

At 8.30 P.M., a reading of only nine metres caused alarm; the engines were stopped and the ship allowed to drift, until the next reading recorded a depth of 180 metres. Captain MacKenzie, who lately had been showing signs of strain, accused Sir Douglas of running the ship into danger. At 11 P.M. the ship was stopped and allowed to drift amongst a group of grounded bergs. The wind, still blowing from the south-east, had moderated to about 40 kilometres an hour.

On the morning of February 14, the ship was standing about 25 nautical miles out from the coast. Clearly visible about 14 kilometres inland, were four distinct mountain ranges extending from the coast in a south-westerly direction and with elevations from 820 to 1200 metres. These proved to be the Henderson, David, Casey and Masson Ranges, sighted on our first voyage.

The wind was freshening from the south-east and bad weather was expected. Coming abreast of the mountain ranges but well offshore, we came to a large number of rocky snow-covered islets ranging in height from five to 50 metres. Grounded bergs were also scattered in all directions. At 7.30 A.M. the depth of the sea floor rapidly shoaled again from 180 to nine metres. There were many anxious moments until the ship, slowly moving ahead, was again in 180 metres.

The wind had freshened considerably at midday and we continued south-west towards a section of the coast showing rocky outcrops and two outstanding rocky headlands. Far away inland to the south-south-west three more high peaks were seen and were estimated to be at least 1500 metres high.

By mid-afternoon the wind had increased to full gale force and a rough, turbulent sea was running. Surrounded by islets, grounded bergs and occasional shoaling waters, the ship was in a dangerous position. During the rest of the day and night the scientific staff took watches, lookouts were doubled and help was given on the lee helm. The ship was pitching and rolling madly with big seas breaking on board and sweeping the decks. An uncomfortable night was spent with little or no sleep.

The gale still raged the next day. Battling against 100-kilometre-an-hour winds with much stronger gusts, the ship sheltered in the lee of grounded bergs. The rest of the day and night was spent drifting away with the wind and then steaming back again to the bergs' shelter.

There was no change in the weather the next day. We were about 40 miles from the coast. At 10 A.M. a dredging was carried out in 180 metres and completed in an hour. The result was a net full of grey mud and very few organisms.

Eleven tonnes of coal briquettes were transferred from the sail locker to empty bunker pockets. Coal shortage was now a serious problem with our stock down to 120 tonnes. We were told by Sir Douglas that he had planned to remain in our present sheltered position until the weather improved, then return to the coast for a day or two before setting a course home to Australia.

MacKenzie had agreed to continue work on the Antarctic coast until our coal stock was down to 100 tonnes. On our return to Australia the previous year we had more than ample coal to spare. It was important that a correct tally of our coal supply be kept as every five tonnes over the agreed amount meant an important extra day's work in the Antarctic.

At 7 P.M. preparations were under way to fish with the large otter trawl in the sheltered water. Six hundred metres of cable was paid out and the trawl was then towed for an hour at a speed of little more than a knot. A magnificent catch resulted, including a variety of most interesting creatures. Outstanding specimens were an octopus with short tentacles and a body about 60 centimetres thick; 108 fish, similar in shape to a flathead except for a larger head; a variety of echinoderms, siliceous sponges and a profusion of bryozoa (sea-mats). A start was made sorting and preserving the material, which kept the zoologists working until near midnight.

The ship was still maintaining position behind the grounded bergs on the 17th. The barometer, which had started to rise the previous afternoon, was steady and the heavily overcast sky showed signs of clearing. The wind had eased slightly and fine weather was expected.

A start was made to transfer the remainder of the coal briquettes, estimated at 11 tonnes, from the sail locker to the bunkers. Professor Johnston was exempt; he was busily engaged in sorting the residue of the previous day's trawling.

Hurley, Simmers and Oom volunteered to form the first links in a working chain below while the rest of the staff completed the chain on deck. We had been throwing briquettes to one another for a surprisingly long time before the sail locker was emptied. Simmers explained later that the locker had originally held 42 tonnes instead of the 26 tonnes listed on the ship's loading papers. We had therefore handled about 25 tonnes.

At daybreak the ship was headed south towards a rocky cape. Although the wind had increased during the night, conditions were improving and visibility was perfect. At 10 A.M., about 30 miles from the coast, we came to a large area of numerous small rocky islets and grounded bergs. Soundings on the way in indicated an undulating sea floor with depths regularly changing between 1575 and 246 metres. Several shallow banks with readings as low as 80 metres were passed over.

Approaching the coast we had a good view of the mountainous Mac Robertson Land. This was the land seen from a distance the previous year, but not reached because of a vast area of solid pack-ice. The four mountain ranges inland, previously sighted and named, stood out in marked relief from the glistening ice-cap. Among the numerous scattered nunataks, one very prominent one, about 50 kilometres from the coast, was named the Mill Peak after a noted Antarctic historian. Its height was estimated to be about 2000 metres.

When the ship was about six miles from the coast, MacKenzie, obviously worried, wanted to stop the ship and suggested that the shore party proceed by motor boat. He was prevailed upon by Sir Douglas to move in closer. After slowly steaming past many islets and grounded bergs the ship was stopped in a sheltered position.

The shore party, accompanied by Second Officer Colbeck, set out in the motor boat towards the prominent cape, still a few miles away. It was named Cape Bruce by Sir Douglas.

A moderate swell was coming in from the north and difficulty in landing was anticipated. However, this did not eventuate. The coast was a magnificent sight with sheer ice-cliffs and many imposing rocky outcrops. We came to a narrow channel running between two rocky cliffs, which, on investigation, led into a beautifully protected small harbour about 100 metres across. On landing we discovered we were on an island separated from the mainland by a strip of water covered by loose ice-floes. It was impossible to cross. We stayed on the island for about 20 minutes while Sir Douglas made notes of the rock structures and Falla collected an emperor penguin and two Adélie penguins.

We left the small protected harbour and set out to find a landing spot on the mainland. After running west for about 30 minutes, along a coast on which it was impossible to land, we turned back to the east and finally came across a snug little harbour by passing in between two imposing steep rocky outcrops. Gliding across the millpond surface, we landed on a coarse gravel beach facing a narrow valley gradually rising inland.

At this stage we were told by Sir Douglas that Captain MacKenzie had been adamant that the shore party return to the ship within two hours. He was very worried because the ship was in uncharted waters and the great diversity of soundings, the many islets and grounded bergs made him determined to leave the coast well behind before the dark hours.

We were surprised and dismayed at this news and hurried up the valley to a height of about 60 metres, built a cairn and raised the flag while Sir Douglas read the same proclamation as on January 13. We then formed a hollow square and sang "God Save the King", which was followed by three cheers. Sir Douglas produced a bottle of champagne after the ceremony; some was sparingly poured over the cairn, the rest was drunk by expedition members and the empty bottle then placed in a crevice in the cairn. Campbell hoisted a flag of the RAAF.

The party now separated to make the most of the time at our disposal. Hurley, Simmers and Howard climbed inland to a height of about 150 metres, from where they enjoyed a panoramic view of the coast and adjoining sea. They observed the mountain ranges inland and innumerable mountain peaks projecting through the ice-cap. Bird life was scarce. Falla and I found only a single emperor penguin and about 50 Adélie penguins scattered around on the rocks. There was no sign of a rookery on Cape Bruce, but some distance to the east, several large Adélie rookeries were visible with the aid of binoculars. A varied series of rock specimens was collected: gneisses and schists, that is, altered granites and sedimentary rocks, of Pre-Cambrian geological age. They were extremely ancient rocks, deposited at least 3000 million years ago.

At last our time ashore was up and we set off down the valley to the boat. On the way Sir Douglas questioned a bulge in Campbell's Burberry. It was the empty champagne bottle that he had souvenired from the cairn. It was an unsuccessful attempt because he was told to return it.

We returned to the ship about an hour overdue and were faced with a hopping mad captain. Heated words passed between him and Sir Douglas, and even Colbeck, for no reason at all, received a tirade.

A Last Look at Antarctica

N O TIME WAS LOST in getting the ship under way and very soon we were heading north on the start of our long voyage to Tasmania. Late in the afternoon we were fortunate enough to witness the unusual spectacle of a large, tabular, green and white banded iceberg capsizing. As we passed close by, the berg began to slowly roll over until its flat surface was perpendicular and then, tilting a little further, it suddenly turned turtle with a loud splash and a great disturbance of the sea. It was still oscillating in the water until lost to sight about 20 minutes later. By 9 P.M. darkness was setting in but having reached fairly ice-free waters, we steamed slowly north through the night.

The weather was perfect on the 19th, with bright sunshine, a light breeze and a calm sea. In the distance, prominent nunataks and inland mountain ranges were still visible, but gradually disappearing from view. It was our final sight of the Antarctic and it was very doubtful whether any of us would ever see it again.

On account of our depleted coal stock, the lower and upper yards on the mainmast were rigged to increase the ship's sail area. These had been taken down to lessen wind resistance before leaving Cape Town on the first voyage and had been lashed on deck alongside the bulwarks. It was a hazardous task to be carried out at sea on a rolling ship, but it was successfully accomplished under the direction of Chief Officer Max Stanton.

Our position at midday was 66°29'S, 61°04'E. At 4.30 A.M. the ship passed over the last of the shallows — a depth of 150 metres; at midnight the depth had increased to 3815 metres.

Late in the evening we saw a magnificent auroral display of pale greyish beams of light shooting up high in the sky from the southern horizon. Changing into curtain-like drapes, they gradually faded only to be replaced by others.

The weather remained unchanged the next morning as we proceeded on a north-easterly course. Falla and I finished skinning the last of the penguins collected on Cape Bruce. The complete bird collection secured during both voyages totalled 300 skins, 67 spirit speci-

The Discovery *is seen in the distance from the inside of an iceberg cave.*
(By courtesy of the Mawson Institute. Photo: F. Hurley.)

mens, 105 eggs, samples of stomach contents and comprehensive field notes compiled by Falla. Most of the zoological specimens had been packed in cases and stowed in a hold. Work in the laboratory was now at a standstill until further specimens came to light from further dredgings and plankton stations.

At midday our distance run for the 24 hours was 107 miles. During the afternoon the wind from the east-north-east came in with increased strength, lifting the seas into racing high waves. Meeting these head-on, the ship's forecastle was continually submerged and tonnes of water swept aft along the decks before returning to the sea through the overworked scuppers.

The course decided on was to continue north-east which would take us across the Banzare Rise, discovered and named on our first voyage, and up to the Roaring Forties where prevailing westerly winds would assist our easterly passage to Hobart.

The north-east wind had increased to half-gale force next morning and the ship was battling to maintain a speed of little more than a knot against it. By midday we had logged only 56 miles for the distance run. The ship, now rid of the 140 tonnes of consumed coal, was in light trim and acted accordingly in the rough seas. Bad weather continued without signs of easing throughout the day and night.

On the 22nd, exactly three months since we had left Hobart, conditions remained unchanged. There was no respite from the ship's erratic and convulsive movements and the decks were continually awash. There was a strong smell of petrol and a check was made of the stock of aviation fuel stowed on the poop deck. Cases were examined and two 18-litre tins, found to be leaking, were thrown overboard. Smoking was then forbidden aft of the fiddley and MacKenzie threatened that anyone caught smoking in the forbidden area would be thrown overboard. We felt that in his agitated state of mind he would not have hesitated to do just that. The captain ordered the seaplane to be dismantled but Campbell refused because of the strong wind and severe rolling of the ship. Our distance run was 103 miles and our position at midday was 62°52'S, 66°02'E. A sounding of 4473 metres was recorded.

Early next morning the north-easterly wind had freshened and by midday it was blowing a full gale. We continued on course. A few icebergs caused some concern as the nights were now pitch black between 9 P.M. and 3.30 A.M. The wind began to moderate late in the afternoon and the two airmen dismantled the seaplane. The crew took down a large boom, weighing about a tonne, from the mizzen mast and stowed it on deck. This helped in a small way to lessen the roll of the ship.

The wind dropped on the 24th and the weather continued to

improve during the day and night. The next morning the wind had swung to the north-west. It was a favourable wind and all sails were set. The ship bowled along on course in fine style in a rather confused but moderate sea. To conserve coal, the engines were cut back and were just turning over. The ship's fresh-water supply was running low and rationing had been introduced. Each man was allowed a quart of water three times a week for all purposes. This was in addition to drinking water at meals and, of course, cooking.

I was awakened early on the 26th by voices singing "Happy birthday . . . ", and with due ceremony received presents of biscuits and sweets. It was my 28th birthday. The weather was unsettled; sky heavily overcast, rain and mist and a confused rough sea. Since 1 P.M. the previous day there had been a gradual rise of the sea floor, from a depth of 4095 metres to only 1195 metres at 10 A.M. We were beginning to cross the Kerguelen–Gaussberg submarine ridge from west to east and 13 soundings through the day registered similar shallow depths.

At midday, 101 miles had been logged for the distance run and our position was 59°30′S, 76°20′E. During the morning we sailed from the degrees of latitude known as the Silent Sixties and entered the Shrieking Fifties.

At 1 A.M. on the 27th, a sounding of 780 metres indicated the shallow bank of the Banzare Rise, discovered and named on December 7, 1929, during our first voyage. On that occasion the recorded depth of the sea floor was only 640 metres. At 8 P.M. we had left the submarine ridge behind and entered deep waters again at a depth of 2190 metres.

With a favourable north-westerly wind, the ship had been running under full sail, assisted by the engines turning over at half speed. At midday we had logged a record run of 148 miles and our position was 57°54′S, 80°E. The engines were then stopped and the ship made four knots under sail alone. The wind sharply veered to the north-east at 4 P.M., sails were taken in and we continued on course under steam.

The following day took us 90 miles closer to Hobart. There was another awe-inspiring auroral display between 9 P.M. and midnight. All hands were on deck admiring the southern sky which, from east to west, was covered with a flickering array of curtains, edged along the underside with a tinge of red. Growing and fading, the luminous curtains rolled and spread, interspersed with curling streamers of faint light and occasional shafts of light flashing high in the sky like searchlight beams. Then, finally, as if by some prearranged signal, the sky suddenly cleared.

On March 1 the wind backed to the west and was soon blowing at full gale force, but later, about midday, moderated to about 50 kilometres an hour. Sails had been taken in with the exception of two jibs and we were proceeding under steam. Hurley was taking cinematograph views of the ship battling her way through the heavy waves. He was clinging to the rigging and was ordered off by MacKenzie who said it was too dangerous and ordered him to remain on deck. Hurley disagreed strongly and the upshot was that he was asked to write a note exonerating the captain if an accident should happen. Hurley complied with the following letter which he handed to MacKenzie:

To Captain MacKenzie.
Dear Sir,
Any risks I may take to secure Kinema films for the expedition aloft or on the decks of the *Discovery* I do so entirely at my own risk.
Your judgement informs me that owing to the state of the seas running it would not be possible to effect a rescue should any person go overboard. I quite understand the position and I accept it. Entirely exonerating you from any blame should any such accident take place.
(signed) F. Hurley

After this document had been handed over, Hurley again climbed the rigging and continued filming.

At 7.30 P.M. all sails were set and with a strong following wind the ship was logging 8½ knots. Soon afterwards the topgallants were taken in and our speed was appreciably reduced. Late in the evening the westerly wind died away, but early the next morning it veered to the north-east and quickly strengthened to gale force with recorded gusts of 110 kilometres an hour.

Enormous waves broke over the ship as she rolled, lurched and pounded into the oncoming seas. Breaking over the gunwales, waves continually swept the deck with great volumes of rushing water that was strong enough to lift anyone on deck clean off their feet. Below deck I was busy chasing articles dislodged by the ship's heavy rolling. Bunk drawers, thought to be securely chocked, were thrown out and their contents scattered around the deck. Sea water, under pressure, had found new places overhead to seep through. The ship's violent movements, the thumping of waves overhead and the shrieking of wind through the rigging, seemed to me a good imitation of a madhouse.

The staff had been delegated watches and we assisted the crew in lookouts, on the lee wheel and deck duties when necessary. To conserve our coal stock, engines were stopped and the ship made good time under two jibs, foresail and topsail. Our course had been altered to the east to take better advantage of the wind. Our coal stock was now estimated to be about 90 tonnes.

Gale-force winds persisted through the night and the seas had developed to a colossal size. Wave crests almost 400 metres apart were separated by great valleys. It was an unbelievable sight. Several of us made our way to the ship's stern to watch her negotiate the mighty seas. Descending the steep side of a following wave she had little more than 30 centimetres of freeboard at the stern. Towering above was a great wall of water, almost vertical, with every appearance of threatening to collapse and overwhelm the ship at any moment. Standing at the ship's stern railing, the sheer wall of the wave could almost be touched with outstretched arms.

In the troughs we were deluged by heavy falls of spray whipped by the wind from the wave crests. Sails idly flapped with the loss of wind and it rested with the engines to drive the ship up the towering wall of the sea fronting her. The masts, 34 metres high, were well below the height of the waves. Ascending the wave, we estimated that the ship's length of 52 metres would fit at least twice in between its base and crest. The seas were by far the highest we had experienced on both voyages of the expedition.

At midday, after an exceptionally good distance run of 173 miles for the 24 hours, we had reached 53°33′S, 93°30′E. Gale conditions continued through the following day until 2 P.M., when the wind suddenly dropped almost to a dead calm. Although conditions were not the best, engines were stopped at 5 P.M. and a full station was carried out. There was an unpleasant confused sea and Doc Ingram, operating the vertical plankton nets from the outboard platform, was more below water than above. When the nettings finished at 8 P.M. he was soaked to the skin. Oblique nets were then towed astern for 20 minutes at a speed of between two and three knots. Heavy rain began to fall, the first for many months, and all hands were on deck catching it in a variety of receptacles to bathe and wash clothes. For some unknown reason, electric lighting was cut off in the wardroom and cabins but the dynamo was still providing lights in the engine room.

Little or no incidents occurred worthy of record during the few following days. Fine weather was being enjoyed and, with a favourable wind, good mileages had been logged each day. The ship was proceeding under full canvas and sailing magnificently. Early on the 8th, we crossed into the Roaring Forties. Our position at midday was 49°38′S, 114°08′E. Later in the day the wind dropped to a dead calm and the ship was becalmed from 9 P.M. to 2 A.M. Electric lighting was restored to the wardroom and cabins with no explanation from the skipper.

A full station was carried out the next day in a depth of 3900 metres. Regular recordings of the echo soundings were almost impossible owing to the heavy rolling and lightness of the ship. Most of the coal that had served as ballast had been consumed and the weight of ashes from the fires, regularly bagged and stowed in the holds, was insufficient to make any marked difference to the ship's stability.

A total of 1800 soundings of sea floor depths in the Southern Ocean were recorded during both voyages of BANZARE. Depths recorded off the Antarctic coast between King George V Land and Enderby Land proved that the Continental Shelf is continuous, thus establishing that Eastern Antarctica consists of a complete and unbroken landmass.

In the afternoon, sails were taken in and the ship stopped to allow Station No. 110 to be carried out. At its conclusion sails were again set and the ship proceeded on course with a favourable strengthening south-westerly wind. At this point we were about 1250 miles from Hobart.

The ship, still under full sail, made good progress through the night and next morning. The weather remained fine and the sea was moderately calm. At midday we had logged 110 miles for the 24-hour run, followed by an exceptionally good run of 167 miles by noon the next day.

The coal situation had become the main topic of conversation amongst the scientists. The consensus of opinion was that at least 75 tonnes were still in stock. Before leaving the Antarctic continent, MacKenzie, in discussing our date of departure with Sir Douglas, had underestimated the remaining coal supply. The captain was obviously anxious to leave uncharted waters. Nevertheless, possibly three or four days' important work on the Antarctic coast had been sacrificed.

A blue sky and bright sunshine heralded the next day. The wind had veered and was now strengthening from the south. Captain MacKenzie was worried about the ship's centre of gravity and coal was transferred from the saddle bunker over the boilers to the bunkers. This work was completed the following morning. According to the ship's coal tally there should have been only 10 tonnes in the saddle bunker, but there were 15 tonnes. The Chief Engineer's figure of coal remaining was 40 tonnes.

The next day we transferred 15.5 tonnes of coal from No. 5 starboard hold to the main bunker. The official figure of our coal stock was now 31 tonnes, but the general opinion was that 70 tonnes would be a correct figure. Another good distance run was made under full sail and 163 miles were logged at midday. Our position was 46°04'S, 131°58'E.

The spell of fine weather stayed with us for the next three days and at 7 A.M. on March 18, we sighted the rugged mountainous Tasmanian coast in the neighbourhood of South West Cape. Moving in closer, sails were taken in and furled. Near Cape Maatsuyker the ship was stopped for a trawling to be carried out. The otter trawl was lowered over the stern and towed for an hour with 105 metres of cable paid out. It was fishing too close to the bottom, which it hit on several occasions. However, a good catch resulted and the zoologists immediately got to work sorting and preserving the specimens. No. 113 station was our last.

The engines were then started and we steamed around the east coast, entering the D'Entrecasteaux Channel at dusk. We anchored off Southport for the night. We had little sleep as all hands worked through the night hauling bags of ashes from the holds and emptying them overboard. Tonnes of ashes were disposed of in a rather confined waterway. It was hard, gruelling work, but made lighter by an array of drinks which were laid on.

While the work was going on Captain MacKenzie invited individual members of the staff into his cabin for a drink and at the same time apologised for his boorish behaviour during the voyage. We all accepted his apology and drank with him except Campbell, who, with the courage of his convictions, refused.

Early on March 19, anchors were weighed and the *Discovery* steamed out of the D'Entrecasteaux Channel into the Derwent River. We expected to reach Hobart about 3 P.M. The latest report on the coal situation was that 50 to 60 tonnes still remained in the bunkers.

Steaming slowly up the picturesque Derwent River, we were escorted by many small craft with their occupants waving and flags flying. At Hobart, ships of the Royal Australian Navy, on their annual visit, signalled a welcome with fluttering bunting while a band on the flagship played us into Queen's Wharf where we berthed at 3.30 P.M. The wharf was crowded with spectators and friends who had been waiting for some time to give us a warm welcome home.

Conclusion

L OOKING BACK over the two voyages of BANZARE, we all felt that a great deal had been achieved. An extensive programme of scientific work and observations embracing many disciplines was successfully carried out. Tonnes of zoological specimens were obtained from deep and shallow dredgings and nettings in little known subantarctic and Antarctic waters.

Geographical work included charting of the Antarctic coastline between the 45th and 180th degrees of east longitude. Lands discovered and named by Sir Douglas Mawson are Banzare Land, Sabrina Land, Princess Elizabeth Land, Lars Christensen Land, Mac Robertson Land, while Kemp and Enderby Lands were visited and charted. Approximately 100 prominent geographical features were named by Sir Douglas during the two voyages. A British Order in Council of February 7, 1933, affirmed that King George V had sovereign rights over a large area of Antarctic Territory. It went on to state: "That part of His Majesty's Dominions in the Antarctic seas, which comprises all the islands and territories — other than Adélie Land — which are situated south of the 60th degree of south latitude and lying between the 45th degree of east longitude and the 160th degree of east longitude is hereby placed under the authority of the Commonwealth of Australia . . ." The Acceptance Bill was passed by the Commonwealth Government and proclaimed in August, 1936.

Since that date this vast area of Antarctica has been the direct concern of the Australian Government. It covers about one-third of the continent with an area of more than five million square kilometres. Wedge-shaped, it extends from the South Pole, 2800 metres above sea level, to the coastline, a distance of about 1280 kilometres.

And last of all comes the parting. Farewells to companions with whom strong bonds of friendship were formed during the expedition. Today, over 50 years later, our members have diminished, but those on deck still meet once a year in Australia to relive our Antarctic days with Mawson.

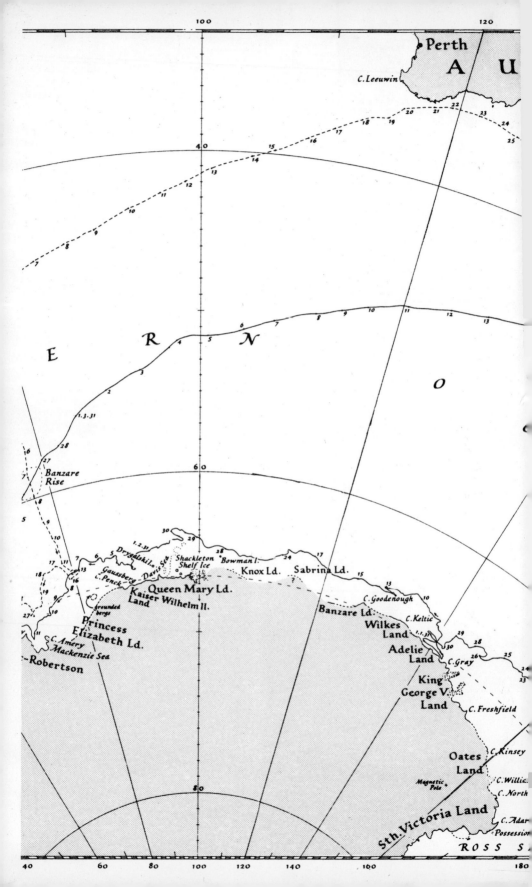